ENTREPRENEURSHIP IN CHINA

To my parents

Entrepreneurship in China

KEMING YANG
University of Reading, UK

Routledge
Taylor & Francis Group

LONDON AND NEW YORK

First published 2007 by Ashgate Publishing

2 Park Square, Milton Park, Abingdon, Oxfordshire OX14 4RN
52 Vanderbilt Avenue, New York, NY 10017

Routledge is an imprint of the Taylor & Francis Group, an informa business

First issued in paperback 2020

British Library Cataloguing in Publication Data
Yang, Keming
   Entrepreneurship in China
   1. Entrepreneurship - China 2. China - Economic policy -
   1976-2000 3. China - Economic policy - 2000- 4. China -
   Economic conditions - 1976-2000 5. China - Economic
   conditions - 2000-
   I. Title
   338'.04'0951

Library of Congress Cataloging-in-Publication Data
Yang, Keming.
   Entrepreneurship in China / by Keming Yang.
      p. cm.
   Includes bibliographical references and index.
   ISBN-13: 978-0-7546-4668-6
   1. China--Economic conditions--2000- 2. Entrepreneurship--China. 3. Business
enterprises--China--Case studies. I Title.

   HC427.95.Y362 2007
   338'.040951--dc22

                        2006039301

ISBN 13: 978-0-7546-4668-6 (hbk)
ISBN 13: 978-0-367-60373-1 (pbk)

Contents

List of Figures

List of Tables

Preface

Two years after the political confrontation at Tiananmen Square in 1989, I started my first job as a lecturer at Nankai University in the City of Tianjin. Very much to my dismay, I was told that I would have to spend the first year of my career in a remote village at the City's outskirts. The arrangement was part of the 'Socialist Education Programme' organized by the Ministry of Education. It was the young academics like me who were to be educated, not the farmers, of course, although university officials claimed that the farmers had a lot to learn from us as well. We were expected to take a hard look at China's reality and consequently, to stop admiring democratic movements. The whole thing might sound preposterous to people in the West, but it was quite successful, perhaps even to the surprise of its organizer. At its completion, many of us were busy helping local officials and nascent entrepreneurs look for opportunities, network with clients and suppliers, or search for a technological patent of promising business value. Money and business, not politics and democracy, dominated our conversations. Some kept their connections with the business world even after returning to their university life; others were even planning to set up their own businesses. Just three years after the democratic protests, entrepreneurial ventures had beaten democracy in popularity among young academics in China.

The importance of business and entrepreneurship was repeatedly reinforced in my mind on the field trips back to China while I was pursuing a PhD degree in sociology at Columbia University from 1994 to 2000. Every time I went back to China, I couldn't help but observe and talk about business: stories about high flying entrepreneurs constantly made the headlines, new books about successful entrepreneurs or how to start your own business were displayed in the most eye-catching positions in bookshops, new businesses were announced and celebrated in newspapers, and people, either those whom I knew personally or those on the street, were talking about their experiences with different kinds of businesses. I had my first dissertation proposal in a bag, which was about a comparative study of democratic development in Russia and China, but it was difficult for me to find an opportunity to pull it out and talk about it with others. I soon realized that I wanted to write another one.

Back in 1986 Stinchcombe observed that 'each choice of a research topic or strategy is a choice of what kind of person to be'.[1] Having decided to write a dissertation about entrepreneurship in China, I was asking myself whether I could make my academic work somehow entrepreneurial. This has turned out to be a very tricky question. On the one hand, all academics are striving to say something 'new', or to be entrepreneurial academically. Some have become academic entrepreneurs by opening up a new research field, institutionalizing a new discipline, or inventing

---

1 'On getting "hung-up" and other assorted illness', in *Stratification and Organization: Selected Papers* (Cambridge: Cambridge University Press, 1986), p. 272.

a new research method. On the other hand, the number of such entrepreneurs has been tiny; it seems to be a business reserved for the very established. Junior academics usually shy away from words like 'invention', 'innovation', 'new', or 'breakthrough'. This is especially true for social science students. Indeed, in today's social sciences, it is all too easy to find a literature, in most cases a large one, on almost any topic that a Ph.D. candidate in sociology can think of. As all candidates know, a big challenge is to argue for what 'new' things one can say after so much has already been said. I find that Ph.D. candidates are more entrepreneurial in terms of dealing with this challenge than they are in terms of conducting the research itself. For example, a popular strategy for candidates whose native tongue is not English is to collect first-hand and large-scale data and to apply highly sophisticated techniques. My English is still far worse than my Chinese, but I have urged myself to say something theoretically interesting.

Not without discouragement, however. A fellow student told me, 'People will certainly want to know what has happened to Chinese entrepreneurs, but no one cares about what you will say about theory'. In the meantime, a senior professor urged me to focus on data analysis because I did not have grey hair yet. (Now I start to have some after finishing this book!)

Sociology is an empirical as well as theoretical discipline. To my understanding, that means that we should constantly go back and forth between theory and empirical evidence, not that any research question accompanied by quality data and excellent technical analysis is worth our time and effort. Rejecting such a way of doing sociology suggested by Ralf Dahrendorf, Merton warned that 'if this formula were sound, problems for sociological investigation could be multiplied at will by turning to any compendium of social data ... and routinely putting the question "Why" to each set of facts reported there'.[2]

In this book, the reader will find some data and data analyses, but my primary objective is to develop theoretical ideas for understanding social processes. And by 'theory' I mean a set of statements that, at least to the satisfaction of the researcher, can meaningfully explain the connection of at least two phenomena. The phenomena under this study are institutional change, economic development, and entrepreneurship in China, with entrepreneurship serving the function of a working mechanism that links the other two. I believe it is safe to assume that entrepreneurship is a key contributor to China's fast economic growth. So, the next but less obvious question is, where does this entrepreneurship come from? Here, several factors (and the theories focusing on them) come in as candidates of explanations, such as historical legacy, financial impetus, personality of the Chinese, the Chinese culture, kinship support and social connections (*guanxi*), political struggles, etc. I see an opportunity to bridge institutional theories and structural theories for identifying the sources of entrepreneurship in China. The explanation that I propose in this book is that it is the 'gaps' between institutional rules (inconsistencies, ambiguities, different

---

2   'Notes on Problem-Finding in Sociology', pp. 17–42 in *Social Research and the Practicing Professions* (Cambridge, Massachusetts: Abt Books, 1982), originally published in Robert K. Merton, Leonard Broom and Leonard S. Cottrell, Jr. (eds), *Sociology Today: Problems and Prospects* (New York: Basic Books, 1959).

ways of enforcement, etc.) that have induced, quite unexpectedly, the emergence and development of entrepreneurship in China.

This is a complete rewriting of my dissertation. It has been a difficult project from its very beginning. Two people have helped me pull through. First, it was impossible for me to complete the first draft of the dissertation without receiving frequent and timely comments from my advisor, Chuck Tilly. Although I have tried to copy him as a model social scientist, I have failed to learn from him how he manages to produce so many publications, advise so many students and junior colleagues, teach courses regularly, and at the same time fight against cancer. The other person who has constantly upheld and boosted my morale is my daughter, Marie. Although her constant but irregular cries during the first six months of her life were interruptions to my writing and thinking, it was in her eyes that I gained courage and saw the value of my work.

I have also been lucky enough to have some practical supports. Harvard-Yenching Institute provided me with a generous three year fellowship for completing my study at Columbia. The Ford Foundation sponsored my fieldwork during the summers of 1996 and 1998. The University of Reading provided a valuable, although small, amount of money that enabled me to purchase the data collected from the National Survey of Private Business Owners in China. The British Academy also offered their valuable financial support. I would like to thank all the entrepreneurs, their managers and employees, local officials, journalists, and many others in China for talking to me in interviews and allowing me to attend meetings and read documents.

Members of my dissertation committee – Allan Silver, David Stark, Andrew Nathan and Douglas Guthrie – offered their help in different ways. From Allan, I can always ask for advice and support without hesitance. I felt settled when Professor Stark told me, twice, that my dissertation was something worth doing. I had a strange feeling of having to be very careful when talking with Professor Nathan about China, who knows so much about the country in which I grew up. I have used Guthrie's book, *Dragon in a Three-Piece Suit*, not only as an excellent study on China's economic development but as a good writing example as well, although I do not have much hope of catching up with his command of English. While working on my proposal, I also had the good fortune of getting some valuable comments and suggestions from Patrick Heller and Wang Nianzu. With unusual courage, I sent a few draft chapters to Andrew Walder, who couldn't join the committee but showed his great generosity by sending many harsh critiques back to me. Roberto Franzosi provided much needed support and encouragement after I took my second job at University of Reading.

Parts of Chapter 3 were adapted from two journal articles: 'Double Entrepreneurship in China's Economic Reform: An Analytical Framework', *Journal of Political and Military Sociology*, 30/1 (2002): 134–147 (© 2002 Sociology Department, Northern Illinois University; all rights reserved) and 'Institutional Holes and Entrepreneurship in China', *The Sociological Review*, 52/3 (2004): 371–389 (© 2004 The Editorial Board of *The Sociological Review*; all rights reserved). I want to sincerely thank the editors and the anonymous reviewers for sending me so many valuable comments in revising the papers.

Had I not met and talked to Mary Savigar, my editor at Ashgate, I would have given up the attempt of publishing this book. I want to thank her and others at Ashgate for polishing the manuscript and bringing it to the reader. In addition, I am very grateful for many useful comments and suggestions made by an anonymous reviewer. Thanks also go to Claire Annals for editing and proofreading the whole draft.

I would never have been able to finish my study, and this book, without the encouragement of my wife, Lixin. During the harsh winter of 1999, she used to ask me to write for several hours in the evening at University of Toronto's Robarts Library; at home, she was suffering from infections and loneliness. She is the kind of woman able to take on a professional career, bring up two kids, and help an academic husband.

Finally, I wish to dedicate this book to my parents, who sacrificed so much of their own lives in order that I could be a well educated person.

Chapter 1

The Puzzle of China, the Puzzle of Entrepreneurship

How the first puzzle leads to the second

At the time of writing (early 2006), that China is on the way to becoming a global power is no longer in dispute. One does not have to analyze complicated economic figures to have a sense of how powerful China's economy has become. We learn from the media that China has overtaken the UK to become the fourth largest economy in the world,[1] something Mao Zedong wished to achieve during his life time. In America, 'The China Price' has become 'the three scariest words in US industry'.[2] Millions of jobs have been lost in the US and recreated in China and India. The US trade deficit with China has been growing at an average rate of 20 per cent per year. With the ambition of building up several business flagships that are internationally visible, China has started a 'Shopping Spree' of American and European companies, including Rover, IBM PC, and some oil producers. Just two decades ago, 'Made in China' was still a synonym of poor quality. Now, it would be difficult for people living in Europe and America to enjoy shopping in supermarkets without clothes, appliances, and many other things made in China. These economic powers will doubtlessly be translated into political, diplomatic, and military ones. True, as China specialists and business analysts have pointed out,[3] both India and China are facing huge obstacles to growth, but it is exactly their growth despite the obstacles that is so remarkable and puzzling.

Most people in the West have now taken China's remarkable economic development as a 'given'. To them, a question of greater urgency is 'What shall we do to deal with China's growth?', not an academic question like 'Why has China been growing in such a speedy manner?'. Even academics seem to have shifted their attention from the triggers and causes to the consequences and implications of China's development. This book, however, sticks to the 'why' question.

But, first of all, let's remind ourselves of what the puzzle exactly is. As far as I know, it was Peter Nolan who initially and most explicitly presented 'The China Puzzle', which obviously troubled the minds of other China specialists and social scientists in the late 1980s and the early 1990s:

---

1 Andrew Peaple, 'China Overtakes UK as World's 4th Largest Economy', *Dow Jones Newswires*, 26 January 2006.

2 *BusinessWeek*, European edition, 6 December 2004.

3 Peter Nolan, *China at the Crossroads* (Polity Press, 2003). Special issue of *BusinessWeek*, European edition, 22–29 August 2005.

Why did China perform so well in the first decade and a half of reform, despite the fact that its economic institutions and policies were gravely inadequate in relation to mainstream Western economic theory and policy?[4]

The puzzle became even more perplexing when Nolan moved on to compare and contrast China's rise with Russia's fall.[5] Whilst the pre-reform conditions in the two nations were different, the two former largest Communist regimes did follow the same line of political ideology for more than two decades, the same reasoning of organizing the economy and, most importantly, the same idea of bringing in market mechanisms to reform their economic organizations in the 1980s. But their paths of economic reforms became divergent later on, apparently leading to two remarkably different economic situations. What's going on?

I would not venture to make a systematic comparison between the two nations' experiences; this book is about China's economic development alone. But the comparison with Russia does highlight the intriguing source of China's economic growth: How could fast economic growth be achieved in a system that is politically authoritarian and economically centralized? Swift economic growth has been going side by side with political reform at a snail's pace. It is perplexing because there has been a popular logic among studies of China: a democratic political system is a prerequisite for successful economic development, no matter at what time or in which country; therefore, either economic reform will lead to the collapse of the communist regime, or the communist regime will suffocate economic growth in its struggle for maintaining political dominance. Gordon White applied the Chinese phrase *qi hu nan xia* (being unable to dismount from a tiger) to illustrate the dilemma: China's economic reform would only lead to 'a political deadlock, reflecting serious contradictions which lie at the roots of the "market socialist" programme'.[6] A more sophisticated version of this 'deadlock' solution to the China puzzle comes from a book by Andrew Walder and his associates:

> This volume's premise is that such departures set in motion a chain of consequences, usually unintended, and if the departures are extensive enough, they eventually alter political institutions and relationships to the point where Communist party rule can no longer be sustained.[7]

In agreement with such prediction, Merle Goldman and Roderick MacFarquhar listed some evidence for China's declining party-state as a consequence of dynamic economy, including the growing independence of the National People's Congress (NPC), the increasing decentralization of power to local authorities, the rigorous

---

4   Peter Nolan, 'China's Post-Mao Political Economy: a Puzzle', *Contributions to Political Economy*, 12 (1993): 71–87.

5   Peter Nolan, *China's Rise, Russia's Fall: Politics, Economies, and Planning in the Transition from Stalinism* (St. Martin's Press, 1995).

6   Gordon White, *Riding the Tiger: The Politics of Economic Reform in Post-Mao China* (Macmillan, 1993), p. 77.

7   Andrew Walder (ed.), *The Waning of the Communist State: Economic Origins of Political Decline in China and Hungary* (Berkeley, California; London: University of California Press, 1995), p. 3.

emergence of the non-state sectors, untameable corruptions that erode the legitimacy of Communist rule, and so on.[8] Some researchers from China have followed a similar line of reasoning.[9]

In short, almost all leading China specialists[10] seem to favour the proclamation that economic development will eventually – although no one would offer a time scale – topple down the political regime rather than that the Communist State will be able to sustain its political dominance by sacrificing economic growth.

To ascertain whether the power of the Chinese State has declined would lead one to get involved in debates over conceptualizing and measuring state power. I am not ready to do that. Nor would I like to engage in the debate over whether (let alone when) the current Chinese State will eventually be replaced by a democratic one for the sake of maintaining economic growth. I simply find those questions too difficult to answer. The fact is, after two and half decades of economic reforms, the Chinese State is still in power, and it is still difficult to completely dismiss an argument for a stronger Chinese State given the increasing amount of economic resources under its control and its growing influence in international affairs.

Whilst pointing out some fundamental problems inherent in China's logic of reform, the leading specialists nevertheless have not taken a head-on approach to solving Nolan's puzzle. Instead of arguing how economic reforms have led, and will lead, to any particular situation, in this book I would go back to Nolan's original puzzle and try to answer a few questions about China's economic growth *per se*: How could China's economic growth occur in the first place? If the Communist regime was so suppressing, where did the products, commodities, services, or in general, China's national wealth, come from? What was the driving force? Would some liberal policies initiated by Deng Xiaoping be sufficient for explaining the establishment of millions of factories, enterprises, and companies? How could profit-hunting individuals and organizations, constantly being labelled in political terms detrimental to their businesses, survive and even thrive on the 'gravely inadequate' institutional structure?

To answer these questions, researchers have picked up their favourite, but different, explanatory variables – including liberal ideology and strategy promoted by political leaders such as Deng Xiaoping[11] and some provincial leaders such as Zhao Ziyang and Wanli[12] at the early stage of reform, pragmatic and ad hoc policies

8   Merle Goldman and Roderick MacFarquhar (eds), *The Paradox of China's Post-Mao Reforms* (Cambridge, Massachusetts and London, England: Harvard University Press, 1999).

9   Pei Minxin, *From Reform to Revolution: The Demise of Communism in China and the Soviet Union* (Cambridge: Harvard University Press, 1994). Zheng Shiping, *Party vs. State in Post-1949 China: The Institutional Dilemma* (Cambridge University Press, 1997).

10   Perhaps an exception is John Burns, 'The People's Republic of China at 50: National Political Reform', *The China Quarterly*, 159 (1999): 580–594.

11   Robert F. Ash and Y.Y. Kueh (eds), *The Chinese Economy under Deng Xiaoping* (Oxford University Press, 1996). Barry Naughton, 'Deng Xiaoping: The Economist', *China Quarterly*, 135 (1993): 491–514.

12   Peter T.Y. Cheung, Jae Ho Chung and Zhimin Lin, *Provincial Strategies of Economic Reform in Post-Mao China: Leadership, politics, and implementation* (Armonk, NY: M.E.

for solving problems such as unemployment in urban areas,[13] decentralization of economic power to local authorities,[14] the symbiotic relations between local officials and private business owners,[15] and so on.

I have learnt a great deal from these studies and I am grateful for their insights in building up my own work. What I am trying to do is no more than adding a bit of theory to the whole business of understanding China's economic development and demonstrating how theoretical mechanisms work with empirical illustrations. Such theorizing will focus on the interactive relationship between institutional rules and entrepreneurship. By doing so I hope we can have a relatively shorter causal chain in our explanation. For example, our chain of explanation will be stretched too long if we start with some grand state policies, because no matter how liberal they are, they remain policies until they are translated into value-producing actions. And even after the translation, there is no guarantee that the actions will be successful. Therefore, it is more manageable to work out the immediate institutional conditions under which productive actions take place.

After years of reading and thinking, I have come to the conclusion that what has not been put at the very centre of current studies and theories, either unwittingly or purposefully, is entrepreneurial opportunities and how these opportunities have been identified, interpreted, and exploited. That entrepreneurship is the eventual driving force of economic development is a well-established insight. It is entrepreneurs who create new jobs by setting up new organizations, increase national wealth by organizing the production of new commodities and by increasing tax revenues.[16] The mechanisms of economic change 'pivot certainly on entrepreneurial activity', which is true not only for capitalist societies[17] but for other types of societies as well. Higgins has offered perhaps the best summary of the importance of entrepreneurship:

Sharpe, 1998).

13 Thomas Gold, 'Back to the City: The Return of China's Educated Youth', *The China Quarterly*, 84 (1981): 755–770.

14 Andrew Walder, 'Local Government as Industrial Firms: An Organizational Analysis of China's Transitional Economy', *American Journal of Sociology*, 101/2 (1995): 263–301. There is also a large literature of local corporatism in China.

15 David Wank, *Commodifying Communism: Business, Trust, and Politics in a Chinese city* (Cambridge University Press, 1999). Bruce J. Dickson, *Red Capitalists in China: The Party, Private Entrepreneurs, and Prospects for Political Change* (Cambridge, England: Cambridge University Press, 2003).

16 S. Birley, 'New Ventures and Employment Growth', *Journal of Business Venturing*, 2/2 (1987): 155–165. P.D. Reynolds, 'New Firms: Societal contribution versus survival potential', *Journal of Business Venturing*, 2/3 (1987): 231–246. President's Commission, *Entrepreneurship and Its Impact on the U.S. Economy* (Washington, DC: President's Commission on Industrial Competitiveness, 1984). Claudia Bird Schoonhoven and Elaine Romanelli (eds), *The Entrepreneurship Dynamic: Origins of Entrepreneurship and the Evolution of Industries* (Stanford, California: Stanford University Press, 2001).

17 Joseph Schumpeter, 'Comments on a Plan for the Study of Entrepreneurship', reprinted in Richard Swedberg (ed.), *The Economics and Sociology of Capitalism* (Princeton University Press, 1991), p. 412.

The key figure in this process of technological advance is the entrepreneur. He is the man who sees the opportunity for introducing the new commodity, technique, raw material, or machine, and brings together the necessary capital, management, labour, and materials to do it ... In any society, the rate of technological progress, and so of economic development, depends greatly on the number and ability of entrepreneurs available to it.[18]

It may sound too commonplace to argue that entrepreneurship deserves a central status in the study of China's economic development, but I don't think I am simply setting up a straw man for the sake of justifying my research when I say that entrepreneurship has not occupied a prominent position in the current studies of China's economic development. In particular, we are short of ideas that theorize the relationship between entrepreneurship and institutional change in this emerging economy. Some researchers have committed themselves to documenting the experience of various types of entrepreneurs,[19] but they do not seem to be interested in identifying the distinctive qualities of entrepreneurship in China, specifying the structural features of institutional rules, and theorizing the interaction between entrepreneurship and institutional conditions.

This less than encouraging situation is reflected in the weakness of specific theories that explicitly connect entrepreneurship with institutional environment in mainstream sociological and economic literature. Although entrepreneurship has established itself in business schools in most western nations, the major concern is ironically with 'routine' practices and strategies in each step of the entrepreneurial process: where to find initial capital, how to network with clients, how to write a business plan, how to organize a team, etc. These issues are of course very important, but they have kept a distance away from some more fundamental ones, such as the social origins of entrepreneurial opportunities, the interpretation and justification of entrepreneurial strategies, the social relations of entrepreneurs among themselves and with others, and cross-national comparisons of entrepreneurial behaviours. While on the one hand it is definitely valuable to take stock of social science studies of entrepreneurship and introduce these insights to students of business schools,[20]

---

18 Benjamin Higgins, *Economic Development: Principles, Problems, and Policies*, revised edition, (London: W.W. Norton and Company, 1968), p. 150.

19 I do not list items published in Chinese here. Malik and Ole studied household business owners; see Rashid Malik, *Chinese Entrepreneurs in the Economic Development of China* (Praeger, 1997). Ole Bruun, *Business and Bureaucracy in a Chinese City: An Ethnography of Private Business Household in Contemporary China* (University of California Press, 1993). Lance Gore studied bureaucratic entrepreneurs in *Market Communism: The Institutional Foundations of China's Post-Mao Hyper-growth* (Oxford University Press, 1999). Two studies of military entrepreneurs: T.J. Bickford, 'The Chinese Military and Its Business Operations: The PLA as Entrepreneur', *Asian Survey*, 34/5 (1994): 460–74. Tai Ming Cheung, *China's Entrepreneurial Army* (Oxford University Press, 2001). Doug Guthrie analyzed entrepreneurship in the state sector: 'Entrepreneurial Action in the State Sector: The Economic Decision of Chinese Managers', pp.159–190 in Victoria Bonnell and Thomas Gold, *The New Entrepreneurs of Europe and Asia: Patterns of Business Development in Russia, Eastern Europe, and China* (M.E. Sharpe, 2002).

20 Richard Swedberg, 'Introduction' to *Entrepreneurship: The Social Science View* (Oxford University Press, 2000).

it is on the other hand equally valuable to derive some theoretical explanations of entrepreneurship across countries at different stages of economic development.

Whether the Chinese State has handled political reforms in a way ideologically acceptable is a matter beyond academic discussion. And even if we do intend to reveal the logical impasse of China's reforms, it is still too early to make any reliable predictions in the foreseeable future. No matter how authoritarian China's political system remains and no matter how poorly designed and enforced the institutional infrastructure has been, it is a matter of fact that the institutional environment in China has offered numerous opportunities for entrepreneurial actions, and when entrepreneurs do take actions to exploit these opportunities, new factories are built up and new products are churned out. Consequently, the economy has grown quickly. As Joseph Stiglitz has correctly noted,[21] China's economic success supplies an important case of focusing on the creation of new enterprises rather than privatizing old ones for making transition economies successful. Douglas North also noted the unique features of the China experience by acknowledging that 'the Chinese developed an incentive structure which managed to produce rapid economic development without any of the standard recipes of the West'.[22] But North is ambivalent about whether China should continue following its own way of development or come closer to the western path, because he does not go one step further to study how that alternative incentive structure works. This whole process is what this book is all about: where did so many opportunities come from, especially during the early years of reform when the whole nation was still against 'capitalist' ways of economic development? Given the less than appropriate environment, how could so many entrepreneurs go about making a huge amount of profit?

No matter how researchers disagree over which aspect of China's institutional framework is the key to understanding the nation's economic development, either fiscal reform, property rights, or central-local relations, few would disagree that it is institutional change that has brought forth the nation's remarkable economic development. Whilst it is doubtless necessary and valuable to study institutional changes themselves, there still exists a black box between what explains and what is explained – if economic development can be understood as the increase of commodities and services, institutional changes cannot directly produce all of these. By focusing on entrepreneurship, we can obtain an intermediate mechanism without leaving too big a black box in between the explaining factor, institutional change, and the target phenomenon, economic development.

Before moving on, I need to make two interrelated points as clearly as possible. First, institutional rules, and the change of these rules, require agents to carry out what these rules are designed to deliver. I am not particularly concerned with whether I have been following the principles of methodological individualism. To me, two other questions for explaining economic development are rather important: who have produced the wealth and how they have done that? It might be obvious that it is millions of ordinary people working in thousands of factories who have made

---

21   Joseph Stiglitz, *Whither Socialism?* (MIT Press, 1994), p. 261.
22   Douglas North, *Understanding the Process of Economic Change* (Princeton University Press, 2005), p. 159.

China's economic growth possible. These people, however, would not have come together without the organization and leadership of entrepreneurs, dubbed *neng ren* ('capable men') in many places within China. It is a simplification – but I believe it is a safe and widely accepted simplification – to see entrepreneurs as the ultimate agents who have translated institutional rules into engines of production.

The second important point is that, entrepreneurial actions should not be seen as automatic responses to rules. Rules do matter, but not in a manner of 'Given rules *R*, there will be actions *A*'. Actions, albeit triggered by rules, may turn out to be unintended consequences of purposefully designed rules. We should start by examining rules and their functions, but what actions people take and how must be taken as open-ended questions.

The puzzle of China, therefore, can be represented in Figure 1.1.

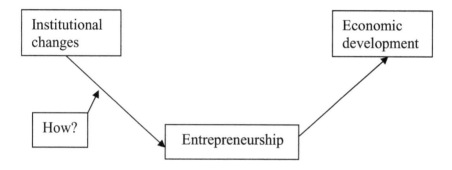

Figure 1.1 Identifying the puzzle

To some readers, the chain of explanation may appear too short as factors looming in the background, such as cultural legacy, connections with other economies, etc., have been purposefully omitted. The omission is justified because there have been many studies about them, whose contribution I need to take for granted in order to keep my own analysis focused. I believe that a specified although short chain of explaining mechanisms is more desirable than a vague but long model.

So, the puzzle of China is fundamentally a puzzle of entrepreneurship: Where did an army of entrepreneurs come from in China? And how could they set up so many profitable businesses so quickly while the nation's whole institutional structure was still murky, fragmented, changing, and even suppressing? Answers to these questions will constitute of the bulk of this book. Not every new business was a success, of course. But the net effect must have been positive; otherwise, there would have been no economic growth in China. Entrepreneurs in China in the late 1970s and the early 1980s knew better than anybody else how constraining the institutional environment was and consequently how high transaction costs could be in such an environment. But still, they decided to go ahead to take the challenge of setting up new factories and companies. Yes, the transaction costs were much higher than those in developed countries, but they would be even higher if no actions were taken – there would be no profits at all. My question is: How could entrepreneurs in China survive and thrive under these institutional constraints?

Answers to some basic questions are in order: Who are entrepreneurs in China? Exactly how fast have private businesses, the most daring group of all entrepreneurial ventures in China, developed? How unfriendly was the whole institutional environment – so unfriendly that the private sector's development becomes a puzzle?

Who are entrepreneurs in China?

As Edwin Harwood acutely suggests,[23] entrepreneurs are elusive animals. Closely examining their habitat and watching how they behave with changing environments are more useful than establishing linguistically seamless boundaries. This does not mean, however, that entrepreneurs have no identities; it is just that their identities are defined by their behaviours, not by the titles that they carry. For instance, the function of an entrepreneur is quite often fused with that of a business owner or a manager. An entrepreneur may carry the title of business owner, but it would be too low a criterion to pass: all petty storeowners in a neighbourhood would be entrepreneurs.[24] It is true that most entrepreneurs become entrepreneurs when they own or manage a business, but owning or managing business itself is not sufficient for one to be qualified as an entrepreneur. According to Schumpeter, an entrepreneur must be innovative in combining various available resources and getting 'new things done'.[25] The 'newness' of the things done can vary dramatically from one case to another, rendering entrepreneurship a variable with some extreme values. Opening a street corner shop is new in the sense of filling out a tiny market niche, but that is far less entrepreneurial than introducing a new way of administering bank loans. By the same logic, a manager is not necessarily an entrepreneur. The former is responsible for making things work smoothly while the later is original in working out how to get things done. Although it is understandable to search for entrepreneurs among top level managers, it would be a conceptual confusion if managers are automatically taken as substitutes of entrepreneurs.[26]

It is difficult to focus on behaviours, however, because they are transient. As no innovations will remain innovative for a long time, entrepreneurs can only be

---

23 Edwin Harwood, 'The Sociology of Entrepreneurship', in Calvin A. Kent, Donald L. Sexton and Karl H. Vesper (eds), *Encyclopaedia of Entrepreneurship* (Englewood Cliffs, New Jersey: Prentice-Hall, 1982).

24 In at least two studies, petty household business owners were selected and interviewed as entrepreneurs. Malik, *Chinese Entrepreneurs in the Economic Development of China*; Bruun, *Business and Bureaucracy in a Chinese City*.

25 Joseph Schumpeter, 'Economic Theory and Entrepreneurial History', in Richard V. Clemence (ed.), *Essays on Entrepreneurs, Innovation, Business Cycles, and the Evolution of Capitalism* (Addison-Wesley, 1949 [1951]), p. 266. Reprinted from *Change and the Entrepreneur*, pp. 63–84.

26 Margaret Pearson, *China's New Business Elite: The Political Consequences of Economic Reform* (University of California Press, 1997).

entrepreneurial for a very short period. Again, as Schumpeter noted, 'No one is an entrepreneur forever, only when he or she is actually doing the innovative activity'.[27] Entrepreneurship presents itself swiftly because once a business innovation is accomplished, the person carrying out the innovation is not an entrepreneur anymore until the next innovation. Thus, entrepreneurs do not constitute a social group as workers, politicians, or homeowners. A person may be an entrepreneur in one situation, but not necessarily so in another. There is no such individual as a career or professional entrepreneur, let alone a life-time entrepreneur. This transient nature of entrepreneurship dictates that we analyze it as an ideal-typical concept, not as a static socio-economic attribute.

In the context of China, a popular but transient behaviour of entrepreneurs is the practice of taking advantage of gaps in both markets and institutional structures (to be discussed fully in Chapter 3). Seen in this light, entrepreneurship is everywhere in China's economic life. Those who know today's China well will not be surprised by the following incidents of entrepreneurship: a high school teacher offers coaching service at weekends, a policeman works as an estate agent, a local official sits in a company's board of directors, several university lecturers are partners of a consultancy company, a group of retired or laid off factory workers run a car servicing shop, etc. Similarly, entrepreneurs in China come from all walks of life: he or she could be a powerful politician,[28] a garbage collector,[29] an individual household business starter,[30] a village party secretary,[31] or even a military officer.[32] To many people in China, being entrepreneurial is a way of life.

Empirical investigation in academic work, however, defies elusiveness. Prior to any analysis, subjects should be clearly defined. So, who are the entrepreneurs in this study? While a more specific answer will be given in a section below on research design, the entrepreneurs in this study can be briefly defined as those who have an experience of starting up their own businesses in China since the end of the 1970s. More specifically, I shall focus on those who started businesses that have been officially categorized as private enterprises or town-and-village enterprises (TVE) in China.

---

27 Richard Swedberg (ed.), *Entrepreneurship: The Social Science View* (Cambridge University Press, 2000), p. 18.

28 Lance Gore analyzed the rise of 'bureaucratic entrepreneurship' in China in his *Market Communism*. In his published PhD dissertation, *Si Ying Qi Ye Zhu (Owners of Private Enterprises)*, She Hui Ke Xue Wen Xian Chu Ban She (Social Science Documentation Publishing House), 2005, pp. 54–58, Liu Peifeng reported many cases of local bureaucrats and politicians 'stepping into the sea' – giving up their political careers to engage in commercial businesses.

29 Ibid., Case 11, pp. 77–78.

30 Thomas Gold, 'Urban Private Business and China's Reforms', in Richard Baum (ed.), *Reform and Reaction in Post-Mao China: The Road to Tiananmen* (Routledge, 1991), pp. 84–103.

31 Bruce Gilley, *Model Rebels: The Rise and Fall of China's Richest Village* (University of California Press, 2001).

32 Bickford, 'The Chinese Military and Its Business Operations: The PLA as Entrepreneur'. Cheung, *China's Entrepreneurial Army*.

The rise of entrepreneurship in China's economic reform[33]

My objective in this section is to concretize the puzzle of entrepreneurship in China's economic reform. It does not mean to provide a comprehensive treatment of the development of entrepreneurship in China. I will, however, analyze the institutional environment for entrepreneurial activities in China in Chapter 4 and present statistical findings on some important steps of the entrepreneurial process in Chapter 5.

The start of a Communist China meant the ending of private enterprises. After the Chinese Communist Party (CCP) came to power in 1949, 'capitalist enterprises' – the domestic ones, to be precise – were not confiscated and banned straight away. That, however, was only an expedient measure, because the co-existence of state enterprises and private businesses was a sign of the New Democratic Revolution, the prelude of the Socialist Revolution, in which the State, in the name of all working people, shall take the ownership of all national resources. Thus came the nationalization of private properties from 1953 to 1956 in all major industrial areas. In rural areas, the elimination of private properties and businesses was carried out at local levels, that is, through the establishment of People's Communes, a movement reaching its peak in 1958. Private businesses then completely vanished during the ten years of the Great Proletariat Cultural Revolution (1966–1976).

One moral justification for terminating the existence of private businesses is to eradicate economic exploitation.[34] Exploitation is a sin because it is unethical for the business owner (or the 'capitalist' in Marxist terminology) to take away the surplus value, which is produced by the employed worker, not the owner. Ownership alone cannot justify the act of taking away enormous profits generated from other people's hard work. Besides, there is a fundamental economic reason for extinguishing private property in China – collective ownership of the means of production is the prerequisite of advanced mass production. According to the Marxist ideology propagated in China, the mode of production should fit the power of production, but because the former can never keep pace with the latter, the former will, sooner or later, have to be altered in order to fit the development of the latter. As the Communist economy promises a much more powerful production, it is economically more effective to establish a corresponding mode of production – i.e., complete collective ownership or state ownership. In short, replacing private property with state ownership is not only morally desirable but economically effective as well.

In this kind of economy, there is no place for entrepreneurship. This is not because no one would have the motivation to become an entrepreneur – in many cases, one may want to be an entrepreneur in order to be a national hero – but because the very condition for the emergence of entrepreneurship, i.e., uncertainty, has been eliminated. The economy is no one else's but the State's business, and the State

---

33 This part draws on a series of reports produced by Zhang Houyi and Ming Lizhi, *Zhong Guo Si Ying Qi Ye Fa Zhan Bao Gao* (*A Report on the Development of China's Private Enterprises*), She Hui Ke Xue Wen Xian Chu Ban She (Social Science Documentation Publishing House), 1999–2005.

34 János Kornai discussed the Marxist ideology against private property in *The Socialist System* (Princeton University Press, 1992), pp. 87–90, 444–447.

can do nothing but make plans. With plans in hand, the State only needs economic soldiers who would strictly follow its orders.

Under two strong conditions, which correspond to the previous two reasons for eliminating private property, such an economic system may function properly, at least for a short period of time. First, the principle of distributing production outputs based on the amount of labor invested rather than on property ownership is deemed to have been fairly enforced in practice. Second, the management of production, which is now centrally controlled by the State, has demonstrated a level of efficiency higher than the level that can be achieved in a capitalist economy. A rare case of the two conditions being largely satisfied is the first Five-Year Plan in China (1953–1957).[35] It has been forcefully argued,[36] and eventually proved by what happened to nearly all Communist economies, that such a system could only lead to an economic dead end.

What makes the case of China truly puzzling is that entrepreneurship experienced striking development *before* state policies suppressing profit-making transactions were publicly and widely denounced. Perhaps the earliest document signalling the State's possible recognition of private business was *Some Specific Policies Regarding Past Business Administrators*, published by the Central Committee of the CCP in December 1979. The first official sanction of private enterprises, with many strict conditions, was *The Tentative Stipulations on Private Enterprises*, published by the State Council in June 1988. Nonetheless, village leaders in rural China had already started their businesses in the mid 1970s, some even before the Cultural Revolution was ended. For example, there were already more than a dozen factories in Xin Hu (meaning, literally, 'New Lake') village in Fujian Province in 1971. Despite several waves of arrests of the mangers and closures of factories, local enterprises flourished. Until 1978, these factories employed nearly 52,000 people.[37] It is next to impossible to make an accurate estimate of the scope and scale of private businesses before 1988, no matter how loosely defined. Such cases, however, are not rare.[38] I shall provide a detailed case study of such an entrepreneur in Chapter 8. The rise of private businesses in urban areas came later in the early 1980s, but also experienced a similarly dramatic growth, mostly encouraged to grow for the sake of solving the employment crisis due to the return of the 'red guards' from the countryside, the

---

35 Denis Twitchett and John K. Fairbank (eds), *The Cambridge History of China*, Vol. 14, *The People's Republic 1949–1979, Part 1: The Emergence of Revolutionary China, 1949–1965* (Cambridge University Press, 1987).

36 That by János Kornai (*The Socialist System*) is perhaps the most notable.

37 Zhang, Houyi and Ming Lizhi (eds), *Zhongguo Siying Qiye Fazhan Baogao (1978–1998) (Report of the Development of Private Business in China)* (Beijing: Social Science Documentation Publishing House, 1999), pp. 28–29.

38 There are many case studies similar to the one cited here. See, for example, John Wong, Rong Ma, and Mu Yang (eds), *China's Rural Entrepreneurs: Ten Case Studies* (Singapore: Times Academic Press, 1995). More are published in Chinese. For those who can read Chinese, see the biographical series published by the Chinese Academy of Administrative Science since 1997. Also, Jia Ting (ed.), *Biographies of Well-Known Private Entrepreneurs in Contemporary China (Dang Dai Zhong Guo Zhi Ming Si Ying Qi Ye Jia Lie Zhuan)* (Beijing: Zhong Guo Cheng Shi Jing Ji She Hui Chu Ban She, 1989).

graduation of millions of high school students, and the migration of surplus labour from rural areas.[39]

The reader can have a sense of the overall pace of growth of private businesses, here produced separately in Table 1.1 for individual household businesses (i.e., sole ownership with no more than eight employees) and in Table 1.2 for private enterprises (with no required limit of number of employees).[40]

Table 1.1 Growth of individual household businesses in China, 1981 to 2002

Year	Number of enterprises (millions)	Percent increase from the previous year	Number of employees (millions)	Percent increase from the previous year
1981	1.83		2.27	
1982	2.61	40.6	3.20	42.60
1983	5.90	133.4	7.46	126.10
1984	9.33	74.60	13.04	58.10
1985	11.71	35.50	17.66	25.50
1986	12.11	4.50	18.46	3.40
1987	13.73	16.90	21.58	13.40
1988	14.53	6.80	23.05	5.80
1989	12.47	−15.80	19.41	−14.20
1990	13.28	7.80	20.93	6.50
1991	14.17	7.90	22.58	6.70
1992	15.34	9.30	24.68	8.30
1993	17.67	19.10	29.39	15.20
1994	21.87	28.50	37.76	23.80
1995	25.28	22.20	46.14	15.60
1996	27.04	8.70	50.17	7.00
1997	28.51	8.50	54.42	5.40
1998	31.20	12.37	61.14	9.44
1999	31.60	2.10	62.41	1.30
2000	26.71	−18.76	50.70	−18.63
2001	24.33	−6.11	47.60	−5.82
2002	23.77	−0.36	47.43	−2.28

39 Dong Fureng, *An Economic History of the People's Republic of China* (in Chinese), volume 2 (Joint Publishing (H.K.) Co., Ltd, 2001), pp. 424–430.

40 Figures in the two tables come from the series of reports on private enterprises in China edited by Zhang Houyi and his associates.

Table 1.2 Growth of private enterprises in China, 1989 to 2002

Year	Number of enterprises (millions)	Percent increase from the previous year	Number of employees (millions)	Percent increase from the previous year
1989	0.09		1.64	
1990	0.10	3.70	1.70	8.30
1991	0.11	8.20	1.84	9.90
1992	0.14	26.10	2.32	29.50
1993	0.24	60.80	3.73	70.40
1994	0.43	73.70	6.48	81.70
1995	0.65	47.50	9.56	51.40
1996	0.82	22.50	11.71	25.20
1997	0.96	15.20	13.49	17.30
1998	1.20	26.67	17.10	25.01
1999	1.51	18.25	20.22	25.64
2000	1.76	18.99	24.06	16.76
2001	2.03	12.80	27.14	15.14
2002	2.44	25.63	34.09	20.05

As indicated in Table 1.1, starting from 1981, the total number of individual household businesses and the total number of people employed by them were both more than doubled in 1983. The summer of 1989 saw waves of political demonstrations in Tiananmen Square and beyond, followed by shrinking of the private sector due to the State's harsher financial and administrative policies.[41] The growth picked up after Deng's talk in 1992 till the end of the last century. The downturn starting in 2000 was caused by a new round of stern regulations aimed to clear up illegal individual businesses. It seems that this time the private enterprises were fortunate enough not to be affected.

Both tables suggest the effect of intervening state policies on the fate of private businesses in China. Researchers have characterized the experience of private enterprises as 'growing out of crevice' or 'emerging from the crevice of traditional systems', indicating the adverse regulatory policies toward them.[42] I think we should take the analogy more seriously: What constitutes a 'crevice' in China's institutional structure? In whatever real sense, how could an entrepreneurial venture grow out of it? Whilst most parts of this book are to answer these questions, here are some examples of 'institutional fissures' (details to be discussed in Chapter 4):

---

41 Such decline also happened to private enterprises as well, which cannot be seen here due to the unavailability of official data.

42 Dong Fureng, p. 215, and 'Preface' of Zhang, Ming and Liang (eds), *A Report on the Development of China's Private Enterprises*, No. 5 (Beijing: Social Sciences Documentation Publishing House, 2003).

- Even long after the publication of reform policies, many local authorities still held the view that private enterprises were less legitimate than state-controlled ones, if not completely illegitimate. Economic punishments on private businesses usually followed political setbacks.
- Although the newly amended Constitution has proclaimed to protect legal income from operating private enterprises, in reality there are few enforceable legal procedures for protecting private property.
- Private enterprises are normally the first to feel the effect of containing economic overheating, strained energy supply, or harsher financial conditions.
- Unlike state enterprises, private ones have to pass through a series of institutional hurdles in order to obtain a legal status.
- The proportion of financial support to the non-state sectors (better for TVEs than for private businesses) by major financial organizations, almost all under complete state control, remains tiny.
- Industries of national importance, such as telecommunications, heavy industries, banking, etc., do not welcome private investments.
- Private enterprises have to put up with higher tax rates and other administrative expense, many times rampantly lavished by local officials.

How could entrepreneurship vigorously develop in such an institutional environment? I hope that the rise of entrepreneurial ventures in China, most astonishingly represented in private enterprises and TVEs, is now puzzling enough to the reader. It is time to set out a plan for solving the puzzle.

Research design

The overall idea

The study of entrepreneurship in China's economic transition requires the analysis of institutional rules and their relations to various aspects of entrepreneurial behavior. The overall idea is to start by deriving some theoretical concepts that will guide the following empirical investigations. The empirical work will then proceed from a qualitative analysis of the national institutional environment to statistical presentation of the entrepreneurial process, focusing on entrepreneurs at the private sector as a whole group, then finally, to a few case studies for illustrating how the mechanisms developed previously work in concrete settings.

To be more specific, after the theoretical discussions in Chapters 2 and 3, the empirical work will start with an analytical survey of the institutional environment for entrepreneurship, especially the entrepreneurship in the private sector in Communist China. Such environment is consisted of different ideological forms, ranging from very general bottom-line principles held by the CCP and the government to detail-oriented regulations created by the State Council, and from spontaneous speeches made by individual political leaders to formal legal codes. I shall also discuss variations of local institutional environments as examples of both opportunities and constraints that every entrepreneur in China has to deal with. The term 'local' is used not only in its geographical sense; administratively, an institutional environment related to a lower bureaucratic level is also 'local'. Evidence for analyzing all of these will come from party and government documents, newspaper reports, research conducted by others, and case studies.

Data from national sample surveys

To understand entrepreneurs in China and their behaviours, a series of questions need to be answered: What are the demographic and socio-economic backgrounds of these entrepreneurs? What did they do before starting up their businesses? What were their motivations? Where did their initial capital come from? What kinds of products or services did they want to make and why? How did they obtain the elements necessary for setting up a new enterprise, such as raw materials, land, employees, information, clients, and technology? If they had any difficulty in this process, what did they do? How did they manage within their companies, such as decision-making, relations with employees, particularly welfare provisions, and the redistribution of profits? How did they manage their relations with organizations outside their companies, including the local authority, local residents, and the mass media? How much did they have to pay for maintaining a hassle-free relationship with local bureaucrats? How much did they contribute, either voluntarily or reluctantly, to public projects – road constructions, schools, hospitals, etc.? Where did they think they were in the society in terms of their political, economic, and social statuses? Did they want to increase their visibility in China's political life? If so, how? And so on.

To answer these questions I need to analyze data collected at the national level on entrepreneurs who have started up businesses outside the sectors dominated by the Chinese state. To my knowledge, *Survey of Private Business Owners* (*quan guo si ying qi ye chou yang diao cha*) is the sole research project that could provide the needed data. The surveys were organized and administered by a team of researchers affiliated with some of the most resourceful organizations in China, including The Institute of Sociology at Academy of Social Sciences, State Administration for Industry and Commerce (*guo jia gong shang zong ju*), All-China Federation of Industry and Commerce (*quan guo gong shang lian*), and The Department of United Front (*tong zhan bu*) of the CCP. These more or less state-supported organizations could not only mobilize sufficient financial and staffing support for conducting the survey but also have good access to the essential information for drawing the sample. Finally, selected respondents would find it very hard to turn down the request to participate in a survey administered by so many privileged organizations. This obviously will help ensure high response rates.

The first survey was carried out in 1993, followed by a survey about every two years, until 2002. I shall analyze the data from five surveys conducted in 1993, 1995, 1997, and 2000, respectively. Note that some questions refer to the situation of the previous year; for example, respondents in the 1993 survey were asked to report their financial situation in 1992. These repeated cross-sectional surveys kept some core questions to allow tracing of the trajectories of important aspects of the entrepreneurial process in China, such as the socio-economic origins of entrepreneurs, the access to bank loans for start-up capital, the nature and structure of ownership, and the relations of these enterprises with some political organizations. In the meantime, questions unique to each year's survey were also created in order to reflect the changing characteristics of entrepreneurs and institutional environments.

There are two major limitations of these data sets. First, the surveys did not start until 1993, one year after Deng Xiaoping's South China tour, in which he endorsed more liberal economic policies for achieving a higher speed of growth. Since then, the overall institutional environment has become much friendlier toward the private sector. Consequently, these data cannot be used for studying the difficult years for private entrepreneurs in China. The harsher institutional structure before 1992 and entrepreneurial strategies for dealing with the harshness will be part of the analysis carried out in Chapter 4, in which I shall review the historical development of institutional rules for entrepreneurship in China, and in the following case studies in Chapters 6, 7, and 8.

The second limitation is rather difficult to handle. Like many other surveys conducted in China, the published information about how these surveys were actually conducted is not enough for making a satisfactory assessment of the quality of the surveys and of the data collected from them. Here I simply point out a couple of problems that may influence the process of drawing substantive conclusions. The first question, perhaps the most important as well as the most difficult, is what constitutes the target population. For many years, even after Deng's speech in 1992, due to their illegitimate (controversial at best) status in China, private enterprises have been an illusive species. If a private enterprise can be understood as an economic organization that is financially owned by an individual or a group of individuals, then many companies in the name of town-and-village enterprises (TVE) are actually private. Also, there are many firms that are nominally affiliated with a state enterprise but actually private. In the end, organizers of the surveys could only study those private enterprises who were officially registered as such at the time each survey was conducted. Consequently, the coverage error could be very large – there could be a substantial number of actual private enterprises that were not included in the sampling frame.

Another problem is that the questionnaire was designed to be filled out by one person, which, as discussed before, raises the difficult issue of identifying an entrepreneur. Presumably, the person who provided the answers should be the entrepreneur who started the firm. A reading of the questionnaire leaves one with an impression, however, that the survey assumes that the respondent is the owner as well as the chief executive officer of the company. To what extent this is true is difficult to know. It should be safe to say that this may not be true for at least a small minority of the respondents, for example, if the respondent in charge of the firm at the time of the survey was an employed manager rather than the original entrepreneur. Or, the respondent might be the original entrepreneur, but at the time of the survey, he or she had delegated most of the routine managerial tasks to others and therefore might not be the right person to provide the details of the company's current situation. Still another possibility is that the firm was started by not one but a group of entrepreneurs, so the corresponding entrepreneur would not be able to represent the experience or report the characteristics of other entrepreneurs. Although the questionnaire did contain a question about the number of investors when the firm was initially established, the survey essentially assumes the leadership of a single entrepreneur. Some scholars have argued that such an individualist perspective should be put to rest and replaced with a collective one.[43] Again, this is a controversial issue – the entrepreneurs in the minds of the advocates of the collective perspective are mostly in the US; where the entrepreneurship in China stands in the continuum from individuality to collectivity will be a question for future research. Finally, the selection problem is always there for all studies on entrepreneurship in general and sample surveys in particular: those who have been selected into a survey have all been more or less successful, thus excluding those who have failed. This is a problem, however, not unique to studying entrepreneurs in China.

Comparative case studies

The limitations of survey data identified in the previous section go well beyond technical issues of sampling and questionnaire design. Although no one has called for a complete abandonment of the statistical analysis of survey data, many have suggested other approaches to studying social phenomena. The main charge is too much focus on variables rather than on cases[44] and their structural relations.[45] By definition, statistics is concerned with patterns emerging from a large number of cases; one does not need statistical methods if there are only a handful of cases. It should also be noted that some statistical tools, such as cluster analysis, *are* designed to study cases, although eventually they have to reply on information about some variables. A fundamental limitation of statistical analysis is its inability to reveal mechanisms that bring about the observed statistical relations.[46] In other words, 'variable-oriented' analysis describes relations by quantifying them without being able to answer why the relations exist in the first place.

I do not think that the alternative approaches mean to put statistical analysis to permanent rest. I would follow their suggestions in the case studies, but I don't think I could properly answer the questions that I raised at the beginning of the previous section without conducting some preliminary statistical analyses. Statistical analysis of survey data can offer a far more precise estimate of the magnitude of the interested

---

43 Claudia Bird Schoonhoven and Elaine Romanelli, 'Emergent Themes and the Next Wave of Entrepreneurship Research', pp. 383–408 in *The Entrepreneurship Dynamic*.

44 Charles C. Ragin contrasted the 'case-oriented comparative methods' with the 'variable-oriented approach' in *The Comparative Method: Moving Beyond Qualitative and Quantitative strategies* (Berkeley, Los Angeles, and London: University of California Press, 1987). David Byrne has followed this case-centered methodology by claiming 'Down to variables' and 'Up to complexities' in *Interpreting Quantitative Data* (London: Sage Publications, 2002) and by organizing the research program 'Focusing on the Case'.

45 Obviously, the now huge literature of network analysis, as both a method and a theoretical approach, has long been focusing on structural relations rather than variables, although statistical methods are still employed.

46 Peter Hedström and Richard Swedberg summarized the approach to focusing on social mechanisms as against to focusing on statistical associations in their introductory essay of *Social Mechanisms: An Analytical Approach to Social Theory* (Cambridge University Press, 1998).

phenomena, reveal patterns that cannot otherwise be detected when the number of cases involved is limited, and quantify the relations among interested factors for the perusal of substantive considerations. As Merton shrewdly advised,[47] establishing a target of research is something that needs to be done before any explanation can be made.

One big price that one has to pay for relying on statistics is the ignorance of the idiosyncrasies of some important cases. Quantitative studies usually answer 'what' and 'how much', rather than 'why' or 'how', questions. It is usually believed that the 'why' and 'how' questions are more important because they demand explanations by enquiring about the process or the mechanism of statistical quantities and associations. In this sense, case studies are ideal complements to statistical analysis.

Very likely a case is selected due to its importance or uniqueness, but that reduces its comparability with others. The study of this type of cases is 'intrinsic', as opposed to the 'instrumental' ones that are used only as a tool for understanding other cases or something more universal.[48] A case can also be used for developing and testing theories.[49] I would like to characterize the type of case studies that I will carry out as *mechanism-illustrations*. Although the cases themselves may turn out to be interesting to the reader, I analyze them mainly for the purpose of illustrating how certain mechanisms work in a particular context, not merely reporting the details of entrepreneurial experiences. In other words, they are fundamentally instrumental rather than intrinsic, but the instrumentality is about illustrating the working of specific mechanisms, not about suggesting or testing any theories. More specifically, the cases are meant to show when the interaction between double entrepreneurship and institutional holes, the two key concepts of this book to be discussed in Chapter 3, can or cannot work together in eventually shaping the fate of entrepreneurial ventures. Further, they are not used to develop theories because the theories have already been developed based on reviewing other theories; nor can they test the theories because of their limited capability of representing other cases due to their limited number and the way they have been selected. In short, the cases analyzed in this book are used to demonstrate the conditions under which the mechanism identified in theoretical discussions could operate, which is an approach much humbler than the ambition of developing causal mechanism theories based on the analytical study of cases.[50]

I will analyze three cases of entrepreneurs: Mrs. Huo Hongmin (founder of the Huaqi Group in the metropolitan city of Tianjin), Mr. Mou Qizhong (founder of

47 Robert K. Merton, 'Notes on Problem Finding in Sociology', reprinted in *Social Research and the Practice of Professions* (Cambridge, Massachusetts: Abt Books, 1982), pp. 17–42.

48 Robert Stake, *The Art of Case Study Research* (Sage Publications, 1995).

49 Michael Burawoy, et al., *Ethnography Unbound: Power and Resistance in the Modern Metropolis* (Berkeley: University of California Press, 1991).

50 Alexander L. George and Andrew Bennett, *Case Studies and Theory Development in the Social Sciences* (MIT Press, 2005). Although I find many useful guiding principles and methods for conducting case studies in this book, I am still not sure whether they have successfully established a solid foundation for explaining social phenomena with causal mechanisms.

the Nande Group in Sichuan Province and later in Beijing), and Mr. Xu Wenrong (founder of the Hengdian Group in Zhejiang Province).

Strategic considerations have played a bigger role than convenience in selecting the cases. At the beginning, convenience was at work for selecting the Huaqi, in which I worked as a part-time marketing consultant for more than a year, a good opportunity for learning the experience of the entrepreneur and some critical events. As shown with details in Chapter 6, Huaqi's initial success was later spoiled in a dispute with some state bureaucrats. This event, dubbed as the 'Huaqi Affair' in the media, has led me to think about a more general question: How far would the Chinese State allow an entrepreneur to go in pursuing financial profits? Or, where can we find the boundaries for entrepreneurship set by institutional rules? I did not believe that Mrs. Huo had gone close enough to the boundaries because I was aware of some much more daring entrepreneurs at that time.

There were several daring entrepreneurs whose stories were featured in the media in the 1980s, such as Shi Yuzhu, Liu Yonghao, and Mou Qizhong. In terms of innovatively exploiting the opportunities in China's changing institutional environment, I believe Mou was without peer. Through some personal connections, I managed to conduct some interviews and collect some documents in the company before Mou was put in jail and the company was shut down in May 2000.

The study of this case is in line with Harry Eckstein's method of crucial case study.[51] This method focuses on the cases that are extreme in pertinent dimensions so that they become either least-likely or most-likely cases. The underlying logic is that, once this case is properly understood, all other cases can be easily understood as their extensions. Following such logic, I pick up the case of Mou because his experience can most clearly show the extreme strategies of taking advantage of institutional change. In other words, this case is crucial in the sense that, if he is not entrepreneurial enough, then it would be extremely difficult to find any entrepreneurs in contemporary China. In this case, what the institutional environment in China would and would not offer should become clear once Mou's experience is properly presented, because he has gone much further than most of the entrepreneurs would dare to go in making use of institutional rules.

This method of focusing on crucial cases is not without risks, however. First, such cases are selected not at all because they could represent 'an average entrepreneur', if indeed there is such a person, or the whole group of entrepreneurs in China. The cases have been selected not as 'typical entrepreneurs' or 'example enterprises'. Second, such cases are selected for the purpose of demonstrating rather than testing the proposed concepts and theories. It would demand a much refined design to carry out a rigorous test. Third, crucial case studies involve a risky bet on the results. If the findings run counter to expectations, it will be difficult to decide whether we should change our original expectations or select some other cases. In practice, this depends on what cases we come up with and how convincing they are in changing our current theories.

---

51 Eckstein, Harry, 'Case Study and Theory in Political Science', in F.I. Greenstein and N.W. Polsby (eds), *The Handbook of Political Science* (Reading: Addison-Wesley, 1975), pp. 79–138.

A major consideration in selecting these particular cases is that they supplement each other quite well at some points. The cases of Huo and Mou seem to share a similar trajectory: the identification of opportunities in the market as well as in the changing rules of doing business in China led to remarkable success during the early period of their business career, but the expansion of business also brought them closer to the sensitive nerves of state bureaucrats. The two cases diverged, however, into different directions in the middle of their life courses, with Mou's business eventually being terminated by state officials, while Huo survived after making some efforts of mending up her relations with them.

Neither was a story of complete success, which very likely leaves the reader wondering to what extent theirs could represent the experience of a 'typical' entrepreneur in China. Again, I don't know how typical they are, and I don't think anyone else knows, because no information is available for comparing these two cases with other entrepreneurs, particularly those whose businesses were shut down in the end. On the other hand, there are many successful stories both in the media and in academic reports. Therefore, it is desirable to select and analyze a successful case in order to at least indicate the conditions under which some entrepreneurs in China could survive the vicissitudes of their relations with the State with no serious setbacks and achieve sustained growth.

The case I selected in the end is Xu Wenrong, the entrepreneur who started from a small factory as the leader of a remote village in Zhejiang but now controls Hengdian Group, a multi-billion yuan business. So far, the enterprise has enjoyed nearly uninterrupted growth, good relations with local officials, and positive coverage by the media. This case also serves a good comparison with the case of Yu Zuomin, whose story has been much more researched by scholars in the west.[52] Yu is an entrepreneur who is no less successful than Xu on the one hand, while his fate is no less disastrous than Mou's on the other hand. These similarities and dissimilarities between these cases will suggest some interesting insights of how entrepreneurship works while China's institutional infrastructure is undergoing dramatic change. Finally, a practical considerations of studying this case is the existence of a large amount of secondary sources of information, indispensable for my analysis when my access to the entrepreneur was limited.

My objective is to write an analytical case study of each entrepreneur, and I have no intention whatsoever of praising them as China's economic heroes. Following Schumpeter, I hope my analysis 'does not involve any "glorification" of the type'.[53] Rather, these cases are presented to show that, in responding to changing institutional environment, entrepreneurs in China did not faithfully follow the path set forth by state policies. What they actually did was to explore and exploit the opportunities embedded in the environment, and if there were no opportunities, they simply went

---

52 There are many reports and studies on the Yu case published in Chinese. Two major studies in English are: Nan Lin, 'Local Market Socialism: Local Corporatism in Action in Rural China', *Theory and Society*, 24 (1995): 301–54. Bruce Gilley, *Model Rebels.*

53 Joseph Schumpeter, *The Theory of Economic Development*, 2nd edition (Cambridge: Harvard University Press, [1926] 1934), p. 90.

ahead to create one. What was particularly entrepreneurial was their imagination and bravery in their actions.

Outline of the book

In this chapter I have presented the central questions that I would like to answer in this book: Where do the opportunities for entrepreneurship come from in China? And how could the entrepreneurs survive and even thrive in a constraining institutional environment, particularly at the early stages of the China's economic reform? I have searched for answers to these questions in area studies on China, institutional economics, entrepreneurship studies, and economic sociology. My ideas and analysis will draw heavily on these studies.

In Chapters 2 and 3 I try to lay a theoretical foundation for the following empirical studies. Chapter 2 is a critical review of the relevant theories and studies, explaining why I don't think the issues in understanding China's economic development have been settled. What has puzzled me is essentially the missing link between the dominant theories in economics and sociology when I put them to the context of China's economic development. Institutional theories, such as that advocated by Douglas North in economics, or those promoted by Paul DiMaggio and Walter Powell and later by Mary Brinton and Victor Nee in sociology, have successfully established the important function of institutional rules in shaping human behaviours and social structures. The question is, if institutional rules are so important in bringing about economic development, this would imply that economic development would not be on a fast track until institutional structures have been put into a proper shape. But this is not what has happened in China. China has put all other countries behind in terms of the rate of economic growth for several decades now, but the economic and political institutions are still far from 'appropriate' in the eyes of institutional theorists. As discussed in the early parts of this chapter, if entrepreneurs are the key players in developing China's economic potential, we have to ask why entrepreneurs, especially those working in the non-state sectors, could set up so many businesses when so many state policies were so immature and hostile? The importance of entrepreneurship in economic development and its institutional conditions have been best theorized and argued by Joseph Schumpeter. Therefore, the ultimate objective of Chapter 2 is to identify the gap between institutional theories and theories of entrepreneurship. Studies of entrepreneurship, albeit offering great details of how some key factors in the entrepreneurial process contribute to entrepreneurial success, take the well functioning of institutional environment for granted. Opposite to such business-school type of analysis is the institutionalist argument which attempts to show that every entrepreneurial action is meant to signal legitimacy. In Chapter 2 I will identify the assumptions and limitations of each group of theories, and then show that such theoretical confrontation is unproductive and demands a coherent connection between the two.

The task of Chapter 3 is to develop a theory that could bridge the gap between the business theory of entrepreneurship and the institutionalist theory. I have found Ronald Burt's theory of structural holes very useful in understanding the sources of entrepreneurial opportunities. Disappointingly, however, he seems to have no serious interest in incorporating features of institutional environment into his structural theory of entrepreneurship. The purpose of this chapter is to extend Burt's theory in order to obtain a generalized structural theory of entrepreneurship, in which structural characteristics of institutional rules are essential components. This is done by generalizing three assumptions implicitly embedded in Burt's theory: (1) The reason that A is isolated from B is a trivial matter; (2) Non-redundant connections will be necessarily complementary; (3) For the entrepreneur, constraints on making connections with A and B are insignificant. Then the twin concepts of institutional holes and double entrepreneurship are developed. Double entrepreneurship incorporates two dimensions: an entrepreneur has to be innovative in both identifying (or creating) a promising market and to be talented in making use of institutional rules. Institutional holes are structural gaps between at least two organizations that are located in respectively different institutional fields and are in control of potentially complementary resources for a future business enterprise.

Chapters 4 and 5 analyze entrepreneurship in China at the national level. Chapter 4 is the empirical extension of the previous theoretical analysis of institutional holes. It demonstrates the construction and reconstruction of institutional rules in economic reforms, which are the very sources of institutional holes. Starting with a vision great but vague, the reformers would like to 'cross the river by touching the stones', a process that cultivates institutional flexibility as a mechanism of promoting business entrepreneurship. This mechanism is illustrated by brief but analytical history of ideological principles and state regulations on private businesses.

Chapter 5 then moves on to the analysis of the entrepreneurial process in China. How do entrepreneurs in China respond to the double demand of institutional legitimacy and economic profitability, and to the opportunities in institutional holes? This chapter answers these questions by looking at how entrepreneurs deal with the following issues: obtaining starting-up capital, recruiting and managing employees, maintaining a good relationship with local authorities, etc. Analyzing the data collected from Survey of Private Business Owners, this chapter firstly depicts a profile of entrepreneurs in reform China and then presents the effects of a variety of factors on the success and failure of private enterprises during the entrepreneurial process, including financial situation, social relations, and political affiliations.

In Chapters 6, 7, and 8, I present an analysis of each of the three cases to show what entrepreneurs actually do – the practice of double entrepreneurship in exploiting institutional holes. I shall also point out the risks and traps in this whole process. Mrs. Huo's story in Chapter 6 will exemplify the near impossibility of always being able to get out of the trap, especially when state officials in charge of institutional rules are ready to prey on budding entrepreneurs. In the confrontation between Mrs. Huo's beverage firm and the officials of the National Bureau of Technology Supervision, we can see how the trajectory of an entrepreneur's business life course can be determined by the levels of profitability and legitimacy. Details of original correspondence between Mrs. Huo and state officials, including records of conversations and letters, will be presented in support of the narrative.

Chapter 7 shows that double entrepreneurship and the exploitation of institutional holes are risky business. The story of Mou Qizhong is an ideal example of how entrepreneurs in China have manipulated institutional changes. Obviously, this is hardly representative of most private business entrepreneurs in China. But, that is exactly the function this case can perform – it tells us where the institutional limits are. Stories about Mou's innovative business theories (the fourth industry, the one-degree theory, steady tillering, etc.) and amazing transactions (desk clocks, Russian airplane project, satellite project, special economic zones, etc.) not only document the strategies entrepreneurs in China could use but also illustrate the potential risks in playing with institutional holes.

Chapter 8 presents the success story about Mr. Xu Wenrong, the founder of the Hengdian Group. It not only illustrates how industrial enterprises took off in rural China but also how the success has depended upon the firm's relations with local communities and governments. In short, in this case we can find some of the conditions under which double entrepreneurship can successfully and safely rip the benefits of institutional holes.

It is always necessary to recap previous points in the last chapter, but I will try to do a bit more by highlighting the context of entrepreneurship, discussing the effects entrepreneurship has made on the Chinese society as a whole, and pointing out the challenges facing the next generation of entrepreneurs in China.

Chapter 2

Rules and Entrepreneurship

China's recent experience, as we have seen, involves a fundamental tension between entrepreneurship's rule-breaking nature and institution's reduction of uncertainty in economic development. How can any economic system, including China's, reconcile entrepreneurial innovation with institutional continuity? Given the enormous weight of China's existing institutions, how has the robust growth of entrepreneurship been possible? There are at least two possibilities: first, that China's institutions actually and surprisingly promote entrepreneurship; second, that entrepreneurs have somehow bypassed the resistance built into China's political and economic institutions. This chapter will lay out the background for concluding that the second is more likely.

What makes entrepreneurship in China an interesting case is the resilient and rapid development of entrepreneurial ventures, *despite* a changing, unstable, and even hostile institutional environment. It suggests that there be no presumed connection between any institutional structure and entrepreneurship. Therefore, we need to clearly identify and then to bridge the theoretical gap in between the entrepreneurial approach, of which Joseph Schumpeter is widely acknowledged as the foremost representative, and the institutionalist one, of which Douglas North has been a leading advocate. To establish a useful and plausible connection is the task of the next chapter.

Making comparison and contrast arguments based on the ideas of a single theorist for each perspective runs the risk of simplification, but I hope that the reader will find it strategic and meaningful. First, this strategy keeps my analysis focused. Next, North and Schumpeter share the common goal of explaining economic development, which provides a basis for making meaningful comparisons. Furthermore, both Schumpeter and North have attempted to bring the favourite variable of the other perspective into their own analysis but eventually failed to complete the mission – the status of the other's variable is only marginal at best. Some economists have long recognized the gap between these two approaches,[1] but focused analyses that integrate the uneasy relationship between entrepreneurship and institutional rules in

---

1 James Buchanan urged economists to include both entrepreneurship and rules in economic analysis back in 1979 (*What Should Economists Do?*, Indianapolis, IN: Liberty Press, pp. 281–282). Recently, Dan Johansson points out the 'dual lacunae' of entrepreneurship and institution by analyzing the key words of textbooks used in PhD economics programmes in Sweden ('Economics without Entrepreneurship or Institutions: A Vocabulary Analysis of Graduate Textbooks', *Econ Journal Watch*, 1(3) (2004): 515–538). Such 'dual lacunae', however, does not touch on the more serious problem discussed here: economists will have to face the challenge of integrating entrepreneurship and institutions even after they fill in the 'dual lacunae'.

a single conceptual framework remain rare. I will, however, consider some theories and studies that have suggested useful ways of bridging the gap in the later sections of this chapter.

Do entrepreneurs follow rules?

Schumpeter has been identified as '*the* main figure in the literature on entrepreneurship'[2] and entrepreneurship as a field of research:

> has borrowed a great deal from Schumpeter, but the field has also forgotten much of what he proposed ... Today, few academic researchers studying entrepreneurship refer to Schumpeter, and fewer still actually use his ideas to study the creation of new enterprises.[3]

To me, the sharp discontinuity between Schumpeter's original ideas and later developments in entrepreneurship as an academic discipline can be easily explained away with two reasons. First, what Schumpeter achieved was establishing the role of entrepreneurship as a driving force of economic development within the economic system. After Schumpeter, that has become a common sense. Second, Schumpeter was one of the last few grand theorists, asking big 'why' and 'what' questions. Today's professional researchers, particularly those in business schools, care much more about practical procedures that work for nascent entrepreneurs and venture capitalists, trying to answer specific 'how' questions.

Interestingly enough, these explanations point to a direction in which we could expand Schumpeter's legacy. Whilst the importance of entrepreneurship in economic development has been established, it is not so obvious how entrepreneurs deal with changing institutional rules, because economic development is essentially a process of transforming rules of the game. In my view, we should go back to Schumpeter for understanding this grand 'how' question. To put this discussion in context, however, I shall start by briefly reviewing some of his general ideas.

Entrepreneurship and economic change

We now know that Schumpeter's theory of entrepreneurship originated from his dissatisfaction of Léon Walras's explanation of economic change.[4] To Walras, economic equilibrium is the normal situation because an economic system is self-sustained by the market. Therefore, the move from one equilibrium to another can only come from the forces external to the system, such as population change, technological inventions, war, etc. Although Schumpeter didn't completely dismiss

---

2   Swedberg, 'Introduction' to *Entrepreneurship: The Social Science View* (Oxford University Press, 2000), p. 12, emphasis original.

3   Howard Aldrich, 'Entrepreneurship', in Neil Smelser and Richard Swedberg (eds), *The Handbook of Economic Sociology*, 2nd edition (Princeton University Press and Russell Sage Foundation, 2005), pp. 454–455.

4   Richard Swedberg, 'The Man and His Work', 'Introduction' to Richard Swedberg (ed.), *The Economics and Sociology of Capitalism* (Princeton University Press, 1991), p. 39.

this model, he 'felt very strongly that this was wrong and that there was a source of energy within the economic system which would of itself disrupt any equilibrium that might be attained'.[5] Schumpeter, however, did not do much justification for such a big conceptual leap – why has there to be an internal force, or why cannot an economic equilibrium move to a next one when only external forces exist? Schumpeter's insight was very important, but it came abruptly; in other words, he pointed out an alternative possibility – a different theory of economic change – without explaining why it has to be the case.

There is another question about Walras's theory, which, I think, is even more fundamental than explaining economic change: where does the economic equilibrium come from in the first place? To resort to market mechanisms is too structural a point of view because the market is essentially a set of principles and rules with regard to how transactions should be made. These principles and rules themselves need an explanation before they could explain economic equilibrium. Something is still missing to connect the employment of market principles and rules to the eventual realization of economic equilibrium. Schumpeter focused his attention on explaining the change of economic equilibrium, but he could have offered a more powerful theory of not only economic change but also economic equilibrium *per se*: entrepreneurship is the actual agent of pushing economic transactions to an equilibrium, because economic equilibrium prerequisites the production of commodities and the organization of commodity exchanges.

For now, let's stay with the theoretical focus of his own. To Schumpeter, the dynamics of Western capitalism lies in its capacity of 'incessantly destroying the old one [economic structure], incessantly creating a new one'.[6] And the causes of such 'creative destruction' function[7] should not be searched from outside the economic system under study because 'we shall understand only such changes in economic life as are not forced upon it from without but arise by its own initiative, from within'.[8] Schumpeter then identified entrepreneurs as the agents who carried out this changing function. Entrepreneurs may not possess any special intellectual gift, nor do they have to be technological inventors, but they must exercise 'practical initiative' in combining various resources and organizing producers. The primary function of the entrepreneur 'is deciding what to do and how to do it' rather than doing it.[9] Five representations of the entrepreneurial function were identified: producing a new commodity, introducing a new production method, opening a new market, acquiring a new source of supply, and reorganizing an industry.[10]

---

5   Joseph Schumpeter, 'Preface to Japanese Translation of *Theorie der Wirtschaftlichen Entwicklung*', quoted in Swedberg (ed.), *The Economics and Sociology of Capitalism*, p. 39.

6   Joseph Schumpeter, *Capitalism, Socialism and Democracy* (New York: Harper and Row, 1942 [1975]), p. 83.

7   Ibid., pp. 81–86.

8   Joseph Schumpeter, *The Theory of Economic Development*, 2nd edition (Cambridge: Harvard University Press, [1926] 1934), p. 63.

9   Frank Knight, *Risk, Uncertainty and Profit* (Boston, Mass.: Houghton Mifflin, 1921), p. 268.

10   Schumpeter, *Capitalism, Socialism, and Democracy*, p. 132.

Researchers have discovered a significant change in Schumpeter's understanding of entrepreneurship. For example, Richard Swedberg noted that:

> while entrepreneurship had been described in terms of creativity and intuition in the first edition of *The Theory of Economic Development* (1911), Schumpeter now [in the second edition of the book] spoke of entrepreneurship in a considerably more technical and dispassionate manner. Innovation, which the young Schumpeter in 1911 had described in a nearly dionaysian manner, had now become more apollonian in nature, and it is simply defined in *Business Cycles* as 'the setting up of a new production function (Schumpeter, 1939: 87).[11]

More recently, Markus Becker and Thorbjørn Knudsen, while making the first English translation of Schumpeter's article 'Entrepreneur',[12] firmly and systematically established the depersonalization of entrepreneurship in Schumpeter's changing conceptions. Schumpeter's notion, and consequently, the focus of his analysis, has changed from the entrepreneur as a person of unusual will and power to the entrepreneurial function that is disconnected from any particular individuals.[13] This conceptual change is significant in the sense that the personal and psychological characteristics of the entrepreneur have become much less important than the entrepreneur's actions. Previously, the chain of explanation is from personal attributes to entrepreneurial behaviours, and finally to new products and businesses. Later, Schumpeter shortened the chain by focusing only on behaviour and new ventures, putting the entrepreneur's personal attributes to the background. As the 'essence of the entrepreneurial function lies in recognizing and carrying out new possibilities in the economic sphere',[14] anyone who can deliver the 'new possibilities' is an entrepreneur. The five major representations of the entrepreneurial functions, however, remain the same.

Entrepreneurship as a mechanism

Besides the contrast between personality and function, there is another distinction that Schumpeter emphasized in his work, which is related to the previous distinction and of no less importance. By seeing entrepreneurship as a function of recombining resources for achieving new business possibilities, Schumpeter actually treated entrepreneurship as a mechanism rather than a contributing factor in the dynamics of economic development. Schumpeter was eager to remind his readers that his theory 'is not at all concerned with the concrete factors of change, but with the method by which these work, with the *mechanism of change*. The "entrepreneur" is

---

11 Swedberg, 'Introduction' to *Entrepreneurship*, p. 15.

12 Joseph Schumpeter, 'Entrepreneur', translated by Markus C. Becker and Thorbjørn Knudsen. *Austrian Economics and Entrepreneurial Studies, Advances in Austrian Economics*, 6 (2003): 235–265.

13 Becker and Knudson, 'The Entrepreneur at a Crucial Juncture in Schumpeter's Work: Schumpeter's 1928 Handbook Entry *Entrepreneur*', *Austrian Economics and Entrepreneurial Studies, Advances in Austrian Economics*, 2003, 6: 199–233.

14 Schumpeter, 'Entrepreneur', p. 250.

merely the bearer of the mechanism of change'.[15] The notion that entrepreneurship is a mechanism of economic change, albeit embodied in the entrepreneur as a human being, was emphasized in his later works. In 'Comments on a Plan for the Study of Entrepreneurship', a lecture delivered in 1947 at the Economic History Association, he claimed that 'What else it may be, enterprise is essentially part of the mechanism of economic change'.[16] It is extremely important for economists to study the role of entrepreneurship because 'the mechanisms of economic change in capitalist society pivot certainly on entrepreneurial activity'.[17] Two years later, in 1949, he again came back to this idea of entrepreneurship as a mechanism:

> We can then attempt to construct an analytic model of the mechanism of economic change or else, for different countries and periods, different such schemata or models ... What we observe is rather a behaviour pattern, possibly supplemented by a schema of motivation; a typical way of giving effect to the possibilities inherent in a given legal and social system both of which change in the process; the effects of entrepreneurial activity upon the industrial structure that exists at any moment; the consequent process of destruction and reconstruction that went on all the time. All these things may be conceptualized in a more or less complicated schema, every item of which has to be nourished with facts and corrected and amplified under their influence. And this is all.[18]

To Schumpeter, the mechanism approach is so important that it should be followed not only for the study of entrepreneurship but for economics as a whole. The discipline is 'the interpretive description of economic mechanisms that play within any given state of those institutions [studied by economic sociology], such as market mechanisms'.[19] In analytical terms, the shift from personal attributes as factors to the entrepreneurial process as a mechanism is a significant progress. Factors could be of a variety of types, and what they could most effectively prove is associations, no matter how sophisticated they are. In contrast, mechanisms constitute the process of change.

Nevertheless, Schumpeter did not elaborate on how the entrepreneurship mechanism works. First, as Hedtröm and Swedberg point out, a mechanism must have an input and an output.[20] We know that the output of Schumpeter's mechanism is new business possibilities, created by combining available resources. It is not clear, however, what the input is. If the input is not the personal characteristics of the entrepreneur, then we need to know the conditions needed for entrepreneurship to work. Even more specifically, the opportunity for the entrepreneurship function to

---

15 Schumpeter, *Theory*, p. 60, emphasis original.

16 Schumpeter, 'Comments on a Plan for the Study of Entrepreneurship', p. 408.

17 Ibid., p. 412.

18 Schumpeter, 'Economic Theory and Entrepreneurial History', reprinted from *Change and the Entrepreneur*, pp. 63–84 in Richard V. Clemence (ed.), *Essays on Entrepreneurs, Innovations, Business Cycles, and the Evolution of Capitalism* (Addison-Wesley, 1949 [1951]), p. 266. Reprinted from *Change and the Entrepreneur*, pp. 63–84.

19 Ibid., p. 293.

20 Peter Hedtröm and Richard Swedberg, 'Social Mechanisms: An Introductory Essay', in Peter Hedtröm and Richard Swedberg (eds), *Social Mechanisms: An Analytical Approach to Social Theory* (Cambridge University Press, 1998), pp. 1–31.

arise needs to be identified. To some extent, Schumpeter did address the supporting conditions for entrepreneurship, which I shall discuss in detail soon, but he only touched the question in some very general terms. Second, as all theorists in favour of the mechanism approach have pointed out,[21] a mechanism is in between universal laws and *ad hoc* stories. As a 'sometimes true' theory, a mechanism has a middle range of generality as well as application. Schumpeter never specified the boundaries of generalization of the entrepreneurship mechanism, nor did he provide a systematic discussion of the conditions under which the mechanism will, or will not, work. It is quite clear, however, that the importance of these questions was very much in Schumpeter's mind. This is most clearly represented in his historical approach to the analysis of entrepreneurship:

> In the enterprise economy the entrepreneur will inevitably exert some influence on things in general; hence the study of his interests, positions, and so on necessarily constitutes one of the possible approaches to an understanding of economic history or even of history in general.[22]

Therefore, in his late career, Schumpeter became more interested in *the interaction* between entrepreneurship and its historical conditions than in entrepreneurship itself. For future researchers of entrepreneurship, Schumpeter made it extremely clear that '[t]he interaction of institutional forms and entrepreneurial activity – the "shaping" influence of the former and the "bursting" influence of the latter – is, as has already been stated, a major topic for further inquiry'.[23] On the one hand, he urged researchers of entrepreneurship to carefully investigate 'into the conditions that call forth, favour, impede entrepreneurial activity', which is 'an essential part of the plan and may conceivably produce its most valuable results'.[24] He then listed some conditions studied by J.S. Mill and Alfred Marshall, including location, physical properties of the environment, social organization, 'good government', freedom, and racial qualities, to which he then added inflation, wars, religion, taxation, and administrative protection. On the other hand, because he saw entrepreneurship as the eventual driving force of economic change, it became natural for him to emphasize the importance of analyzing the extent to which 'entrepreneurial activity impresses the stamp of its mentality upon the social organism'.[25] Seen in this light, Schumpeter's theory of entrepreneurship is more than taking entrepreneurship as a driving force of economic change through setting up new businesses. As a new way of thinking and organizing economic activities, entrepreneurship will show its effect of shaping current beliefs, practices, and norms. In short, entrepreneurship is the source of revolutionary change in institutional terms as well. I believe this is one of Schumpeter's most important legacies.

---

21 See the essays in Hedtröm and Swedberg (eds), *Social Mechanisms*.
22 Schumpeter, 'Economic Theory and Entrepreneurial History', p. 268.
23 Schumpeter, 'Comments on a Plan for the Study of Entrepreneurship', p. 414.
24 Ibid., p. 409.
25 Ibid., p. 270.

Schumpeter's flirtation with institutional rules

No matter how strongly he urged others to study the interactive relationship between history and entrepreneurship, Schumpeter himself is famous for a theory lopsided to the side of entrepreneurship. In order to restore the balance between the two, we need to find out where Schumpeter has left only a light touch of historical conditions in general and institutional structures in particular. To make my analysis focused and to dovetail this part nicely to the rest of this chapter, I take institutional rules of entrepreneurship as a representing piece of historical conditions.

When we bring institutional rules into Schumpeter's theory of entrepreneurship, we start to gather a sense that the role of entrepreneurship has become more and more marginal. As pointed out in the previous discussion, accompanied to Schumpeter's conceptual shift from the entrepreneur as a person to entrepreneurship as a function was an analytical transfer from seeing entrepreneurship as a factor to a mechanism. Although he didn't explicitly define what he meant by mechanism, it should be clear that he used mechanism interchangeably with procedures of change. There is no doubt that the mechanism is indispensable for making new combinations possible. For example, business opportunities will not be realized without the entrepreneurial function – 'in capitalist society objective opportunities or conditions act *through* entrepreneurial activity'.[26] But, it is also doubtless that something behind the mechanism (by Schumpeter's implicit understanding) is more fundamental than the mechanism itself. What does the agent of entrepreneurship represent? Whose effects does it carry? What was in Schumpeter's mind seemed to be the general institutional environment of entrepreneurship. If this understanding is correct, for which I will provide some supporting evidence below, then the depersonalization of entrepreneurship from a heroic individual to functions makes the entrepreneur subjective to institutional arrangements.

I think that Schumpeter had two understandings of institutions, one narrow and the other broad. The narrow understanding refers to specific organizations and concrete procedures that entrepreneurs have to encounter and deal with throughout the whole process of establishing new business ventures, including financial and taxation institutions,[27] governments, property inheritance, regulations of contract, and so on.[28] If the distinguishing quality of entrepreneurship is to get new things done, then the things are new not only in terms of organizing a business but more importantly new to current routines, practices, assumptions, and institutional rules as well. Therefore, Schumpeter was clearly aware of the entrepreneur's liability of newness, which was later systematically elaborated by Stinchcombe, 'to cope with the resistances and difficulties with which action always meets outside of the ruts of established practice'.[29]

---

26 Ibid., p. 412, emphasis original.

27 Schumpeter, *Theory*, pp. 86–87.

28 Schumpeter included these 'social institutions' when he defined the scope of economic sociology in *History of Economic Analysis* (Allen & Unwin, 1954), p. 21.

29 Schumpeter, 'Comments on a Plan for the Study of Entrepreneurship', p. 413.

By contrast, institutions in the broader sense include social customs,[30] established practices,[31] or the so-called 'social climate'.[32] Benjamin Higgins offered a concise presentation of Schumpeter's notion of 'social climate':

> a complex phenomenon reflecting the whole social, political, and socio-psychological atmosphere within which entrepreneurs must operate. It would include the social values of a particular country at a particular time, the class structure, the educational system, and the like. It would certainly include the attitude of society towards business success, and the nature and extent of the prestige and other social rewards, apart from profits, which accompany business success in the society. A particularly important factor in "climate" is the entrepreneur's understanding of the "rules of the game", the conditions under which he must operate. Sudden changes in the rules of the game are particularly deleterious to an increasing flow of enterprise.[33]

It should be obvious that such 'social climate' will affect the supply of entrepreneurs, but that does not say very much because the concept vaguely includes almost everything that is either hostile or friendly to the entrepreneurial behaviour. Therefore, we need to find out which components in the climate are hostile and which are friendly. According to Higgins, Schumpeter provided some indicators or 'thermometers', including distribution of income, rationalization, democratization, legal and political impediments, social ostracism, and so on. But these are barely better than the above general definition – not only are terms like rationalization still too vague to be useful but also it still remains unclear *how* each component of social climate works in either promoting or impeding the emergence and growth of entrepreneurial ventures. The analytical progress of bringing in the effect of institutional environment has been achieved at the price of making the whole analysis much less tractable.

But by now it should be extremely clear that Schumpeter's theory is not one that exclusively focuses on the function of entrepreneurship. He repeatedly rejected the interpretation that *The Theory of Economic Development* viewed economic development as a result of entrepreneurship alone. For him, entrepreneurship is only one half of the whole story of economic development. The other half is institutional conditions, a critical point that, unfortunately, was not developed very much during his lifetime. He claimed that:

> the entrepreneur's role is to be investigated because it constitutes an avenue to the study of economic change and besides, presents many interesting problems, but not because there

---

30 Schumpeter, *Theory*, p. 87.

31 Schumpeter, 'Comments on a Plan for the Study of Entrepreneurship', p. 413.

32 Schumpeter, *Business Cycles: A Theoretical, Historical, and Statistical Analysis of the Capitalist Process* (New York: McGraw-Hill, 1939; reprinted by Porcupine Press, 1982), vol. 1, pp. 30–35.

33 Benjamin Higgins, *Economic Development: Principles, Problems, and Policies*, revised edition (W. W. Norton and Company, 1968), p. 94. Note that such an understanding of the institutional environment for entrepreneurship includes exactly what later Douglas North will pay special attention: 'rules of the game'.

is a theory *a limine* to the effect that entrepreneurship is the motive power or creation of "economic progress".[34]

Therefore, Vacchi is correct in pointing out that 'analyzing the entrepreneur is subordinate to his theory of economic change and only when the latter does the former retain the meaning which Schumpeter intended.'[35] The intrinsic feature of a rigorous capitalism, for Schumpeter, is an interactive, dynamic relationship between innovative behaviours and supporting institutions. During the entrepreneurial process – from the moment of recognizing an opportunity to the realization of profits, the entrepreneur has to constantly resort to technicians, state officials, suppliers, employees, and distributors, each of which is located in a different institutional setting. However, analysis on these groups and the institutional rules that govern their relations with the entrepreneur is perhaps the weakest part of Schumpeter's whole theoretical edifice.

Thus, it makes good sense to note that, while searching for the most hospitable social climate for entrepreneurship, Schumpeter started an enterprise that later Douglas North and other institutionalist economists will be operating: the search for an optimal, if not the best, institutional structure for economic development.

What are the optimal rules for entrepreneurship?

The importance of rules

With Schumpeter, Douglas North shares the interest in understanding and explaining economic development, or economic change in general. More importantly, both have identified and emphasized the importance of the interaction between entrepreneurship and institutional environment. We have seen how Schumpeter reached this point in previous discussions. The following arguments by North are in absolute agreement with Schumpeter's:

> It is the interaction between institutions and organizations that shapes the institutional evolution of an economy. If institutions are the rules of the game, organizations and their entrepreneurs are the players.[36]

Nevertheless, both of them have never been fully committed to focusing on the *interaction* – while Schumpeter devoted much of his attention to entrepreneurship, North has devoted his almost exclusively to institutions. Although Schumpeter made a strong proposal of combining economic, sociological, statistical and historical perspectives for analyzing entrepreneurial behaviours, the change of institutions and their connections to economic performance were not what he was truly interested in. I understand that North has emphasized institutions so strongly because he

---

34 Schumpeter, 'Comments on a Plan for the Study of Entrepreneurship', p. 409.

35 Nicoló De Vecchi and Anne Stone, *Entrepreneurs, Institutions, and Economic Change: The Economic Thought of J.A. Schumpeter (1905–1925)* (Edward Elgar, 1995), p. 17.

36 Douglas North, 'Economic Performance Through Time', *American Economic Review*, 84/3 (1994): 361.

takes a much broader view of economic change. The scope of his analysis is as vast as covering all societies throughout the entire human history. The study of entrepreneurship is simply far from being able to help explain the huge variation of economic performance across so many societies and so long a historical period. But, the enormous scope of North's theory enables it to shed light on economic development of a particular country at a particular time. In short, the two theorists' shared interest in the interaction of entrepreneurship and institutions make the comparison of their theories possible and meaningful.

I must present North's definition of institutions before moving further, which does not differ very much from Schumpeter's. Recall that Schumpeter would see values, norms, social attitudes, and supporting organizations all as institutions that entrepreneurs will have to deal with. North focuses on rules as well, both formal and informal, but he explicitly excludes organizations from his definition. To North, institutions are:

> the rules of the game in a society or, more formally, are the human devised constraints that shape human interaction. In consequence they structure incentives in human exchange, whether political, social, or economic.[37]

In explaining economic development or different levels of economic performance, Schumpeter was searching for a carrier or an internal driving force of economic development, but North has paid much of his attention directly to the rules that the carrier and other economic players have to comply with.[38] In other words, a key difference between the two theoretical approaches is that, although Schumpeter attempted to incorporate institutional rules in his theory of entrepreneurship, most of the times the rules play only a supporting, and thus minor, role in entrepreneurial ventures, while North sees the rules the most fundamental because all economic activities will have to follow the tracks set up by the rules.

To North and many other institutionalist economists, rules are so important because they can reduce transaction costs, which occur in the process of measuring, specifying, monitoring, and enforcing contracts. Contracts are rules that regulate relations of economic entities with different property rights. Assuming that property rights are the foremost important interests for all economic players, rules about property rights thus become the most important. Institutions vary in terms of their effectiveness in clarifying and regulating property rights, which is measured by the ratio of the amount of transaction costs given the institutions to that without the

---

37 Douglas North, *Institutions, Institutional Change, and Economic Performance* (Cambridge University Press, 1990), p. 3. He offered a very similar definition in *Structure and Change in Economic History* (W.W. Norton and Co., 1981: 201–202): 'Institutions are a set of rules, compliance procedures, and moral and ethical behavioural norms designed to constrain the behaviour of individuals in the interests of maximizing the wealth or utility of principals.'

38 It should be added that North also include the enforcement of rules as an important part of his explanation of economic change. 'It is the admixture', North insists, 'of formal rules, informal rules, and enforcement characteristics that shapes economic performance.' 'Economic Performance Through Time', p. 366.

institutions. 'Institutions arise and persist when they confer benefits greater than the transaction costs.'[39] Therefore, institutions are at the root of differential economic performances. No one has more powerfully argued than Douglas North for the role of institutional rules in economic development:

> It is the structure of political and economic organization which determines the performance of an economy as well as the incremental rate of growth in knowledge and technology. The forms of cooperation and competition that human beings develop and the systems of enforcement of these rules of organizing human activity are at the very heart of economic history. Not only do these rules spell out the system of incentives and disincentives that guide and shape economic activity, but they also determine the underlying distribution of wealth and income of a society.[40]

These words suggest that, although North clearly emphasized the important interaction between institutions and entrepreneurs as quoted before, institutions and entrepreneurs are not at all on an equal footing. North sees institutions much more fundamental than entrepreneurship, so fundamental that one has to wonder how seriously he is interested in the interaction. Entrepreneurs and their organizations, according to him, only 'reflect the opportunities provided by the institutional matrix'; consequently, whether it is piratical or productive organizations that will come into existence all depends on what institutional framework is at play.[41]

Implied in this theory is a strong assumption that human beings are rational in the sense that the calculation of the expected incentives and disincentives determines how entrepreneurs will behave. But North makes a claim that his historical and institutional perspective modifies the rationality assumption of the neoclassical economic theory.[42] The modification is made, however, not by dismissing the rationality thesis – economic actors make calculations of input and output with sufficient information and competence – but by adding the constraining effects of institutions and time. Left intact is the economic actor's ultimate concern over incentives and disincentives (gain or loss). Calculative actors cannot avoid institutions because transaction costs are almost always positive and the actors are strongly motivated to reduce them. The other side of the coin is that institutions cannot work either without rational actors. While emphasizing the power of rules, North would not want to go as far as acknowledging that institutional rules exercise their effects regardless of individual actors' calculations, a point founding fathers of sociology, Emile Durkheim, Max Weber and Karl Marx, made many years ago. To North, rules are powerful not because they are essential to collective solidarity, legitimate, or crucial to the formation of class structure, but because individual actors care about incentives and penalties. In short, consequential rationality is the very reason why institutions are so important. One of North's key insights is that self-interest oriented individuals do not have complete control of their economic choices

---

39 Robert Bates (ed.), *Toward a Political Economy of Development: A Rational Choice Perspective* (University of California Press, 1988), p. 387.

40 North, *Structure and Change in Economic History*, p. 17, also p. 201.

41 North, 'Economic Performance Through Time', p. 361.

42 Ibid., p. 359.

and exchanges because the market itself is a set of rules. By putting a limit on the number of choices, institutions may reduce overall transaction costs and bring order to economic life. Why a particular set of institutions have fulfilled such a function while others not have constituted the core of North's and his associates' research enterprise. What North has achieved is going beyond the neo-classical assumptions of rational behaviour without actually dismissing them. And this is done by setting up the institutional boundaries of rational choices:

> When economists talk about their discipline as a theory of choice and about the menu of choices being determined by opportunities and preferences, they simply have left out that it is the institutional framework which constrains people's choice sets.[43]

Rules and entrepreneurship

Although North has argued for the fundamental or even determining power of institutional rules over organizations and entrepreneurs, perhaps because the interaction between institutions and organizations is still in his mind, he has not completely ruled entrepreneurship out. In relation to institutional rules, entrepreneurship has two representations. First, there are some political entrepreneurs who drive institutional change by setting up new rules or changing old rules; these 'institutional entrepreneurs' 'enact policies to improve their competitive position'.[44] Because '[t]he key to understanding the process of change is the intentionality of the players enacting institutional change and their comprehension of the issues',[45] we need to understand the ideas of these institutional entrepreneurs. They are the ones who control Schumpeter's 'social climate' for business entrepreneurs, or entrepreneurs in the traditional sense.

The second type of entrepreneurial behaviour in North's theory is more directly related to Schumpeter's notion:

> Sometimes that recontracting can be accomplished within the existing structure of property rights and political rules; but sometimes new contracting forms require an alternation in the rules. Equally, norms of behaviour that guide exchanges will gradually be modified or wither away. In both instances, institutions are being altered.[46]

North does not explicitly characterize these rule-changing behaviours as entrepreneurial, but to me, this is a very important insight because it links business entrepreneurship with institutional change. Here, North opens up the possibility that business entrepreneurs do not always have to follow institutional rules; if 'they perceive that they could do better by restructuring exchanges (political or economic)', they could make modifications to rules.[47] Consequently, this opens up an enormous

---

43 North, *Structure and Change in Economic History*, p. 201.
44 North, *Understanding the Process of Economic Change*, p. 3.
45 Ibid.
46 North, 'Economic Performance Through Time', p. 361.
47 Ibid.

institutional space for entrepreneurship, an insight that I shall build on in the next chapter.

From the above discussions, one cannot help but wonder: to North, exactly how constraining are institutional rules for entrepreneurship? He is quite ambivalent about this. Sometimes, his theory seems to argue that we could nearly predict what entrepreneurs would do because they have no other choices but to follow rules. Other times, his theory leaves some space for entrepreneurs or allows them to leave their marks on the institutional structure. If the general point is that most of the time entrepreneurs have to comply with rules and only occasionally could they alter the rules, then we need to know the conditions under which they could make those alterations. In the end, North moves away from entrepreneurship because he does not believe it determines the level of economic performance. To him, economic performance is largely determined by transaction costs, and because institutions matter greatly for reducing or increasing the amount of transaction costs, eventually it is institutions, not entrepreneurs, that matter.

But there are some even more fundamental questions than whether entrepreneurs can change institutions. For example, why would entrepreneurs have to follow the rules in the first place? Again, North goes back to the rationality answer: entrepreneurs follow rules because they believe that there will be a net gain. Other possibilities exist, however. Like political authority, rules are followed probably because they are perceived as more or less legitimate. From Max Weber we learn that legitimacy could have different bases, such as tradition, affection, and value-rationality.[48] An important implication of the various bases of rule-conformity is that different basis may entail different levels and ways of conformity, thus questioning the overall effectiveness of institutional rules. The variations of when and how strictly entrepreneurs follow rules of the game are the key questions for analyzing the interactive relationship between institutions and entrepreneurship.

North does not follow the line of reasoning from institutional rules to behaviours and then from behaviours to economic performance. He has expanded his theory in the opposite direction. That is, because institutions are only part of human made devices for comprehending and controlling the natural environment, we should be able to understand all these devices. Under the assumption that human behaviours result from their own devices, which North thinks reasonable, a good understanding of these devices will lead to a powerful theory of economic change. The cognitive science of human mentality therefore constitutes the foundation of theories of economic change. What becomes important now is the whole process of cognition and decision-making. Even his understanding of institutional functions seems to have changed from providing rules of the game to filling 'the C-D gap' (competence and decision) by 'restricting the flexibility of choices in such situations'.[49] The world of cognitive process is much more comprehensive, and entering it would enormously increase the scope of application of North's theory of economic change. It includes not only rules of the game but also knowledge, technology, social networks, and many other things. Not surprisingly, this world is much less tractable as well, which

---

48 Max Weber, *Economy and Society* (University of California Press, 1978), p. 36.
49 North, *Understanding the Process of Economic Change*, p. 14.

is why North has repeatedly reminded us how little we know about it. In the 1980s and the early 1990s, he was still searching for the institutional structure that could most effectively promote economic performance. Writing his latest book, in 2005, he retreated to the conclusion that 'there is no set formula for achieving economic development. No economic model can capture the intricacies of economic growth in a particular society'.[50]

North has set a research agenda for the coming generations. I know just how little that I can do in that direction, so the best strategy for me is to stick to the original plan of looking at the interaction between institutional rules and entrepreneurship. In the early 1980s, North's analysis left room for business innovations, but that generosity was offered out of institutionalist considerations: innovations would come only after the institutions of property rights had been properly set up. This clearly assumes that, once the rules of providing higher rewards for entrepreneurship are in place, entrepreneurs will certainly be motivated to innovate because of the expected higher rewards, and the market will take care of the rest. At the beginning of this century, by vastly expanding his view of economic change, North has actually increased the flexibility of institutional structure, thus unwittingly leaving a bigger room for entrepreneurship. In the 'non-ergodic' world of continuous novel change, '[t]he best recipe … is the maintenance of institutions that permit trial and error experiments to occur'.[51]

But who shall do the experiments? I believe North would say, entrepreneurs of all sorts. As Tilly has put it succinctly, 'institutions supply the rules, but organizations do the crucial behaving'.[52] Whilst it is absolutely worthwhile to study how institutions are created, maintained, enforced, and changed, it is no less worthwhile to discover how entrepreneurs have interpreted, followed, and made use of institutions. If we invest more effort in understanding the use of rules, not merely the rules themselves, then we should be in a better position of understanding at least some of the complexities of institutional changes and their effects on organizations and entrepreneurs.

Paradoxically, North's broad understanding of institutional change takes up a quite restricted view of institutional functions. A central argument of economic institutionalism is that institutional rules are needed almost exclusively for reducing uncertainty. North claims that economic history 'is a study of the perception that induce institutional innovation intended to reduce uncertainty or convert uncertainty into risk'. 'What is the deep underlying force driving the human endeavour – the source of the human intentionality that comes from consciousness?' he asks, and then answers by saying: 'It is the ubiquitous effort of humans to render that environment intelligible – to reduce the uncertainties of that environment.'[53] Again, North is right if we take a broad view of human history: scientific knowledge is developed to understand and then control nature, organizations are created to provide services at minimal costs, and rules are designed to achieve social order. Nevertheless, there

---

50 Ibid., p. 165.

51 Ibid., p. 163.

52 Charles Tilly, 'Review of *Understanding the Process of Economic Change*', *Perspectives of Politics*, 4/3 (2006): 616–617.

53 North, *Understanding the Process of Economic Change*, p. 2.

are many complexities in the whole process of reducing uncertainty with rules, such as the absence of rules, contradictory rules, ambivalent rules, and unexpected consequences of rules. I would argue that, if our ultimate concern is to promote economic change, and if we agree with Schumpeter that entrepreneurship is a key driving force of economic development, then we should study how these complicated situations of rules and rule-followings shape the growth of entrepreneurship.

Let's consider, more specifically, the concepts of uncertainties and opportunities, the intersection where we most likely meet both institutions and entrepreneurship at the same time. In economic institutionalism, uncertainty is assumed to be detrimental to economic performance. The difficulty with this argument is that, uncertainty is very often linked to opportunities. If everything is certain, then economic performance will be simply a result of rule-following. But a rule-follower will not score well in competitions because competitive advantage often comes from highly skewed distribution of rare opportunities and resources. It is different perceptions and uses of uncertainty that explain relative competitiveness and therefore differential economic performance. Similarly, one of the functions of institutions is to curb opportunism. This explains, at least in part, why entrepreneurship cannot find its place in economic institutionalism. As entrepreneurs constantly search for opportunities, the line between entrepreneurship and opportunism becomes very thin. At least in principle, effective institutions, therefore, are inimical to entrepreneurial behaviours. In an environment with extremely effective institutions, the only foreseeable entrepreneurship is the classic Cantellon's notion of dealing with uncertainties in market prices. What the entrepreneur can do is therefore very limited, i.e., making confident but arbitrary prediction of where the price is going. No opportunities are rising because all other issues have been firmly settled by institutions.

Entrepreneurship and institutional ambiguities

To understand and then to effectively promote economic development is the ultimate goal of academic studies of institutions and entrepreneurship. I believe that North, Schumpeter, and others would all agree that institutional rules are more fundamental than entrepreneurship because entrepreneurs react to, although not necessarily always comply with, institutional rules.[54] Institutions draw up the field in which entrepreneurs play. But then we must face several very difficult questions: What are the best institutions, if there are any, for promoting entrepreneurship? Or more generally, is there any way that we can assess and determine the effectiveness of institutions in terms of their power of encouraging entrepreneurship? And if entrepreneurs do not always comply with the rules, what else can they do? Here are some possibilities: they may modify the rules, re-interpret the meaning of the rules, find loopholes in the rules, or perhaps even create new rules. If we look at each of the combinations between institutional effectiveness and entrepreneurial behaviour,

---

54 Frederic Sautet has provided a succinct summary of this point in 'The Role of Institutions in Entrepreneurship: Implications for Development Policy', Mercatus Center, George Mason University, February 2005.

then we end up with many complicated relations between the two. We are in great shortage of good theories of these relations.

In particular, I see a deep dilemma arising from the previous discussions of entrepreneurship and institutions. Entrepreneurs are by definition explorers and routine-breakers, but they need a supporting environment; otherwise, their newness will kill them. Rules can bring predictable behaviours and thus reduce uncertainty, but they need to be flexible as well so that routines will not suffocate entrepreneurial discoveries of new territories. It is truly a challenge to strike a good balance between the two, both in theory and in practice.

In this final section of the chapter, I discuss some insights that have highlighted these complexities. This review will not be comprehensive at all, especially to the specialists in institutional economics and business-school entrepreneurship, but my discussion should be sufficient for getting across two messages: (1) although ubiquitous, rules can never be perfect – which has many repercussions for entrepreneurship; and (2) how to deal with rules is an essential part of entrepreneurship.

Institutional ambiguity

Rules are powerful tools for achieving social organization. Like it or not, bureaucratization helps us clarify who should do what and when; therefore, no confusions arise. Various economic organizations allow many people to work together to generate maximum benefits by sharing a limited amount of resources. Rules like legal codes and political regulations maintain social order, of course. Human beings have created a great variety of rules for constraining their own behaviours – conventions, codes, values, norms, procedures, practices, routines, beliefs, and so on. Rules are ubiquitous.

But their ubiquity does not mean that they are always perfectly designed and followed. As March and Olsen have pointed out: 'Rules are codified to some extent, but the codification is often incomplete. Inconsistencies are common. As a result, compliance with any specific rule is not automatic'.[55] Just like the number of roads built can rarely catch up with the growing number of cars, rules are always struggling to cope with exceptional cases, strong conditions, and conflicting demands. This is so not only because rules are most often designed retrospectively but also because rules are designed to deal with general types of cases rather than any particular one. Indeed, it is a tricky business to define the type without unbearably leaving out some important cases. 'The history that generates and changes rules', March and Olsen move on further, 'is not a single cohesive history but consists in a variety of experiences in a variety of places under a variety of situations'.[56] However, if the coding of rules has to be an experiment with many trials and errors, then rules cannot exercise their full power before they reach their maturity. Finally, March and Olsen discussed a more widely recognized imperfection of rules – their ambiguity:

---

55 James G. March and Johan P. Olsen, *Rediscovering Institutions: The Organizational Basis of Politics* (The Free Press, 1989), p. 20.

56 Ibid., p. 24.

Moreover, rules and their applicability to particular situations are often ambiguous. Individuals have multiple identities. Divisions of labour sometimes break down. Situations can be defined in different ways that call forth different rules. Rules are constructed by a process that sometimes encourages ambiguity.[57]

March and Olsen do not say much about what behaviours rules will encourage, nor do they explain whether the ambiguity would be an unavoidable consequence of some special features of rules or a product of purposeful design. Since rules are so important for the purpose of explaining entrepreneurship and economic development, we need a more systematic examination.

I find the analysis by Robert Merton the most relevant. It was Merton who, very likely for the first time, brought social relations to the centre of the analysis of psychological ambivalence. Although he was not studying the ambiguity of rules, his ideas about ambivalence in general and ambivalence in organizational leadership are of great value because he attempted to show how ambivalence resulted from social relations, mostly represented in roles, statuses, and social structures.

'Sociological ambivalence', according to Merton, refers to incompatible expectations of a social role or a status.[58] Examples of the roles that Merton analyzed include scientists, physicians, and organizational leaders. Entrepreneurs could be another, of course. Psychological ambivalence occurs to the people who occupy these roles because they receive incompatible expectations. Such ambivalence is sociological as well because the expectations come from social norms and structures. Therefore, 'sociological ambivalence is one major source of psychological ambivalence'.[59] Here, it is important to note that, understood as such, sociological ambivalence is exactly institutional ambiguity discussed previously. No matter what exact form they take, if institutional rules send out inconsistent expectations of how an entrepreneur should behave, the entrepreneur will experience a certain level of psychological ambivalence and, very likely some ambivalence of decision-making as well. Merton then identified six types of sociological ambivalence, or institutional ambiguity in our terminology:

1. contradictory demands upon the occupants of a status;
2. conflict of interests or of values incorporated in different statuses;
3. conflict between several roles;
4. contradictory cultural values;
5. the disjunction between culturally prescribed aspirations and socially structured avenues for realizing these aspirations;
6. differing cultural values from two or more societies.[60]

---

57 Ibid.

58 Robert K. Merton, 'Sociological Ambivalence', pp. 3–31 in his *Sociological Ambivalence and Other Essays* (The Free Press, 1976).

59 Ibid., p. 7.

60 Ibid., pp. 8–11. More relevant to the study of entrepreneurship, in another essay in the same book, 'The Ambivalence of Organizational Leaders', Merton listed and analyzed a variety of ambivalences facing business leaders.

Theories of institutions, either economic or sociological, rarely take institutional ambiguities seriously, let alone incorporate them explicitly into their models. Much of the attention has been given to uncertainties due to market fluctuations rather than ambiguities, inconsistencies, or conflicts embedded in the institutional structure that surrounds the entrepreneur. The institutional ambiguities discussed by Merton, however, could lead to a series of questions highly important for understanding the interaction between institutions and entrepreneurship: How would entrepreneurs cope with different or even conflicting demands to the role of an entrepreneur and to another role such as a political party member? (This is the extended sense of Merton's sociological ambivalence.) How would they cope with incompatible expectations to different aspects of the role of an entrepreneur, such as creating a cost-saving management structure versus the social responsibility of protecting employee welfare? (This is the restricted sense of Merton's sociological ambivalence.) What strategy would they adopt when they find their aspirations barely acceptable either to formal economic procedures or to implicitly accepted cultural practices? How would immigrant entrepreneurs or entrepreneurs opening businesses across multiple countries deal with different, many times conflicting, cultural values or even legal codes? We need theories and empirical investigations of rule-dealing entrepreneurship.

Entrepreneurship as an adventure of dealing with rules

In both North's understanding of institutional rules and Schumpeter's model of innovative combinations, entrepreneurship is a process separate from institutional structures and changes. Both have been searching for the optimal institutional environment that effectively induces productive actions. Therefore, rules and their constructions, interpretations, and manipulations are *not* part of the entrepreneurial process. On the one hand, either entrepreneurs follow rules, or they don't. Institutions, on the other hand, either encourage or discourage entrepreneurship. Few alternative possibilities with regard to the relationship between entrepreneurs and rules have been explored and seriously considered.

That organizations and entrepreneurs, especially the nascent ones, have to deal with institutions – both formal and informal rules – is not an insight new to sociologists. As Howard Aldrich summarized in a recent review, sociologists starting from Talcott Parsons in the 1950s and Arthur Stinchcombe in the 1960s have long analyzed how legitimacy has made an imprint on the fate of new organizations and industries.[61] Researchers in the following generations have specified different types of legitimacy, including cognitive, political, and social legitimacies, and they have studied different factors that affect the level of legitimacy, such as industry, life course, etc. Shared in these studies is an image of adaptive entrepreneurs and new organizations – how they have made their effort to appear legitimate or even truly become legitimate, a central theme running across many institutional studies of organizations.

---

61 Aldrich, 'Entrepreneurship'.

Obtaining legitimacy, however, is just one of the many possible ways that organizations and entrepreneurs deal with institutional rules, but the institutionalist argument has played a quite passive tone – new organizations are either to become legitimate or to perish. We should explore other possible scenarios so that we can detect emerging patterns that connect the various entrepreneurial strategies to different characteristics of rules. At least, we should distinguish the appropriateness of rules from the logic of choosing a particular rule, as March and Olsen have clearly stated:

> To say that behaviour is governed by rules is not to say that it is either trivial or unreasoned. Rule-bound behaviour is, or can be, carefully considered. Rules can reflect subtle lessons of cumulative experience, and the process by which appropriate rules are determined and applied is a process involving high levels of human intelligence, discourse, and deliberation.[62]
>
> The criterion is appropriateness, but determining what is appropriate in a specific situation is a nontrivial exercise. One possibility is that rules are followed but choice among rules and among alternative interpretations of rules is determined by a consequential logic.[63]

Again, the consequential logic might be only one way of reasoning that entrepreneurs follow when they deal with rules. The general message is that it is hard to link rules and their characteristics to people's perceptions, interpretations, and behavioural reactions, because there exist a whole range of situations in which we can find different forms of connections. For instance, inspired by Harold Garfinkel's ethnomethodological analysis of *ad hocing*, Howard Becker has reminded social science writers that:

> rules are never so clear and unambiguous that we can simply follow them. We always have to decide whether a rule exists at all, whether what we have is really covered by the rule, or whether there might not be some exception that isn't in the book but one the rulemakers, we think, must have intended. We also need to interpret rules so that the result we get is reasonable, not some foolishness resulting from blind rule-following.[64]

This insight does not deny the effect of rules; it is just that we should not assume that institutional rules always exist, that when they do exist, they will always take the originally designed or desired route, and that people will hold the rules sacred and bow to them without resistance. We have seen a number of studies arguing for and illustrating the ambiguities of rules before in this chapter, and some studies have documented that 'Entrepreneurs can take advantage of the inherent ambiguity in interpreting new behaviours by skilfully framing and editing their behaviours and intentions *vis-à-vis* the trusting parties'.[65] One of the key capacities of a leader or an entrepreneur is 'to offer a convincing interpretation of reality, an attractive vision

---

62 March and Olsen, *Rediscovering Institutions*, p. 22.
63 Ibid., p. 25.
64 Becker (ed.), *Toward a Political Economy of Development*, p. 69.
65 Aldrich, 'Entrepreneurship', p. 468.

of the possible future, and a prescription on how to reach that vision'.[66] In doing so, 'entrepreneurs not only create rational and tangible aspects of organizations, but also "symbols, ideologies, languages, beliefs, rituals, and myths, aspects of the more cultural and expressive components of organizational life"'.[67] In short, besides discovering new opportunities or innovating new ways of doing business, entrepreneurs have to be entrepreneurial on the institutional front as well. And this is true not only for developing and transitional economies but for mature market economies as well.[68] As Paul DiMaggio and his associates have shown, across the West and the East, in both old and new capitalist economies, organizations have been dragged into fierce competitions of bending old rules and creating new rules to their own interests:

> Within corporations, consultants, pundits, and new MBAs are telling seasoned managers to violate helter-skelter the rules they learned in business school. In the sphere of employment, less secure internal labour markets, more fluid job definitions, and more ambiguous reporting relationships replace the rules of clarity and commitment.[69]

Unfortunately, so far the business side of entrepreneurship is still kept apart from its institutional side; we need theoretical frameworks that seriously incorporate the two as essential components of a single process.

In terms of emphasizing the exploratory nature of entrepreneurship, the Austrian School has offered perhaps the most powerful arguments. Although scholars within this School have some disagreements, they all start with the following point of view: uncertainty is a fact of life. 'The term entrepreneur as used by catallactic theory means', Mises said, 'acting man exclusively seen from the aspect of the uncertainty inherent in every action'.[70] As opposed to risk, which is measurable, uncertainty is not. In other words, if risk is due to imperfect information, then uncertainty is 'sheer ignorance'.[71] It is so uncertain that people do not even know what the possible consequences are and how likely each of them will happen. The only way of dealing with uncertainty is to learn by trial and error, which is why knowledge, alertness,

---

66 Barbara Czarniawska-Joerges, *Economic Decline and Organizational Control* (New York: Praeger, 1989), p. 7, quoted in Aldrich, 'Entrepreneurship', p. 464.

67 Aldrich, 'Entrepreneurship', p. 468, quoting Andrew Pettigrew, 1979, 'On Studying Organizational Culture', *Administratively Science Quarterly*, 24: 574.

68 In his review, Aldrich cited several studies of how economic corporations deal with regulatory rules in western developed countries, such as the life insurance industry, the newspaper industry, bioindustry, etc.

69 Paul DiMaggio, 'Introduction: Making Sense of the Contemporary Firm and Prefiguring Its Future', p. 5 in *The Twenty-First-Century Firm: Changing Economic Organization in International Perspective* (Princeton University Press, 2001).

70 Ludwig von Mises, *Human Action: A Treatise on Economics* (Irvington: Foundation for Economic Education, 1996), p. 254. In terms of dealing with uncertainty, entrepreneurship is not something peculiar to entrepreneurs. The distinction between entrepreneurs and other people is therefore a matter of degree: 'In any real and living economy every actor is always an entrepreneur' (ibid., p. 253).

71 Israel Kirzner, 'Entrepreneurial Discovery and the Competitive Market Process: An Austrian Approach', *Journal of Economic Literature*, XXXV (1997): 62.

and the capacity to make good judgements rather than innovative productions are so important in the Austrian portrait of the entrepreneur. Entrepreneurship is thus a discovering rather than an innovating process.[72]

The theoretical target of the Austrian School is the neo-classical and other mainstream economics. But I think it may also become a serious blow to institutional theories of all types. If we have no way of escaping from our 'sheer ignorance' of at least some aspects of our economic life, then institutions, although designed to reduce uncertainty, will sooner or later reach their fatal limitations. As far as I know, the Austrian scholars have not specified where the uncertainties may come from. However, as their perspective has often been presented in quite general terms, there are no reasons for ruling out institutional rules as one source of uncertainty. This clearly brings us back to the previous discussions of the ambiguities of rules and their utilizations by entrepreneurs. Putting all these points together, we come to the understanding that entrepreneurship is a process of discovering and acting upon opportunities in multiple arenas, including the market, the management, and the matrix of rules.

Concluding remarks

My thinking has become focused on the interaction between institutions (rules) and entrepreneurship while mulling over the China puzzle presented in the previous chapter. The two phenomena – institutional change and development of entrepreneurship – stand out together during China's experience of reforming its economy. The first generation of entrepreneurs have demonstrated how much China's economic growth comes from their boldness, wit, and hard work. The reader will see much more evidence of this in Chapters 4 to 8. We simply cannot afford ignoring entrepreneurs in order to have a proper understanding of China's economic development. Note that these entrepreneurs were born in the context of China's economic transformation. Economists and other social scientists all have been amazed or dismayed by the fact that China seems to have defied the usual wisdom of getting institutions right. The simultaneity of the emergence of an entrepreneurial army and institutional reconstruction in China strongly suggests that it is the interaction of the two that are at work in pushing the country's economy forward. Our task is to find out how the interaction works.

This observation, however, poses the theoretical challenge of incorporating entrepreneurship and institutional structure into a single analytical framework. By contrast, to most economists, the biggest challenge is how to go beyond the neoclassical model without losing its analytical rigour. For example, William Baumol has tried to stay in the neoclassical tradition as long as he could while bringing entrepreneurship

---

72 Following Mark Casson and others, I also think that Schumpeter's notion of entrepreneurship and the Austrian notion mostly represented by Israel Kirzner are complementary in the sense that they have emphasized different aspects or situations of a single process. See Casson, 'Entrepreneur', in J. Eatwell, M. Milgate and P. Newman (eds), *The New Palgrave: A Dictionary of Economics*, London: McMillan, 1987, p. 151; P.J. McNulty, 'Competition: Austrian Conceptions' in the same collection.

into the mainstream economic model, but he has ended up with a very sceptical prospect for the mission because of the difficulty of putting entrepreneurship into a mathematical equation.[73] More recently as well as interestingly, he has analyzed the institutional conditions of entrepreneurship in comparative historical studies. His overall conclusion is very much in line with what North has argued. That is, the growth of entrepreneurship largely depends on how the rules of the game have been designed – if 'social payoff structure' is right, then entrepreneurship will grow, and if not, rent-seeking behaviours will creep in.[74] Oliver Williamson has reached the same conclusion strictly from a transaction cost perspective. Although he seldom addresses entrepreneurship, his theory has left some room for entrepreneurship if entrepreneurship is understood as a process of searching for the most optimal organizational structure that curbs opportunism and reduces uncertainties,[75] but his understanding of institutions is restricted to the specifications of contractual relations.

My review of the theories of both entrepreneurship and institutions is obviously highly selective, but I think the reader by now should agree that there has been a convergence of different theoretical lines for constructing some meaningful connections between entrepreneurship and institutional structures. No one has found it an easy task. In this chapter I have tried to identify the sources of this difficulty. Here I suggest two solutions of taking a step further. First, our understanding of entrepreneurship should go beyond the conceptualization in most business-schools, according to which entrepreneurship is basically a process of identifying new markets or products and then mobilize resources to produce the supply. Added to the business side is an institutional one. We should not, as economists commonly do, let institutions (in the Northian sense) 'only emerge when markets cannot be constructed or when traditional rational choice analysis fails'.[76] Rather, we should see institutions as an inherent aspect of the entrepreneurial process, not just an exogenous condition. We may not be able to insert entrepreneurship as a parameter in a mathematical equation, but analyzing how entrepreneurs understand and react to (not just simply comply with) the rules of the game should be a routine in our research on entrepreneurship. I am not saying that entrepreneurs can do whatever they like to institutions, but if we agree that eventually it is the entrepreneurs who do the acting, then we need to know how they act upon the institutions and the implications of their actions.

---

73   William J. Baumol, 'Entrepreneurship in Economic Theory', *American Economic Review*, 58/2 (1968): 64–71. For a more recent but similar statement, see Sherwin Rosen, 1997, 'Austrian and Neoclassical Economics: Any Gains from Trade?', *Journal of Economic Perspectives*, 11 (4): 139–52.

74   Baumol, *Entrepreneurship, Management, and the Structure of Payoffs* (Cambridge, MA: MIT Press, 1993).

75   See Chapter 10 of *Markets and Hierarchies: Analysis and Antitrust Implications* (New York, Free Press, 1975) and Chapter 9 of *The Economic Institutions of Capitalism: Firms, Markets, and Relational Contracting* (The Free Press, 1985).

76   Neil Smelser and Richard Swedberg, pp. 5–6 in 'Introduction' to *Handbook of Economic Sociology*, 2nd edition (Princeton University Press and Russell Sage Foundation, 2005).

Second and following the previous point, we should be clearly aware of how far we can go in searching for the 'best' institutions. We have learnt that institutions are shrouded with ambiguities, and if we accept the above point that entrepreneurs can do something to institutions, then it follows that the 'best' institutions may not work as they are expected to. After broadening his view of institutions, North has reached the conclusion that the 'best' institutions are those that allow trials and errors. Arthur Stinchcombe has offered almost the same insight by showing that rules even as formal as legal codes work most effectively when they can correct their own mistakes.[77] We may have learnt some lessons of how to make institutions work, or not work, from history, but in principle we should keep in mind that institutions work by exploration, not by design. David Stark and others have shown that this is particularly true for post-socialist economies.[78] Indeed, the entrepreneur's encountering of rules will produce different patterns and paths, and to figure out what the patterns are and where their paths lead to is a daunting task. Perhaps we can only follow an inductive process: coming up with some ideas based on careful observations. I shall verify the usefulness of this exploratory notion of entrepreneurship and institutions by examining the experience of entrepreneurs in China. This will be done by firstly proposing a couple of theoretical notions, 'institutional holes' and 'double entrepreneurship'.

77 Arthur L. Stinchcombe, *When Formality Works: Authority and Abstraction in Law and Organizations* (University of Chicago Press, 2001).
78 David Stark and László Bruszt, *Postsocialist Pathways:Transforming Politics and Property in East Central Europe* (Cambridge University Press, 1998). See also David Stark, 'Ambiguous Assets for Uncertain Environments: Heterarchy in Postsocialist Firms', pp. 69–104 in Paul DiMaggio (ed.), *The Twentieth-Century Firm*.

Chapter 3

Institutional Holes and Double Entrepreneurship

The previous chapter shows that rules and entrepreneurship have not enjoyed an amicable relationship in theories of both institutions and entrepreneurship. Some economic and sociological theories have highlighted the gap between rules and entrepreneurship, and some scholars have even suggested the conditions under which a useful theory could be constructed. Still, I have found few serious attempts to put the two phenomena into one analytical framework. The unique path of China's economic development provides an empirical focus for such a theoretical exercise. By relating to the case of China, in this chapter I shall propose some theoretical notions through which rules and entrepreneurship can in a way be meaningfully connected together for understanding economic development.

I think that it is more challenging to discover and theorize opportunities for entrepreneurship in rules (or institutional structures) than to argue for the rule-dealing aspect of entrepreneurship. Therefore, I shall start with concepts of institutions and pay more attention to them. All theories emphasizing the effects of institutions seem to share the following point: social actions avoid uncertainty, so institutions are created to reduce it. These theories suggest that, without a well constructed framework of institutional rules, economic development will be fragile at best. It is here that all species of institutional analysis are not amenable to the role of entrepreneurship. In sharp contrast, it has been identified for a long time that uncertainty is the very starting point of entrepreneurial action. Entrepreneurs understand that they cannot escape uncertainty while chasing after profits. If institutional theories cannot incorporate an element of uncertainty in the functioning of institutions, then we will have no hope of explaining entrepreneurship from an institutional perspective.

Back to the case of China, few would agree that a clearly defined and well enforced institutional framework has been established in China. It is all too easy for one to find many drawbacks, loopholes, problems, and even unjust regulations in China. Corruption arises where different state policies are executed for the same economic activity. Particularistic interests sabotage fair competition. Many policies have to be suspended because of unexpected problems. Nevertheless, it is against such a backdrop of deficient institutions that we have witnessed the birth and growth of a new generation of entrepreneurs in China (as shown in the following chapters). So, the question is: how could institutional transformations with so many setbacks provide so many opportunities and strong incentives for profit-seeking activities? It is very unlikely that entrepreneurs have simply followed the new rules. Particularly for those not working in the state sector, following the new rules will most likely arouse confusion and frustration. But the change of institutional rules must have played a significant role in the dramatic development of entrepreneurship in China since the end of the 1970s; otherwise, entrepreneurs would not have waited for so long. Ultimately, there must be something in the changed institutional structure that entrepreneurs in China have found exploitable in venturing on new businesses. While certainly not everyone has been successful in exploiting the opportunities embedded in the changing structure, many of them have, and their work has turned to be a key driving force of the economic boom in China.

The central concepts and theories in this chapter assumes that entrepreneurs do aim at achieving economic efficiency (in the sense of being able to earn sufficient profits to survive and thrive). I believe that most entrepreneurs care about their interests most of the time. Institutions matter as well, but they matter not because entrepreneurs would give up efficiency for legitimacy, as many institutional theorists have argued, but because entrepreneurs draw on available institutional structures to legitimize their strategies and practices for improving economic efficiency. Therefore, entrepreneurship is an *active translation* rather than a loyal reflection of institutional demands. For entrepreneurs, uncertainties in institutional changes are mixed blessings, but that is a fact of life that they have to learn to live with. Discriminating rules and unexpected setbacks could suddenly put new businesses in a devastating position. Manoeuvring skilfully, however, entrepreneurs could take advantage of the changing and ambiguous institutional rules to increase the likelihood of success.

A uniqueness of the China case is that neither the Chinese state nor the Chinese entrepreneurs have much interest in searching for the best institutional rules. Rather, they prefer to explore what they can do with the suggestive but ambiguous rules and policies. The limitations of the search for the most appropriate institutions have illustrated themselves in the less than successful experience of the shock theory in most Eastern European nations. The frustrating experience there 'has pointed to the intractable nature of social arrangements embedded in interpersonal ties, cultural beliefs, norms, and old regime institutional arrangements studied by economic sociologists'.[1] Such a shift of attention has evolved into a competition of arguing for the relative importance of formal versus informal norms. But we should look for answers in the very nature and structure of formal rules themselves. For a long time sociologists have tended to tackle an economic question by resorting to a 'social' factor, fighting against the economic perspective but virtually leaving it untouched, rather than directly providing sociological framework that could incorporate the economic point of view. For example, North asked, 'What is it about informal constraints that gives them such a pervasive influence upon the long-term character of economies?'.[2] Clearly, the question was raised because some sociologists have forcefully argued for the effect of social ties, which are informal in contrast to laws, state policies, and organizational procedures. The question, however, clearly implies

---

1   Victor Nee, 'The New Institutionalisms in Economics and Sociology', in Neil Smelser and Richard Swedberg (eds), *The Handbook of Economic Sociology*, 2nd edition (Princeton University Press and Russell Sage Foundation, 2005), p. 54.

2   Douglas North, 'Institutions', *Journal of Economic Perspectives*, 5 (1991): 97–112, p. 111.

that how formal institutions work is a question that has pretty much been resolved. A key point of this chapter is that there is still a lot to be done, even on the effect of formal institutions.

A final note is needed before moving on to detailed discussions. I do not aim to argue that institutions do not constrain social actions or they do not store up shared values and norms. What I am arguing for is that in reality there are many situations in which institutions cannot fulfil their duty assigned by the institutionalists of putting actions under control; the processes of creating, modifying, and enforcing institutions would prove this. We should take the variation of the effectiveness of institutional rules and the entrepreneur's constant search for opportunities as normal situations, especially when rules are under dramatic change.

A gap between structural and institutional theories

How do entrepreneurs obtain a legitimate competitive advantage? While some answers are available, they do not lead toward a consistent explanation. Ironically, Ronald Burt's theory of structural holes[3] provides an analogy that helps identify and repair a defect of that very theory. In Burt's analysis, structural holes exist when complementary resources remain at poorly connected or unconnected sites. Economic players whose own positions connect them to many such sites enjoy significant competitive advantages, since they can construct closer connections between weakly linked sites, organize the synergy of complementary resources, and seize benefits from the resulting new productivity; their locations, observes Burt, provide them with extensive social capital. For them, entrepreneurship involves knowledgeable creation of effective links, with themselves as mediators and beneficiaries. Burt's analysis of organizational structure adds a crucial element to Schumpeter's old, wise conceptions of the entrepreneur:

> We have seen that the function of entrepreneurs is to reform or revolutionize the pattern of production by exploiting an invention or, more generally, an untried technological possibility for producing a new commodity or producing an old one in a new way, by opening up a new source of supply of materials or a new outlet for products, by reorganizing an industry, and so on.[4]

Burt's structural and organizational perspective places Schumpeter's individual entrepreneur in a network of social connections. Although it does not rule out individual genius, it also permits specification of the sorts of structural environments in which brilliant entrepreneurs are more likely to succeed.

Nevertheless, Burt's formulation ignores the insights of another perspective on organizational dynamics that was gaining strength as Burt was pursuing his own analysis of structural holes. The new institutionalism of Powell, DiMaggio, and

---

3　Ronald Burt, *Structural Holes* (Harvard University Press, 1992).

4　Joseph Schumpeter, *Capitalism, Socialism and Democracy* (New York: Harper and Row, 1975), p. 132.

others[5] helped to resolve a puzzle that became increasingly urgent as state socialist regimes began to collapse or mutate: contrary to the hopeful idea that integration of firms into national and world markets would induce them to perform efficiently, forms of organization that worked more or less well in well developed capitalist environments failed miserably elsewhere. New institutionalists called attention to the crucial importance of the socially constructed normative environment within which entrepreneurs and firms actually operate. They argue that organizations obtain legitimacy – and hence viability – by conforming to widely recognized rules and rituals. They argue further that the chance of survival increases as organizations and entrepreneurs conform to widely adopted rules rather than merely accumulating various types of capital, including social capital. Yet new institutionalists themselves recognize that firms and entrepreneurs do not simply conform to rule-bound environments, but reshape those environments through their own actions. 'Under what conditions', ask DiMaggio and Powell, 'are challengers and entrepreneurs able to refashion existing rules or create new institutional order?'.[6]

More recently, after refusing the definitions by North and Greif, Nee argues that institutions fundamentally:

> involve actors, whether individuals or organizations, who pursue real interests in concrete institutional structures. An institution in this view is defined as *a dominant system of interrelated formal and informal elements – custom, shared beliefs, conventions, norms, and rules – which actors orient their actions to when they pursue their interests.*[7]

While I appreciate his intention of integrating the constraining function of institutional structure and the active role of individual pursuit of interests, it is not clear how the circle has been squared – what if the interest-searching individual finds the institutional rules too constraining? Is he going to follow the rules or to continue to pursue his interest? 'As economic sociology move beyond the earlier perspective on embeddedness', he argues, 'the challenge is to specify and explicate the social mechanisms determining the relationship between the informal social organization of close-knit groups and the formal rules of institutional structures monitored and enforced by organizations and states'.[8] While an integrated perspective to looking at the link between formal and informal rules is definitely much needed, such a call implicitly accepts the spontaneous effectiveness of formal institutions, which, to me, is still pretty much an open question.

Hence the irony. Burt's structures consist of personal connections among organizationally situated economic actors; they form networks, and lend themselves splendidly to the formalism of network analysis. But the institutional environment also consists of incompletely connected understandings, practices, rules, and organizations. The more incompletely connected those institutions, the greater the

---

5   Walter Powell and Paul DiMaggio (eds), *The New Institutionalism in Organizational Analysis* (University of Chicago Press, 1991).

6   Ibid., p. 28.

7   Nee, 'The New Institutionalisms in Economics and Sociology', p. 55, emphasis original.

8   Ibid.

opportunities for institutional entrepreneurs to create productive connections between poorly linked sites, and thus to reap gains for themselves. Indeed, in environments characterized by extensive institutional disjunctions, only entrepreneurs who can create new connections are likely to escape from segmented niches. Institutional holes, relatively disconnected sets of rules, practices, norms, and values that harbour and segregate complementary resources, provide splendid, if risky, opportunities for daring, perspicacious entrepreneurs. Economies in rapid transition from one set of institutional arrangements to another generally feature many more institutional disjunctions and segmented niches than do extensively connected capitalist economies. They therefore provide significant opportunities for entrepreneurs who can identify and fill institutional holes. The complementary strengths of Burt's structural theory and the new institutionalism point toward an analytic synthesis that combines insufficiently connected intellectual resources.

The gap between the structural and the institutional perspectives demands a coherent conceptual framework for analyzing how entrepreneurs simultaneously obtain institutional legitimacy and competitive advantage. To accomplish such a framework, we should understand institutions as more than a set of rules that entrepreneurs have little choice but to follow. Here I aim to develop a theoretical idea of the conditions under which institutional structures can become sources of entrepreneurial opportunities. My central argument is that reconstruction of national economic systems causes valuable resources to become more institutionally segregated, thereby creating a situation in which entrepreneurs are more likely to find opportunities. Somewhat analogous to the concept of structural holes, non-redundant connections to economic sectors that have been kept apart by institutional rules could therefore become competitive advantage. However, since entrepreneurs must cross different institutional boundaries in order to establish connections, they must also take particular care not to precipitate legitimacy crises by either deliberately or inadvertently violating institutional rules. They will seek business opportunities heavily bounded by institutional rules under constant reconstruction. As a consequence, access to economic resources remains restricted not because of any failure to establish social connections but because of various national and local state policies.

Structural holes and institutional holes

That entrepreneurial opportunities arise from gaps in the market has almost become an economic common sense. An entrepreneur fulfils such a gap by establishing a new business that will supply the demand for a particular product. As we have seen in the previous chapter, the gap and its fulfilment can take a variety of forms.

However, the great variation of entrepreneurial competitiveness – why are some people more successful in initiating and maintaining a new venture than others – is still a puzzle for economists and business specialists.[9] Here I would draw on

---

9   Scott Shane, *A General Theory of Entrepreneurship: The Individual-Opportunity Nexus* (Edward Elgar, 2003).

Ronald Burt's theory of 'structural holes' as it is more than an explanatory factor, i.e., it suggests a mechanism by which conditions of differential performance by entrepreneurs can be clarified. Burt argues that:

> much of competitive behaviour and its results can be understood in terms of player access to 'holes' in the social structure of the competitive arena ... The holes in social structure, or, more simply, structure holes, are disconnections or nonequivalencies between players in the arena. Structural holes are entrepreneurial opportunities for information access, timing, referrals, and control.[10]

That is, in market competition, players' structural positions in social relations matter because information is never evenly distributed throughout the relations; competitive advantages therefore rely not only on financial and human capitals but also on structural positions in social relations, a valuable form of social capital. Those who have access to a variety of social connections enjoy a higher level of structural autonomy and competitive advantage.

Take the simplest case of structural holes from which more complex situations can be derived. Consider three players: A, B, and the entrepreneur. The entrepreneur would be in a structural hole when all the following three conditions are satisfied:

a. A and B have no direct contact with each other;
b. A and B possess different kinds of information;
c. the entrepreneur has contacts with both A and B.

An entrepreneur 'plays conflicting demands and preferences against one another and builds value from their disunion'.[11] He or she thus maximizes not only the total amount but also the scope of information and social support from such position.

I believe that institutional rules should be brought into the notion of structural holes in order for the full potential of this idea to be developed, because institutions are created and designed to shape and regulate social relation.

But before going any further, let me make it extremely clear what I mean by 'institutions', often been confused with organizations or professions. Here I adopt Douglas North's definition of institutions, that is, institutions are 'the rules of the game in a society or, more formally, are the human devised constraints that shape human interaction. In consequence they structure incentives in human exchange, whether political, social, economic'.[12] Thus by imposing rules on the distribution of widely demanded resources, institutions help construct social connections by determining who has the privilege of making what kinds of connections and with whom.

Among economic players who are potentially able to acquire structural holes, only some are eventually able to occupy the holes. Social connections based on friendship, kinship, membership, etc., cannot guarantee an optimal realization of

---

10 Burt, *Structural Holes*, pp. 1–2.

11 Ibid., p. 34.

12 Douglas North, *Institutions, Institutional Change, and Economic Performance* (Cambridge University Press, 1990), p. 3.

advantage. Many institutions other than outside the realm of inter-personal relations regulate the distribution of valuable resources. Entrepreneurs often have to find space between institutional rules to take full advantage of a structural position. To show why a perspective on the structure of institutional rules may lead to some useful insights of entrepreneurship, it is thus necessary to explicate the assumptions underlying Burt's analysis.

The idea of 'structural holes' implicitly assumes the following three conditions:

1. The reason for A's isolation from B is trivial. To identify their structural relations, we don't have to know *why* there is no direct contact between A and B.
2. Non-redundant connections will be necessarily complementary. In other words, the combination of resources previously possessed by A and B respectively will generate new benefits. Otherwise, it is not rational for the entrepreneur to make simultaneous contact with A and B no matter how much non-redundant information they can provide.
3. There are no significant institutional barriers (constraining rules) for the entrepreneur to make connections with A and B.

These assumptions are strong and leave many important questions unanswered. Why couldn't A and B make direct connection and reap the potential benefits without the entrepreneur? What has prevented them from doing this? Also, for separated resources to be complementary, they demand extra conditions than merely non-redundant connections. For example, A may offer help in getting loans, while B can advise on legal matters; it is still a long way to go to link those resources together in a complementary manner. Last but not least, it is unrealistic to assume that the hurdles for the entrepreneur to make connections with A and B are ignorable. But if the entrepreneur cannot afford to ignore them, what must be done to overcome them?

I suggest that we redefine the concept of 'institutional holes' for analyzing entrepreneurship in institutional settings.[13] However, I must introduce the concept of 'institutional fields' before defining 'institutional holes' as the latter is also an extension of the former. Powell and DiMaggio used the term 'organizational field' to refer to an aggregate of organizations that share a common institutional life.[14] In competing for legitimacy, organizations in the same organizational field become structurally similar to one another because they tend to adopt the same organizational form. Institutional fields differ from organizational fields in that the former are systems

---

13 I say 'redefine' because Burt used this term in his book (1992: 148–149). However, he didn't provide an explicit definition. For him, institutional holes are a natural extension of structural holes. He understands institutional holes as structural positions that have contacts with different formal roles within an organization. The formal roles fulfil the same function of providing non-redundant information as those of players A and B in structural holes. While analyzing China's labour market, Bian (2002) used the term 'institutional holes' to refer to 'a state of labour markets in which formal mechanisms are either unavailable or insufficient in connecting job seekers and prospective employers' (p. 117), which clearly has little affinity to the structural properties of either organizational positions or institutional rules.

14 Powell and DiMaggio, *The New Institutionalism in Organization Studies*, pp. 64–66.

of institutional rules set up for controlling and distributing valuable resources. For example, institutional rules manifest their functions when people attempt to obtain a variety of resources, such as political power, licenses, information, etc. For the case of China, access to valuable resources such as bank loans and raw materials is still in most cases determined by an enterprise's ownership, i.e., whether state-owned or privately owned.

Unlike those in an organizational field, organizations in the same institutional field may or may not orient themselves to the same organizational structure for the sake of legitimacy. What they compete for is the control of resources, and being or at least appearing legitimate is just one step on the way of achieving such control. Because there is always a set of institutional rules regulating the acquirement of resources and evaluating the appropriateness of organizational behaviours, organizations have to innovatively make use of the rules in order to get control of resources.

I thus define institutional holes as structural gaps between at least two actors (persons or organizations) that are located in respectively different institutional fields and are in control of potentially complementary resources for a future business enterprise. For three reasons, institutional holes are structurally non-equivalent and thus may contain opportunities for entrepreneurs:

1. institutional rules in different institutional fields cover different resources and actions;
2. organizations in a particular institutional field may enjoy unique resources (either economic or non-economic), especially designated by institutional rules;
3. rules, either formal or informal, may prevent currently unconnected economic players from exploiting the potential benefits if they were connected.

When these conditions exist, it is then up to the entrepreneur to recognize the opportunities and take actions (see the following section on double entrepreneurship). Because institutional structures could be perceived from different perspectives and there are multiple ways of recombining resources in different institutional fields, institutional holes only emerge when the entrepreneur is confident of obtaining a satisfactory amount of profits derived from institutional structure.[15]

We should specify the exact boundaries and structures of institutional fields and thus institutional holes on a case-by-case basis for each empirical investigation, as we do in studying organizational fields.[16] We can advance our understanding of the institutional conditions of entrepreneurship, however, by conceptualizing entrepreneurial opportunities as institutional holes defined before. Firstly, the concept of 'institutional holes' pays serious attention to the institutional origins

---

15 Obviously, there is a great variation in how the entrepreneur perceives institutional structures and how much the perceived opportunity will be eventually realized. The perceived opportunity could be just an illusion without sufficient level of legitimacy (see the section on double entrepreneurship), or it could arise as an unexpected consequence of rational calculations. I shall discuss some illustrative representations in the following chapters.

16 Powell and DiMaggio, *The New Institutionalism in Organization Studies*, p. 65.

of why potential economic players cannot make direct connections without the entrepreneur. There are many situations in which connections are difficult to establish due to institutional barriers, such as cultural taboos, historically inherited practices, political affiliations, etc. A Chinese entrepreneur will have to convince local authorities and residents that it is politically correct and ethically acceptable to bring in money and technology from a Japanese company to a community occupied by the Japanese during the Second Wold War. Unlike what happens in organizational fields, where legitimacy is pursued for its own sake, legitimacy problems arise in institutional fields only when the entrepreneur violates institutional rules in order to make connections.

Secondly, besides possessing non-redundant information, organizations in different institutional fields could be institutionally complementary to one another. For example, privileges are rare resources in any society. Institutions set up frameworks in regard to who can enjoy certain types of privileges, how the privileges should be exercised, and what will happen if someone breaks the rules. Each privilege defines special rights and obligations. Organizations are institutionally complementary when the entrepreneurs who are short of certain privileges for conducting businesses recognize that, by combining the respective privileges of those organizations, they can make their business dreams come true. An example in China is the popular strategy of registering an actually private business as a joint-venture with a local authority by paying a certain amount of money to the authority as 'administration fee'. Tax deduction and access to a larger number of employees are the privileges a private enterprise cannot enjoy. In the meantime, the entrepreneur can still keep the privilege of laying off employees at will. I shall discuss these issues in detail in the next two chapters.

Finally, everywhere entrepreneurs are under the constraint of institutional rules when they try to take advantage of structural positions, either structural holes or institutional holes. Their strategy of dealing with the constraint is very often reflected in constant reinterpretations of institutional codes and negotiations with policy-makers and other players. Therefore, institutional holes are always in the process of reconstruction, because the great variation in the ways in which social actions are bounded by institutions leaves an ample space for entrepreneurs to exploit. For instance, ambiguity in institutional rules lends entrepreneurs the flexibility to reinterpret and manipulate the rules. Ambiguities and inconsistencies may come from different versions of rules that are applicable to different groups or sectors of society, such as geographical areas, demographic groups, industries, etc. When policy makers twist the production, enforcement and application of institutions toward their own interests, entrepreneurs may recognize business opportunities if they understand how policy makers' interests are involved. The reader can find further discussions and empirical evidence in the following chapters.

Some representations of institutional holes

Let me remind the reader of an important point that I made in the previous chapter: North is absolutely right in that, by controlling the distribution of incentives and penalties, institutional rules shape people's motivations and thus their actions, but that should not lead us to an automatic view of such process. In reality, institutional effects are not so deterministic. The deterministic understanding of institutional effects is in part due to the lack of a more comprehensive analysis of the nature of the rules and of the process through which they exercise some impact on human actions. Rules are different along a variety of dimensions and their values along each dimension should obviously be taken as variables rather than fixed values. The effectiveness of rules, therefore, differs from one dimension to another. Consequently, there will be many scenarios in which institutional rules show different ways of affecting social actions. It is a great and exciting challenge for social scientists to analyze these scenarios and derive middle range theories based on empirical and logical studies.[17]

It is not the task of this book to carry out such comprehensive analysis. Some dimensions of institutional rules, however, represent situations in which institutional holes can be identified. After previous discussions of institutional holes, it helps further the understanding of this concept with a few more specific extensions. Again, these extended concepts of institutional rules are only ideal-types and these dimensions are intertwined with one another.

A first dimension of institutional rules is the *presence or absence* of institutional rules, which may vary from a vacuum, where no rules whatsoever can be found for a particular action, to saturation, where all aspects of an action are under the constraint of a set of institutional rules. An institutional vacuum may exist because sometimes rule-makers fail to anticipate the necessity of making the rules, and other times they may purposefully avoid producing or publishing the rules for a variety of reasons, such as lack of sufficient information, or anticipation of an adverse consequence. If the rules are potentially relevant to the business venture under consideration and the time of publishing the rules plays a key role in the execution of the project, the absence or development of institutional rules will become an institutional hole.

An in-between situation would be that formal rules are only developed *ex post* some informal rules have already been adopted in practice – there is a temporal lacuna in which no formal rules can be found, let alone, applied or enforced. Several consequences will follow in such a circumstance: (1) the actors involved have to invent the rules by themselves; (2) an old rule has to be revived and used; (3) actors follow different strategies.

The next dimension of institutional rules relates to their *clarity*, that is, once the rules are published, how clear they are for people to understand, and this may include the underlying logic or reasoning, the ultimate objective, conditions of application, reinforcement procedures, penalties of non-conformity, and so on. Ambiguities of rules may increase transaction costs and thus hinder the emergence and growth of

---

17 For example, Ostrom discovered the importance of social learning, trust, external authority, structural inertia, and incremental change in successful institution building and socially derived incentives as a motivational force (Elinor Ostrom, *Crafting Institutions for Self-Governing Irrigation Systems* (San Francisco, California: Institute for Contemporary Studies Press, 1992)). See also, Elinor Ostrom, Larry Schroeder, and Susan Wynne, *Institutional Incentives and Sustainable Development: Infrastructure Policies in Perspective* (Boulder; Oxford: Westview Press, 1993).

entrepreneurship. For the entrepreneur, the ambiguities may become an opportunity when the entrepreneur believes that either conforming to the rules will result in a desirable amount of benefits or making a case for an exception to the rules will avoid a likely penalty.

A third dimension is the *flexibility* of institutional rules in their reinforcement. By definition, rules are general principles that are supposed to cover a variety of circumstances whose differences are at a tolerable level. In reality, however, the variation of the circumstances may be so large that either the rules contain some statements for flexible applications and reinforcements at the moment when they were initially designed, or the rules will be manipulated or forced to change with respect to some situations that are claimed to be beyond the original domain of coverage. Similarly to what they would do to ambiguous institutional rules, entrepreneurs will point to the flexibilities or inflexibilities of the rules when they are twisting the rules toward their own interests.

Nee seems to emphasize the uniformity of formal rules and ignore the local variations:

> Despite differences in local and regional history and culture, the laws and regulations monitored and enforced by the federal government apply to all regions of the United States, with very few exceptions. Variations in locality and region may limit the effectiveness of monitoring and enforcement, but they do not give rise to different underlying rules. Not only is the constitutional framework invariant, but federal rules aim to extend the power of the central state uniformly.[18]

This points to a difficult issue of the uniformity and variation of rules – on the one hand, he is right in recognizing the uniformity of federal laws and rules, but on the other hand, it is also true that, even in the US, different states have different laws, such as the death penalty, suitable to each state's unique conditions. Therefore, not only is it nearly impossible to make rules absolutely universal, but also that leaving some room for variation and flexibility is a wise or desirable thing to do.

A last dimension constitutes a continuum with complete *consistency* among the rules at one hand and complete *inconsistency* at the other. Although all rule-makers aim to achieve complete consistency, inconsistency or even conflicts among rules seems to be unavoidable for a number of reasons: different agencies may produce different sets of rules, all targeting the same group of social actions, without being aware of each other's different principles; new rules are produced to replace old but still effective rules; or the underlying idea of one set of rules may be in conflict with another idea, for example, economic development and environment protection. Entrepreneurs, if we can assume that most of them would put their own interests at the top priority most of the time, will extol the merits of the set of rules from which they could develop their business while downplaying or even denouncing the appropriateness of another set.

---

18 Nee, 'The New Institutionalisms in Economics and Sociology', p. 59.

Double entrepreneurship under institutional change

According to Schumpeter, the entrepreneur, while venturing on a new business, has to deal with two tasks:

> The entrepreneurial performance involves, on the one hand, the ability to perceive new opportunities that cannot be proved at the moment at which action has to be taken, and, on the other hand, willpower adequate to breaking down the resistance that the social environment offers to change.[19]

In a transitional economy like China, entrepreneurship incorporates two dimensions. The first one is economic – an entrepreneur has to be innovative in identifying or creating a promising market. Second, there is a socio-political dimension. To become a successful entrepreneur, one has to be talented in making use of institutional rules, frequently represented as contingent government regulations, and manipulating those rules. An entrepreneur in China is someone who can handle the two missions of making profits and obtaining socio-political security in a way that the two can mutually benefit from rather than destroy each other. Just as the price system and market mechanisms are not sufficient for inducing economic development, it is naïve to draft a business-school new venture plan and then go about implementing it in reality.[20]

We need a more general theory that specifies the link between institutional rules and entrepreneurship. The theory starts by recognizing that entrepreneurship varies along the dimensions of the extent it exploits institutional rules, the level of legitimacy of exploiting strategies and practices, and the likelihood such entrepreneurship shall survive (measured by economic profitability). In the following pages I shall try to spell out the relationships between these dimensions.

First, because entrepreneurship varies from one institutional setting to another, I examine the relationship between rule-exploitation and legitimacy in a general context of profit-seeking activities. Some common types of such variations are accordingly mapped out in Figure 3.1.

Starting from the lowest left corner, activities involved in black marketing, underground transactions, smuggling, and embezzlement are the least legitimate and demand the least exploitation of rules. They are entrepreneurial in the sense of ruthlessly violating formal legal codes. There are no fewer rules for these illegal activities than there are in legal businesses. Nevertheless, to finish any transaction in these highly risky activities, the first thing that one has to do is follow, not exploit, the rules.

---

19 Schumpeter, 'Comments on a Plan for the Study of Entrepreneurship', p. 417, in Richard Swedberg (ed.), *The Economic and Sociology of Capitalism* (Princeton University Press, 1991).

20 This does not suggest that social science knowledge about entrepreneurship should not be translated into advice for business school students. On the contrary, it is to serve such a function that we need to ensure that our knowledge is realistic and useful. Richard Swedberg argued for this point in his book *Entrepreneurship: The Social Science View* (Oxford University Press, 2000).

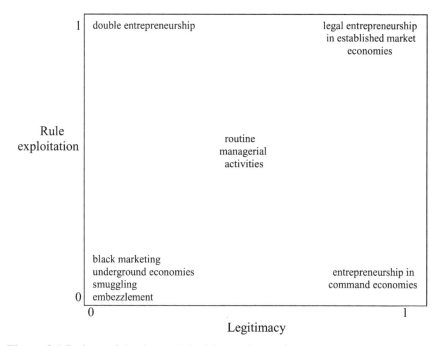

Figure 3.1 Rule-exploitation and legitimacy in profit-seeking activities

To the right is entrepreneurship in Communist command economies, which enjoys a high level of legitimacy but suffers from the lack of autonomy in exploiting rules. Like underground economies, command economies survive by demanding strict conformity to rules. Unlike those in the illegal world, entrepreneurs in former Communist economies do not have to worry about the legitimacy of their activities because they are already in the sector supported by the state. Working under strict regulations, however, does not mean that there is no room for entrepreneurship. Entrepreneurs in China and the former USSR were highly innovative in carrying out state plans of building an industry and launching out new enterprises. As a matter of fact, Communist states were heavily dependent upon such entrepreneurship in maintaining their political dominance.

At the top of the diagram are double entrepreneurship and legal entrepreneurship. The major difference between the two is the degree of legitimacy, which, in turn, is determined by the source of the autonomy of exploiting institutional rules. In transitional economies, autonomy comes from a changing institutional environment. The institutional environment is changing because the institutional rules are not yet effective enough. Deficient institutional rules, however, invite interpretations and exploitations that are actively initiated by entrepreneurs. In other words, it is due to the impotence of changing institutions in reinforcing rules that entrepreneurs become autonomous. In contrast, in well established market economies, the institutional boundaries for economic activities are so clear, stable, and subject to predictable reinforcement that, although entrepreneurs could make profits by exploiting institutional rules, in most situations it is economically more rational for them to play within legitimate fields. In this sense, transforming a Communist economy into a market-oriented one is about turning double entrepreneurship into legal entrepreneurship.

In a nutshell, double entrepreneurship is about simultaneously getting maximum economic rewards and minimum socio-political risks by taking advantage of changing institutions. Entrepreneurs seek promising economic niches from outside the current institutional boundaries, but they also have to acquire political and administrative protection from within the previous and current institutional boundaries. Successful entrepreneurs connect business opportunities in the market to institutional holes so that opportunities can be seized without provoking political, administrative, or public-relations problems. Legitimizing business innovations therefore becomes a constant and essential part of the entrepreneurial process (see the cases of entrepreneurs in Chapters 6, 7, and 8). This is especially true when entrepreneurial ventures are deemed as potentially threatening to the dominant political ideology and system, to administrative authorities, or to widely accepted moral codes. In the context of China, legitimacy of entrepreneurship means establishing ostensible consistency between rule-exploitation and state regulations, smoothing relationships with local authorities and bureaucrats, bettering connections with business partners, and improving management-employee relations.

More generally, institutional effects should not be left untouched in the background when attention has shifted to entrepreneurship alone. Institutions do not emerge in vacuums and they cannot work on their own.[21] They are interpreted and acted upon by economic actors, among which entrepreneurs are the most active and strategic. Consequently, the original meaning and functions of institutional rules will be modified, if not completely changed, during their 'use'. A very important potential of the concept of 'double entrepreneurship' is that it calls for a model that addresses socio-political legitimacy and economic profitability simultaneously. The following figure suggests a possible framework that may help us understand how the balance between legitimacy and profitability shapes the viability of entrepreneurial ventures.

The whole figure is divided into several areas with two dimensions, legitimacy and profitability, ranging from low to high. In between are the minimum and limit levels. The 'minimum' indicates the required level for entrepreneurial ventures to be viable. The 'limit' level refers to the upper points beyond which entrepreneurship will enjoy the additional probability of remaining viable. Below a minimum level of either legitimacy (area II) or profitability (area III), no entrepreneurship is viable. Below the minimum level of profitability, firms will find themselves either hardly able to financially support themselves or with no grounds for bargaining for administrative protection. If a firm's legitimacy is below the minimum level, entrepreneurship is not viable, regardless of its level of profitability, because in this situation the requirement for high legitimacy either cramps entrepreneurship

---

21 Arthur Stinchcombe, 'On the Virtues of the Old Institutionalism', *Annual Review of Sociology*, 23 (1997): 1–18.

or drains profits into administrative payoffs. State authorities, the media, or interest groups could all seriously damage profit-seeking enterprises if entrepreneurs fail to establish that their profit-making businesses are at worst of no harm to the interests of the public, no matter how 'the public' is claimed. If they fall into legitimacy crisis, entrepreneurs will have to pay a dear price for reclaiming their legitimate status, sometimes dear enough to terminate their financial viability. Obviously, enterprises with legitimacy and profitability levels both below the minimum (area I) will be the least viable.

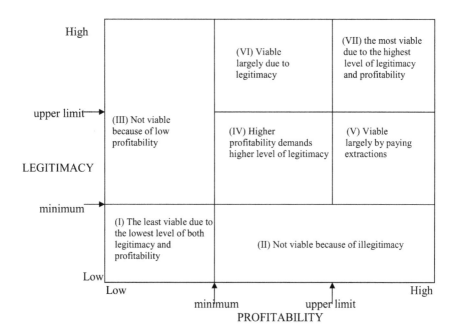

Figure 3.2 The influences of legitimacy and profitability on the viability of entrepreneurship

Beyond the minimum levels, there are four possible scenarios. Within the boundaries of minimum and limit levels (area IV), the demands of legitimacy and profitability constitute a positive relationship – the more legitimate an enterprise wants to be, the more profitable it has to become, and *vice versa*. This situation differs from the above three in that entrepreneurs are largely able to handle the dual requirements of legitimacy and profitability with the resources available to them. None of the two imposes unbearable burdens upon the other. Firms have a better chance of surviving and thriving if they can go beyond the upper limit of either or both dimensions. For the enterprises with economic resources above the average level (area V), legitimacy crisis could be resolved simply by paying off state bureaucrats or powerful interest groups. Naturally, financial costs rise, but so does the probability of survival. Those with better access to socio-political assets enjoy higher chance of viability by successfully obtaining political and administrative privileges and protections (area VI). Clearly, an enterprise resourceful in both profitability and legitimacy will be at the top among viable firms (area VII).

Theoretical implications

I aim to use the twin concepts of 'institutional holes' and 'double entrepreneurship' to make a useful link between institutional rules and entrepreneurship in China's economic reform. The first concept identifies the potential opportunities embedded in the structure of institutional rules. The second one points out what kind of entrepreneurship is needed in order for the potential opportunities to be realized. They also suggest that, to take advantage of institutional holes, an entrepreneur must find, build up and maintain multiple connections by not only innovatively dealing with institutional rules but also watching out for constraints and threats in the structure of institutional rules.

The significance of these ideas for the study of entrepreneurship is that they explicitly bring the institutional conditions of the emergence and growth of entrepreneurship directly to a centre of our understanding of entrepreneurship. As discussed in the previous chapter, Joseph Schumpeter brought entrepreneurship to the centre of the analysis of economic development. According to him, it is entrepreneurship that fulfils the 'creative destruction' function by pooling various resources together to create new business ventures, which are the driving force of any economic development.[22] What has been far less appreciated in Schumpeter's theory, unfortunately, is that entrepreneurship is only half of the story. Schumpeter himself has to take some responsibility for this under-appreciation, because his discussion of institutions ends with no more than a brief account of how entrepreneurs rely on credit organizations such as banks. In fact, his ultimate purpose is to offer a theory of economic development with a focus on the institutional conditions for entrepreneurship.[23] The intrinsic property of the capitalistic economic system is supposed to be an interactive, dynamic relationship between innovative individuals and supporting institutions.[24]

I believe such an approach to studying entrepreneurship is more fundamental than psychological and cultural approaches.[25] If psychological characteristics and cultural legacies can in any sense transcend particular institutional settings, it is so only when we can make at least two assumptions: the institutional structures never change and

---

22 Schumpeter, *Capitalism, Socialism and Democracy* (New York: Harper and Row, 1975).

23 N. De Vechi and A. Stone, *Entrepreneurs, Institutions, and Economic Change: The Economic Thought of J.A. Schumpeter (1905–1925)* (Edward Elgar, 1995).

24 Schumpeter, 'Comments on a Plan for the Study of Entrepreneurship'.

25 Scott Shane, 'Cultural Influences on National Rates of Innovation', *Journal of Business Venturing*, 8 (1993): 59–73; K.G. Shaver and L.R. Scott, 'Person, Process, Choice: The Psychology of New Venture Creation', *Entrepreneurship Theory and Practice*, 16/2 (1993): 16–22.

institutional changes can never change people's psychology or a society's culture, which are of course unsustainable.

As shown early in this chapter, a serious discussion of the institutional conditions for acquiring competitive advantage is weak at best in Burt's structural theory as well. The effect of institutional rules have been put into such a far away background that structural positions among personal or organizational relations can do all the trick in increasing competitiveness; it seems no need to understand the institutional settings in which the structural relations can be functioning.

The marginal position of institutional rules in entrepreneurship studies is in sharp contrast to the overwhelming effect of institutions in neo-institutional economics and organizational theories. There, it is entrepreneurship that has been marginalized. The new institutionalism in economics made a theoretical breakthrough by replacing individual rational choice and market equilibrium with institutional structure. Nonetheless, if there is no room for entrepreneurship when information is complete and everyone is capable of conducting rational calculation, then nor can entrepreneurship find its place either if organizational decisions are made by copying dominant institutional norms and practices. It is the required consistency between institutional structure and economic actions that leads to the marginality of entrepreneurship. Although North later acknowledges that entrepreneurs may in turn 'influence how the institutional framework evolves', 'the focus on organizations (and their entrepreneurs) is primarily on their role as agents of institutional change'.[26]

Such institutionalist perspective poses a paradox to understanding economic development: economic development can only be on the right or fast track when institutional structures have been set up properly, but economic development, by definition, means that institutional structures are still underdeveloped. One way of breaking the circle is to discover entrepreneurial opportunities right in the still inefficient institutional structures, which is exactly what the concept of institutional holes has suggested.

Similarly, the new institutionalism in organization studies maintains that choices are made not based on individual preference but channelled through institutions.[27] Perhaps it is not completely fair to criticize institutionalism for having 'a tendency to enslave individuals to the social structure in which they are embedded',[28] but scholars following this line of thought should openly claim where they put innovative and manipulative behaviours in their analyses. To be sure, for the sake of survival, entrepreneurs have to comply with cultural values and norms, government regulations, and legal codes. Little discussion, however, has been devoted to analyzing the relationship between such institutional demands and the inherent adventurous nature of entrepreneurship. In other words, we should expect to see very

---

26 North, *Institutions, Institutional Change, and Economic Performance*, p. 5.

27 A later, more rounded, version of the new institutionalism in sociology has started to focus on how institutions and organizational actions interact with each other by emphasizing their mutual effects (Nee and Brinton, 2001; Oliver, 1991; Scott, 1994). More needs to be done, however, to clearly specify the mechanisms through which the interactive process takes place.

28 Lance Gore, *Market Communism* (Oxford University Press, 1999), p. 26.

few new business ventures, especially those truly innovative ones, if institutional legitimacy is taken as an overriding consideration in the minds of entrepreneurs. More fundamentally, institutional legitimacy is not as clear-cut as it is usually expected, more so in transitional economies than in mature market economies. Instead of a one-off provision, legitimacy is made through actions. At least for the entrepreneurs in China, the best strategy is to simultaneously acquire legitimacy and profits by making the two processes contribute credits to each other. As previously shown in the discussion of double entrepreneurship, the best strategy for entrepreneurs is to look for business opportunities that could earn them credits of legitimacy, which in turn helps them gain access to future opportunities and protect them at difficult times. In the case studies presented in Chapters 6, 7, and 8, the reader will see how the fate of entrepreneurial businesses varies with the level of success of striking a balance between the two demands. In some situations, legitimacy becomes not merely a *sine qua non* to survive institutional isomorphism but actually a valuable asset in order to thrive. When the rules are not absolutely clear, entrepreneurs procure legitimacy not only by following rules but also by accumulating profits as long as they can justify the nature and sources of their profits.

The disconnection between the power of institutional rules and the adventures of entrepreneurs seems to exist in area studies of China as well. On the one hand, some leading researchers of China have concentrated on the institutional changes in China as the ultimate driving force of the country's economic development. For example, Victor Nee and his students have argued for the effect of the introduction of market mechanisms on individual social mobility and organizational economic performance.[29] Others have focused on the effect of fiscal reforms on local authorities' leadership in establishing economic organizations.[30] On the other hand, as we have seen in Chapter 1, there are a few studies that have documented the experience of entrepreneurs in China, mostly in the non-state sectors. While these studies cannot avoid relating the Chinese entrepreneurial process to the macro economic conditions, they analyze institutional rules as backgrounds rather than as an explicit element of theoretical framework.

All in all, the challenge is to incorporate both institutional effect and entrepreneurship in a coherent analytical framework without overemphasizing any of them simply for the sake of theoretical preference. Taking institutions as the sole dominant force of economic development will make our research reify institutional effects, leading to the unjustifiable statement that economic growth will automatically take place once the rules of the game have been set up properly.

---

29 Victor Nee, 'A Theory of Market Transition: From Redistribution to Markets in State Socialism', *American Sociological Review*, 54/5 (1989): 663–681. Victor Nee and Cao Yang, 'Path Dependent Social Transformation: Stratification in Hybrid Mixed Economies', *Theory and Society*, 28 (1999): 799–834.

30 D.J. Solinger, 'Urban Entrepreneurs and the State: The Merger of State and Society', pp. 121–141 in Arthur Lewis Rosenbaum (ed.), *State and Society in China: The consequences of Reform* (Boulder, CO: Westview Press, 1992). Andrew Walder, 'Local Government as Industrial Firms: An Organizational Analysis of China's Transitional Economy', *American Journal of Sociology*, 101/2 (1995): 263–301. J. Oi, 'The Role of the Local State in China's Transitional Economy', *The China Quarterly*, 144 (1995): 1132–1149.

Nor should we simply replace the craving for economic efficiency (the neo-classic economic assumption) with the desire to appear legitimate as the primary rationale behind organizational decision-making; otherwise, the interactive process between institutions and entrepreneurial behaviours will be very likely left in the dark. Like it or not, most of the time and for most economic organizations, being competitive in the market has been, and will still remain, the first objective. No matter how powerful institutional rules are, legitimacy alone will not help organizations survive increasingly fierce business competition. This does not imply that institutional rules do not matter. They do matter, but not because entrepreneurs would like to give up competitiveness for legitimacy, but because, to improve competitiveness, they must draw upon available institutional structures to legitimize their profit-making strategies and practices. The dual task of procuring legitimacy and competitiveness do not necessarily contradict to each other. Rather, under some conditions, they reinforce each other in promoting organizational competitiveness.

While discussing 'Organizational Isomorphism in East Asia', Orrù, Biggart, and Hamilton challenged the 'presumption of the dichotomy or necessary antagonism of technical and institutional environments'.[31] I totally agree with their arguments. I have attempted to go further by making two important points. First, the mutually beneficial relationship between technical efficiency and institutional legitimacy is a source of entrepreneurship and competitive advantage. Second, by connecting the levels of legitimacy to the degrees of technical efficiency we can map out and compare the life cycles of different firms, which is represented in the earlier model of double entrepreneurship.

Toward a comparative sociology of entrepreneurship and institutional change

Institutional holes exist in all types of economies and everywhere entrepreneurs look for opportunities embedded in institutional structures. What varies is the specific representations of institutional holes and the way double entrepreneurship is practised. Indeed, enterprises in mature market economies are experiencing changes that are no less dramatic than those in transitional economies.[32] This does not mean, however, that differences between institutional conditions don't matter anymore. Quite to the contrary, it is by looking at how institutional holes and entrepreneurship work differently in a variety of institutional settings that we can advance our understanding of each phenomenon. If these points are acceptable, then we can make some suggestive observations for comparing entrepreneurship and institutional change in transitional and mature market economies.

---

31 Marco Orrù, Nicole Woolsey Biggart, and Gary Hamilton, 'Organizational Isomorphism in East Asia', pp. 361–389 in Walter Powell and Paul DiMaggio (eds), *The New Institutionalism in Organizational Analysis* (University of Chicago Press, 1991).

32 See the chapters in Paul DiMaggio (ed.), *The Twenty-First Century Firm: Changing Economic Organization in International Perspective*, especially Chapters 2, 3, and 4 (Princeton University Press, 2001). See, also, R. Greenwood and C.R. Hinings, 'Understanding Radical Organizational Change: Bringing Together the Old and the New Institutionalism', *Academy of Management Review*, 21/4 (1996): 1022–1054.

First of all, institutional holes are expected to be more prevalent in transitional economies than mature market economies. By definition, institutional rules in transition are more often incomplete, ambiguous or conflicting with one another – the establishment of any institutional framework has to be a historical process. The scale and scope of applicability, the exact meaning and relations with other rules, etc., are all to be clarified and verified in practice. Thus more gaps will emerge when the new rules have not completely replaced the old ones, when the general principles have not exhausted the specific conditions, and when different administrative authorities have their own ways of interpreting and reinforcing the new rules. Enticed by the opportunities embedded in those gaps, entrepreneurs in transitional economies thus search for institutional holes more often, and more earnestly, than those in mature market economies. Standard structural holes are not sufficient in understanding their competitive advantage since changing institutional rules always reorganize the positions of different social groups.

Institutional holes in transitional economies will also produce more short-term returns than those in mature market economies. In transitional economies the average life expectancy of institutional rules, often represented as policies at different government levels, is considerably short. On the one hand, the consequences of new state policies are not clear. In the context of China, a key strategy adopted by policy makers for coping with uncertainties is to repeatedly test the political, economic and social implications of each policy on a small scale. Other factors that make state policies short-lived include regional disparities of economic development, political conflicts among policy makers, and ordinary people's opposition to some policies. On the other hand, most entrepreneurs react by taking a short-term, exploitive approach to business transactions, which again makes it hard for the state to enact long-term policies. Extending institutions' life expectancy actually has become a top concern for state leaders of China.[33] For entrepreneurs, opportunities become transient not merely because soon competitors will bring a similar or even better product to the market but more importantly because state policies are frequently changing and organizations in the same institutional field will try to exhaust all the resources when they are in advantageous positions.

Finally, entrepreneurs in transitional economies are more adventurous in taking advantage of institutional holes than those in mature market economies. Transitional economies are full of institutional fields with boundaries that are hard to identify. For example, the Chinese state policies on private enterprises during the period from the

---

33 One interesting case in point is 'the fool's watermelon seeds'. Before private enterprises were allowed to run as legal economic organizations, a man nicknamed 'fool' in Jiangxi province made millions of Chinese yuan by selling toasted watermelon seeds based on a family recipe. It was especially illegal because he employed several assistants in his workshop, an evidence of exploitation. Some local officials proposed to put him in jail. Then Deng Xiaoping intervened by saying 'My opinion is to wait and watch. Will he do any harm to our socialist mission? If you remove him, people will say our policy has changed'. Zhang Houyi, 'The Upsurge of a New Force: The Re-emergence and Development of the Private Economy after Economic Reform and Opening', pp. 3–59 in Zhang Huoyi and Ming Lizhi (eds), *Report of the Development of Private Enterprises in China (1978–1998)* (in Chinese, Beijing: Social Science Documentation Publishing House, 1999).

end of 1970s to the end of 1980s were especially ambiguous: from encouragement of small scale self-employment, to the permission of a limited number of private enterprises in certain industries, to a legitimate status of private business in party resolutions (without specific legal protection of private property, however), etc. As the risk of rule-violations goes when the rules become increasingly ambiguous, changing directions of political winds have made businesses riskier than they are in mature market economies.

In addition, government agencies are far less directly involved in, if not completely prohibited from, profit-making activities in established market economies. By contrast, for government officials in China, it is in the interests of their political careers and personal well-being to improve local economic conditions.[34] This makes playing with institutional holes a riskier game for entrepreneurs because state bureaucrats have the authority to determine the legitimacy of new enterprises. Structural autonomy in social relations will not lead to competitive advantage without a certain level of legitimacy acknowledged by state officials. China's changing economic institutions have promoted entrepreneurship by offering opportunities in institutional holes at high transaction costs.

In short, competitive advantages in transitional economies are therefore determined by how autonomous entrepreneurs are with regard to locating themselves in institutional structures, that is, whether the entrepreneurs have access to different institutional rules and how much they are constrained by the rules, and how successful the entrepreneurs are in legitimating strategies and behaviours of making profits by taking advantage of the changeability of the rules. Those with better access to various resources concerning how the rules will change or how the rules could be manipulated have fewer rules to conform to and thus enjoy more autonomy in combining or recombining complementary elements for a business venture, such as information, finance, services, etc.

Summary

Institutions are still the rules of the game in China. But the way it works is relatively different. In the context of China, uncertainties generated from changing institutional structures are risk factors as well as assets for the development of entrepreneurship. Entrepreneurship in China is about taking advantage of the non-equivalently distributed resources produced by the changing institutional rules and combining these resources into profitable business projects. To a large extent and represented in many cases (some illustrative ones will be presented in Chapters 6, 7, and 8), entrepreneurial opportunities come from the fact that the interpretation of their meaning and application in practice are open for negotiations. If entrepreneurs could successfully negotiate the legitimacy of their strategies and practices with authorities in charge of the rules, entrepreneurial opportunities are then realized.

---

34 Walder, 'Local Government as Industrial Firms: An Organizational Analysis of China's Transitional Economy'. Oi, 'The Role of the Local State in China's Transitional Economy'.

Various situations embedded in changing institutional frameworks have stimulated entrepreneurial ventures to come back and forth across the presumably clearly defined institutional boundaries, many times unexpected to designers and administrators of the institutions and to entrepreneurs themselves as well. This could happen because ambiguity, inconsistency, delay, and incompleteness in institutional rules all offer discriminating rewards and punishments. Viable enterprises are those that can find and occupy the position of institutional holes while at the same time remaining legitimate.

Chapter 4

Institutional Change and Entrepreneurial Strategies

Guided by the conceptual and theoretical ideas developed in the previous two chapters, this chapter starts the empirical study of changing institutional rules and entrepreneurial strategies, which is discussed in two parts. The first part consists of this and the next chapters, which, by taking a quite broad view, examine the interaction between rules and entrepreneurship under China's economic transformation. The second part, in Chapters 6, 7, and 8 is the comparative study of three entrepreneurs.

This chapter traces the change of rules for entrepreneurs, particularly those in the private sector, in the history of the People's Republic of China. It also identifies the strategies adopted by private entrepreneurs in responding to the rules. In contrast, the study in the next chapter will be quantitative and focused on the steps that the entrepreneurs have to go through.

Rules for entrepreneurs in China are concretely represented in forms of different formality, ranging from the most formal, such as legal codes, to the most informal, such as a point made by a political leader in a spontaneous conversation. The most important form of rules is party policies, so it is necessary to begin with a brief account of why this is the case. Then the historical study will follow. Readers with no previous exposure to the history of the People's Republic of China may want to know that the Chinese Communist Party (CCP hereafter) did not eliminate all private businesses straight away after it came to power in 1949; it was at the end of 1956 that nearly all private (or 'capitalist', to use the term in those days) enterprises were transformed into a kind of public company under state control. The private firms that re-emerged in the late 1970s, whose exact nature is to be discussed below, are both new and old. They are new because this generation of entrepreneurs have little connection with the previous one; they have to start their own businesses from scratch. But as a type of economic organization, these businesses are not new to many ordinary people, especially the older generations who lived through the turbulent years of the 1950s and the 1960s. They are also not new ideologically, easily reminding people of some sensitive and difficult issues including, for example, exploitation. The tension between the new and the old is crucially important for us to understand in the construction of new rules, the reconstruction of old rules, and the exploitation of these changes as entrepreneurial opportunities. My ultimate aim in this chapter is to provide a brief but broad view of China's economic reforms from the perspective of examining the interactions between institutional change and entrepreneurship in the private sector.

Party policies as rules

Although more and more policies have been transformed into laws since the Chinese Communist Party (CCP) became the ruling party, more often than not, it has not ruled by law, but by policy. The overall procedure runs as follows: leaders of the Party come up with some ideas, which will be discussed in a wider group, either the Political Bureau or the Central Committee; then the Party will have to collectively reach a final resolution, which will then be specified technically and administratively by the State Council and People's Congress as administrative or legal regulations. The Party found policies more effective than legal codes for turning its political ideas into reality when it was still struggling to fight for political power in the Anti-Japanese War and the Civil War. For one thing, compared with laws, policies are indeed more flexible in coping with problems in such a vast country. Legislation demands many rounds of careful discussion in order to leave as little room as possible for mistakes and manipulations. A legal system is expected to be a set of codes of high logical consistency and to be consistent with the general principles of the larger political system. Party policies also need to be comprehensive, logically coherent and consistent, but they can be produced in a rather short period of time and put into action quickly for tackling a nation-wide problem in an effective and efficient manner. Whilst laws aim to exhaust all important situations, policies supply general principles to be applied in all relevant situations without having to identify what the situations are, thus maintaining a wide range of applications without sacrificing flexibility.

In practice, the flexibility of policies puts policy makers in an advantageous position. Depending on the extent to which a particular consequence of using a policy is to their own interests, policy makers will be able to determine which results should be further promoted or terminated straightaway, without having to make these decisions beforehand. But the flexibility may turn into ambiguities, inconsistencies, or even complete arbitrations. As a foreign investor doing business in China has learnt:

> How easy is it to get your business registered and licensed? How likely is your investment project to be approved? Will you be able to get loans from the banking system? What tax rates will your company be subject to?
>
> The answer to the above questions is: 'it all depends'. In this wonderland of preferential policies, it depends on who you are, where you are from, and who your Chinese business partners are. It depends on which part of China your company is doing the business in and where you intend to invest. Again it depends on which industry you intend to operate in. To make things more bewildering, these policies are dynamic and fast-changing, and often implemented with discretion. Many foreign investors are confused. Some are frustrated. Quite a few, however, have been so far surfing well on these policies and making their fortunes.[1]

---

1 Ding Lu and Zhimin Tang, *State Intervention and Business in China: The Role of Preferential Policies* (Edward Elgar, 1997), p. 4.

Finally, policies are much easier for ordinary people to understand than complicated legal procedures. For millions of people who are barely literate or capable of understanding written documents, ideas formulated in daily spoken languages, such as slogans, short phrases, analogies, and rhyming words are much more effective than carefully worded legal terms for passing a message over to a huge audience. In essence, party policies are forms of rhetoric masquerading as announced principles. Usually, they work brilliantly in describing a general situation rather than offering specific analysis of possible scenarios and corresponding solutions. Consequently and constantly, it is local authorities who have the final say with regard to what the policies really mean, how they should be implemented, and what can be taken as exceptions.

Party policies can take many different forms according to their formality. The most formal policies are obviously legal codes, and the most informal ones are spontaneous talks by top party leaders or an editorial in a state newspaper. The bulk of party policies are in the form of party resolutions and stipulations issued by the State Council. Political resolutions published at national conventions of the CCP are the most important because they set the tone for resolving controversial issues, prioritize the allocations of valuable resources, and point out the general direction in which the Party wants the nation to move. Based on these general guiding points and principles, ministries of the State Council and specialized committees of the People's Congress will produce specific regulations for each particular issue. Those by the ministries may take the forms of official notes, resolutions, reports, conference minutes, or even official letters. Obviously, formality does not always reflect the power of a policy; many times, it is what a top leader said in a conversion that becomes the first version of a new policy. But this observation should not go as far as to say that a top leader is always able to determine an exact policy. The final versions of most policies are actually the results of negotiations and discussions within the Party.

The disappearance of private businesses in the People's Republic of China, 1949–1956

Coming to power in 1949, the Chinese Communists had a very strong sense of moving toward a Communist society in several steps. They realized, however, that they had to work with the capitalists in the early years of the new regime – the so-called 'New Democratic Revolution' – because it took time for the economy to become ready for moving to the Socialist Revolution. They could not jump over this 'New Democratic' period because China's capitalist class was especially weak compared with those in western societies due to the corrupt Qing Dynasty, the war against the Japanese, and the following Civil War. After the wars, the country was in ruins and the most urgent task for the new political administration was to restore order and production in all areas of society. As Mao clearly stated right before the new Republic was formally established:

> China's private capitalist industry, which occupies second place in her modern industry, is a force which must not be ignored. Because they have been oppressed or hemmed in by

imperialism, feudalism and bureaucrat-capitalism, the national bourgeoisie of China and its representatives have often taken part in the people's democratic revolutionary struggles or maintained a neutral stand. For this reason and because China's economy is still backward, there will be need, for a fairly long period after the victory of the revolution, to make use of the positive qualities of urban and rural private capitalism as far as possible, in the interest of developing the national economy.[2]

Crucial distinctions were made between three groups of capitalists, i.e., the bureaucratic, the imperial, and the national. The bureaucratic capitalists were those closely connected to the defeated Guomintang government. The imperial capitalists operated industrial enterprises with the support of western or Japanese military powers. As the previous government and the imperial powers were absolutely the enemy of the Communist State, the new administration had every reason of usurping all their assets. But the national capitalists were different. Some of them might have been forced to support the Guomintang, but their first motivation was to survive, not to fight against the Communists. Some even had helped the Communists during the wars. So they became part of the 'national united front', which included not only workers and peasants as the dominating classes but the petty bourgeoisie (mostly intellectuals and small business owners) and the national capitalists as well.

But everyone knew that such a 'united front' would not last for long. Fortunately to the capitalists, Mao Zedong, Zhou Enlai, Liu Shaoqi all promised in various occasions that the process of socializing their businesses be made as peacefully and reasonably as possible. The overall plan was to establish 'state capitalism', which would make capitalist enterprises phase out of China's national economy by gradually purchasing their assets while in the meantime still letting the capitalists earn a reasonable proportion of profits (about 25 per cent). With orders and sales exclusively made through the State but virtually no further investments, in most industries the proportion of the value produced by capitalist businesses out of the total national value quickly reduced to less than 10 per cent by 1955. Finally, by setting up joint ventures between private businesses and public enterprises, it was clear that private businesses had no other choice but eventually 'sell off' their factories and companies to the new People's Republic. The whole process actually finished at the end of 1956, one year earlier than was planned.[3]

The two decades after the disappearance of capitalist enterprises were dramatic in the new China's history, with the first, the 'Socialist Construction' period (1956–1966) being a success, while the second, the Great Proletariat Cultural Revolution (1966–1976) a complete disaster. During the Cultural Revolution, all private businesses were perceived as sinful; they were 'the capitalist tails' that should be cut off immediately. The business owners were accused, condemned, humiliated, and in many occasions executed. Thereafter, private businesses disappeared, literally.

---

2   Mao Zedong, 'Report to the Second Plenary Session of the Seventh Central Committee of the Communist Party of China' (5 March 1949) http://www.marxists.org/reference/archive/mao/selected-works/volume-4/mswv4_58.htm.

3   Dong Fureng, *An Economic History of the People's Republic of China* (Hong Kong: Joint Publishing Co., Ltd., 2001), vol. 1, Chapter 8.

Two beliefs about private properties and businesses have survived those stormy years, however. The first is ethical: private ownership is morally wrong because it allows capitalists to reap the surplus value produced by workers. This process of exploitation is possible simply because capitalists own the means necessary for production. With private ownership disappearing so goes exploitation. The second belief of eliminating private ownership is economic: advanced and large-scale production requires the centralized management of all necessary resources and means of production, which can only be achieved by state ownership in the name of all working people but is impossible when the resources are in the hands of selfish capitalists. Therefore, managing the economy by a comprehensive plan is another essential feature of the socialist economy. The replacement of private ownership with state ownership will therefore greatly enhance economic development. The several rounds of debate over the legitimacy of private ownership *after 1976* means that, given so many years of political chaos and economic stagnation, many CCP leaders, and most ordinary people, did not realize that there would be no entrepreneurship if the State remained in control of everything and that without entrepreneurship there would be no economic development. Years after the Cultural Revolution, the fright and the hatred of private property were still lingering in people's minds.

New rules, new entrepreneurs

Employment or exploitation? Economic pragmatism in the shadow of Communist ideology

The socialist demands of eliminating private ownership of means of production and organizing the economy by state plans left little hope for people who had the ambition of setting up their own businesses. Nevertheless, the economic conditions for realizing this ambition became favourable at the end of the 1970s: all the Chinese people were highly motivated to get out of extreme poverty, there was a shortage of nearly everything, meaning plenty of opportunities in the market, and the market was huge. But these conditions were not strong enough to force the Chinese State to give up the socialist principles and to lift the ban on private business, which also explains why the Chinese State did not take the shock therapy route applied in the former USSR and Eastern Europe. It was a practical problem that eventually forced a way out for private entrepreneurs: the huge unemployed labour force.

During the movement of 'Up to Mountains and Down to Villages' in the Cultural Revolution, tens of millions of youths went to rural areas to be 're-educated' by the ideologically purer class of farmers. Although some of the youths eventually stayed in the villages because of marriage or for any other personal reasons, most of them wanted to go back to the cities immediately after the movement was over. From 1976, when the Cultural Revolution ended, to 1979, when the State started to take some liberal policies toward economic issues under the leadership of Deng Xiaoping (but not liberal enough to encourage private entrepreneurship), there were more than 10 million young people coming back to urban areas. In the meantime, several million high school graduates in the cities could not find jobs. In 1979, economists estimated that there were 15.38 million unemployed people in cities and towns, constituting about 6 per cent of all the working population.[4] Those at the top were clearly aware of the urgent nature of the problem. As Li Xiannian, then the Vice-Chairman of the CCP in charge of financial affairs, pointed out in a Central Committee meeting in April 1979:

> Now, about 20 million people need to be employed in the whole nation. Among them, 1.05 million are college and high school graduates and demobilized military staffs whose families are in cities, 3.2 million young people staying in cities according to our policies, another 7 million youths returning from rural areas, 2.3 million unemployed labours in cities and towns, 0.85 million wrongly treated during the Anti-Right Movement and the Cultural Revolution who now need to be employed, etc. Out of the 20 million unemployed, 8 million have to be allocated a job urgently this year. This has become a serious social problem, which, if not handled properly, will be easily triggered to break out into a disaster, gravely jeopardizing our nation's stability and solidarity.[5]

Although the unemployment figure decreased to 12 million in 1980,[6] the situation had no sign of improvement. The State could not hold on to its principles anymore – it simply could not send millions of young people to already overstaffed state or collective enterprises. It became obvious and inevitable to let the youths take care of themselves. And the door to private businesses was finally opened in February 1979 when, under the suggestions of some influential economists such as Xue Muqiao, the State Administration for Industry and Commerce (SAIC) told its local branches that they:

> may, according to the needs of local markets and with the approval of relevant departments, give permission to idle labour with registration of permanent residence to undertake individual businesses in repair, service and handicraft industries, but hiring labour shall not be allowed.[7]

As this message is typical of the institutional rules in China, it deserves a careful examination. Firstly, the rules were set out with a general objective and a certain level of flexibility. It seems clear that the objective was to solve the 'idle labour' problem, but it left some important decisions to be made by local authorities. What was a local market? If there were more than one, how to prioritize? How to determine whether a market was in need of labour? What was 'idle' labour? Answers to these questions were not clearly stated. Secondly, the rules laid out some conditions for any actions to be taken. In this particular case, the conditions included (1) the businessman must have permanent residence registration; (2) the business could only operate in three industries, namely, repair, service, and handicraft; (3) the businessman

---

    4   Dong, *An Economic History of the People's Republic of China*, vol. 2, p. 425.

    5   Central Committee of the Chinese Communist Party, *A Collection of Important Documents Since the Third Plenum* (People's Press, 1991), vol. 1, p. 114.

    6   Zhang Houyi and Ming Lizhi (eds), *Report of the Development of Private Businesses in China* (1999), p. 15.

    7   Wu Jinglian, *Understanding and Interpreting Chinese Economic Reform* (Thomson/ South-Western, 2005), p. 181.

was not allowed to hire anybody else. Perhaps most important of all was the rule that individuals should not open their businesses without 'the approval of relevant departments' of local authorities, but it did not (perhaps it could not) say which departments were 'relevant'. All these features show just how supple the rules are.

If the rules' suppleness left substantial power to local officials, it also offered some room for manipulation by potential business owners. Individuals strongly motivated to open their own businesses would find many things that they could do if the rules appeared to be a hurdle: to obtain permanent residence by bribing the local official in charge, to argue that a manufacturing business should fall into the category of 'service', to show that someone was just helping out the business rather than being hired as an employee, and to exercise pressure through personal connections.

Obviously, individual businesses would not remain truly individual for long; even a small operation would require some assistants, let alone when the business expanded into one of some scale. Either by capacity or by luck, or by both, some individuals earned enough money for a bigger business. The market remained huge, and there were many people waiting to be hired. Sooner or later, to employ others, that is, to commit the ethical and political crime of exploitation, became unavoidable. The Central Committee of the CCP was clearly aware of this. In August 1980, it published 'The Guidelines for Combining Employment through Labour Administrations, Employment through Organizing Cooperatives on a Voluntary Basis, and Employment through Establishing Individual Businesses', which required that 'the development of the urban individual business sector be encouraged and fostered'.[8] Still, the guidelines were trying to walk a fine line between employment and exploitation – there was a green light for employing others, but it had to be carried out under government administrative supervision and on a voluntary basis. Again, there was some room for bending these rules, all depending on the attitudes and interests of local authorities or on the relationship between local authorities and businessmen. To strike the balance of keeping these virtually private businesses alive while preserving political correctness, the Party published a baseline for distinguishing acceptable employment from exploitation: it was not a private enterprise (thus, no exploitation) if the business owner hired only seven or less employees.[9]

But even the new rule of 'seven or less' could not hold for long. As researchers in China have reported, many entrepreneurs employed more than eight people in both rural and urban areas after the policy was announced.[10] Of course those hiring a large number of people attracted a lot of attention from the media and local governments. One of the most well-known examples is the case of 'the fool's toasted sunflower

---

8 Ibid., pp. 181–182.

9 According to Wu Jinglian (2005, p. 182), the baseline was initially suggested by the economist Li Zili, who claimed that Karl Marx made such a distinction in *Capital*. Zhang Houyi (1999, 16), however, argued that this was simply because an individual business would need one or two assistants and no more than five apprentices, so the total should be seven or less.

10 Zhang and Ming, *Report of the Development of Private Businesses in China*; Liu Peifeng, *Owners of Private Enterprises* (*Si Ying Qi Ye Zhu*, in Chinese) (Beijing: Social Science Documentation Publishing House, 2005), Chapter 1.

seeds'. Nicknamed 'the fool', the businessman's real name was Nian Guangjiu. Starting from 1972, he operated a successful business of producing and selling toasted sunflower seeds, an extremely popular snack food in China. Initially, to show that they were following the general policy of promoting individual businesses, local officials encouraged him to grow. But soon they came to realize that, politically, this was a risky business – by 1981, 'the fool' had already employed more than 100 people and paid a tax of more than 300,000 yuan, an amount possibly equivalent to a local area's total revenue in those years. No doubt, the business was not 'individual' anymore; it had grown into a 'capitalist' enterprise. Some local officials made the proposal of putting him in jail on the charge of exploitation. Clearly, the rule-makers at that time were not united behind a clear principle. As a matter of fact, they were torn between developing local economies and maintaining political correctness, which we can see in the following document published in 1983:

> We are a socialist nation, and thus will not allow the existence of exploiting institutions. But we are also a developing nation with still a relatively low level of production and underdevelopment of commodity, particularly in rural areas. It is therefore beneficial for the development of socialist economy to allow a certain level of mobility and various combinations of finance, technology, and labour … For those who have employed more than what the regulation has permitted, we should not recommend or disseminate publicly, but nor shall we be in a hurry to eliminate them. What we should do is to provide proper guidance so that they will develop into various types of cooperative economy.[11]

It was Deng Xiaoping who was behind such a 'wait and see' policy and dismissed the hostile approach to solving the case of 'the fool's toasted sunflower seeds':

> With regard to some other problems, we don't have to be impatient for quick solutions. For instance, the emergence of privately hired labour was quite shocking a while back. Everybody was very worried about it. In my opinion, that problem can be set aside for a couple of years. Will that affect the overall situation? If we act on the question now, people will say the policies have changed, and they will be upset. If you put the man who makes 'Fool's Sunflower Seeds' out of business, it will make many people anxious, and that won't do anybody any good. What is there to be afraid of if we let him go on selling his seeds for a while? Will that hurt socialism?[12]

Such tacit consent to private businesses lasted for about four years from 1983 to 1986, during which time only a few ambiguous rules were published. Obviously, to the entrepreneurs, the absence of rules was the amber light, an encouraging sign with great uncertainty: you could go ahead but you had to be cautious. Another implication is that China's top leaders actually put the fate of private businesses into the hands of local authorities. Businesses in the areas with a liberal local leader, mostly in the coastal provinces, enjoyed more friendly policies and favourable

---

11 The Central Committee of the CCP, 'Some Issues Regarding Current Economic Policies in Rural Areas' quoted and translated from Zhang and Ming (1999, p. 36).

12 Deng Xiaoping, 'Speech at the Third Plenary Session of the Central Advisory Commission of the Communist Party of China', October 22, 1984: http://english.peopledaily.com.cn/dengxp/vol3/text/c1280.html.

administrations, while those in areas under conservative leadership suffered from harsher treatments.[13] Overall, the re-emergence, and surprising growth, of non-state enterprises posed a dilemma for many local officials: these enterprises could make enormous contributions to the much needed economic growth, but they were not the type of businesses that the Party was supposed to support according to the ideological principles that it had held for such a long time. Debate within the Party over how to solve the dilemma prevented the formation of a clear policy. As a result, the CCP took a 'watching' strategy, that is, *to allow but not to openly encourage* non-state sectors. From 1978 to 1986, the Party virtually relinquished its responsibility of providing guidance to this part of the national economy. There was no talk, no document, no research, and no signal whatsoever. In short, there was a void of institutional rules in this period of time. With no incentives from institutional rules, most entrepreneurs in China, as we shall see in the following chapters, started their businesses with the motivation of liberating themselves from poverty. What the institutional void provided for entrepreneurs was an institutional space for releasing their energy and realizing their dreams, not direct incentives.

The year 1987 was a turning point for private enterprises in China. Before, the State had few choices but to allow the private sector to fulfil the functions of reducing unemployment rate and improving people's quality of life. In 1987, economic pragmatism gained an upper hand over Communist ideology.[14] The CCP seemed to have finally made up its mind that all forms of economic organization, regardless of their ideological identities, should be encouraged to grow for the sake of developing China's national economy. As a 'supplementary component of China's socialist economy', private enterprises became not only necessary but also desirable. The CCP granted private enterprises a legitimate status in its thirteenth Congress in October 1987, and the issue of exploitation was resolved by pointing out the valuable contributions made by the private sector:

> It is true that employed labour relations exist in the private economy. However, under socialist conditions, it will be necessarily related to, and heavily influenced by, the dominating public economy. Practices have proved that the development of the private economy at a certain level will promote production, enliven markets, expand employment, and better satisfy people's various needs in life, and it is thus a necessary and beneficial supplement to the public economy.[15]

In short, the contributions by private businesses were so overwhelming that exploitation had become an insignificant issue. Their legal status was formally established at the seventh People's Congress on 12 April 1988, when an amendment was added to the Constitution that 'the State protects the lawful rights and interests of the private economy and exercises guidance, supervision, and guarantees the

---

13 Lynn T. White, III, *Unstately Power (I): Local Causes of China's Economic Reforms* (M.E. Sharpe, 1998).

14 In 1986, *The General Principles of Civil Law* (*min fa zong ze*) was published, but it was too simple to be practically useful, only applicable to individual businesses (*ge ti hu*) and not related to the legitimacy of private businesses in general.

15 http://news.xinhaunet.com.

status of private enterprises'. Based on the amendment, the State Council issued a more specific regulation, *The Interim Stipulations on Private Enterprises*, in June. Although there was still a voice within the Party that private enterprises should not be allowed to develop into a threat to the dominance of state enterprises, especially during the aftermath of the political turmoil in 1989, it became very unlikely that the policy set in the thirteenth National Congress could be reversed.

One big lesson that the CCP has learnt from managing economic reforms is that it is vital to keep their policies as stable as possible. Recalling the case of 'the fool's sunflower seeds' in 1992, Deng Xiaoping made this point very clear in his famous South China tour:

> In the initial stage of the rural reform, there emerged in Anhui Province the issue of the 'Fool's Sunflower Seeds'. Many people felt uncomfortable with this man who had made a profit of 1 million yuan. They called for action to be taken against him. I said that no action should be taken, because that would make people think we had changed our policies, and the loss would outweigh the gain. There are many problems like this one, and if we don't handle them properly, our policies could easily be undermined and overall reform affected. The basic policies for urban and rural reform must be kept stable for a long time to come.[16]

And Deng was determined to solve the exploitation issue once and for all:

> The reason some people hesitate to carry out the reform and the open policy and dare not break new ground is, in essence, that they're afraid it would mean introducing too many elements of capitalism and, indeed, taking the capitalist road. The crux of the matter is whether the road is capitalist or socialist. The chief criterion for making that judgement should be whether it promotes the growth of the productive forces in a socialist society, increases the overall strength of the socialist state, and raises living standards.[17]

These are the well-known 'three benefits' (*san ge you li yu*) in China.

Ambiguities remain, however, in these general principles. For example, although private businesses have become a legitimate component of the national economy, it is still not clear whether they should be treated in the same way as the ones owned by the state. The report of the Third Plenary Session of the Fourteenth Congress was quite ambiguous about this, claiming that the public sector should keep its 'mainstay' status for the whole nation, but that can vary from region to region, or from industry to industry. The next significant step was not taken until 1997 at the CCP's fifteenth National Congress where the role of the private sector was elevated to one of parity with the state sector. It seemed, however, that private entrepreneurs were still haunted by their inferior status due to private ownership. What Liu Yonghao, a prominent entrepreneur elected to be a member of the Standing Committee of the People's Political Consultation Assembly (PPCA, or *zheng xie*), would like to see

16 Deng, 'Excerpts from Talks Given in Wuchang, Shenzhen, Zhuhai and Shanghai', January 18–February 21, 1992. http://english.peopledaily.com.cn/dengxp/vol3/text/d1200.html.

17 Ibid.

was to grant private businesses a legitimate status in China's Constitution.[18] That wish was realized soon in March 1999, when the National People's Congress passed an amendment (article 16) to the Constitution to recognize the legitimate status of the private sector.

Ambiguous and discriminating rules for private businesses

It would be naïve to believe that, once a legitimate status of private businesses was ratified and written down in the Constitution, then private entrepreneurs in China did not have to worry about ownership any more and that they could start to behave as state firms or collective enterprises do. Whilst the State promises to protect private rights and properties, it does not specify how it will do it. The Constitution (article 12) clearly states that 'Socialist public properties are sacred and inviolable. The State protects socialist public properties'. To most Chinese, the implications are clear: private properties, albeit legal, are not sacred and, therefore, violable. As presented above, for about two decades, the Chinese State held an ambivalent attitude towards the private sector, recognizing its indispensable contributions while in the meantime worrying about its threat to the socialist nature of China's economy. This attitude was clearly reflected in the discrepancies between the Chinese government's responsibility of supporting private enterprises, repeated many times in the documents of the CCP or the State Council, on the one hand, and the conditions and restrictions for operating private businesses on the other hand. The ambivalence has prevented the State from taking a head-on approach to administering the private sector. At the back of the minds of some Chinese leaders and officials, private ownership remained, for a long time, a circle that could not easily be squared with the socialist nature of China's economy. There has not been any government agency established with the main responsibility for coordinating the administration of private enterprises. This is clearly different from the situation for town-and-village enterprises (TVE). As they are officially defined as 'collective enterprises', TVE enjoy much clearer and stronger support from the State. Administratively, there is a Bureau of TVE in the State Council's Department of Agriculture, but a corresponding administrative body for private enterprises is nowhere to be found, although the State Administration for Industry and Commerce is the most important one in practice. In principle, almost every governmental department has a duty to supervise private enterprises, and all can wield some power over them, but no agency has been designated with the responsibility of speaking on behalf of private business owners. In more concrete terms, as Jian Fu has detailed:

> The State Taxation Bureau assesses and collects tax from private enterprises. The State Pricing Bureau is in charge of pricing certain products, although its power has gradually diminished. The People's Bank of China administers loans to private enterprises and is responsible for accounting issues. The Technology Supervision Bureau is in charge of technical standards and product quality. The Hygiene Inspection Bureau, together with the Administration of Industry and Commerce, licenses enterprises involved in food production and sale. The Environmental and Natural Resources Protection Bureau,

---

18 Interview of Liu Yonghao, *China Economic Times* (11 May 1998).

together with the Administration of Industry and Commerce, licenses and inspects those enterprises whose products may affect the environment. The Ministry of Labour and Social Security is responsible for employment and social security issues. The main problem with this system is the confusion over which rule will prevail if there is any conflict between the rules of the departments.[19]

And we shall see in Chapter 6 how one of these agencies, The Technology Supervision Bureau, could shape the fate of a private firm.

Similarly, legal codes for private enterprises, although carefully drafted and worded by legal specialists, may not be consistent with one another if they are written by different agencies, for example a sub-committee of the People's Congress and a consulting group within the State Council. Here are some examples of inconsistent or even conflicting rules. According to *The Interim Stipulations*, a private enterprise is an economic organization whose assets are owned by private individuals and employ more than eight people, and there are three types of private enterprises: sole individual ownership, partnership, and limited liability. More importantly, only people of the following categories are allowed to open and run a private enterprise: village residents in rural areas, anyone unemployed in urban areas, individual businessmen (*ge ti hu*), retired and resigned staff and others. Nevertheless, such restrictions disappeared five years later in 1993 when the *Company Law* was published. The issue was important in the 1990s because many employees of state enterprises were made redundant, and they could not find clear rules as to whether they were eligible to open a private firm. Another inconsistency between the two regulations is about the number of initial investors. *The Interim Stipulations* allows more than 30, but it would be fine according to the *Company Law* if it is under 50. The difference between the two matters for enterprises with more than 30 but fewer than 50 investors.

Besides ambiguities in the legislation of private enterprises, there are many discriminating and confusing regulations in specific state policies.[20] Private enterprises, for example, face restrictions on entering into some industries and markets that are only open to state enterprises. In particular, private enterprises are not allowed to do business in the following industries: antiques, jewellery, guns and military supplies, telecommunications, steel production, natural resources, automobiles, explosives, medical service, aviation, mass media, etc. Similarly, private firms face severe restrictions on import and export businesses. The *Interim Stipulations* does not allow private firms to import or export commodities. However, the Ministry of Foreign Trade and Cooperation passed a directive in 2000, which permitted them to do so while the *Interim Stipulations* still remain effective.

Another example is China's taxation system, which has been in a constant flux of transformation, especially for the private sector. There has long been the problem of taxes not being distinguished from fees. As much of the right of collecting tax was

---

19 Jian Fu, 'Private Enterprises and the Law', in Ross Garnaut and Ligang Song (eds), *China's Economic Transformation: The Rise of the Private Economy* (RoutledgeCurzon, 2003), p. 175.

20 Based on results of a survey on private business owners, Garnaut and Song (2003) compiled lists of constraints on the private sector.

delegated to local authorities in the 1980s, there have been many arbitrary charges imposed on private businesses, dubbed 'the three relentless charges' (*san luan*) in China – relentless fees, fines, and requests for donations. Different rates of tax have been applied in different areas, industries, and for different firms without much justification. The inconsistent and discriminating rules offer some private business owners a ready excuse of evading tax, which in turn entail severe punishments from local officials when the overall policy is in not in favour of the private sector.

But perhaps the most taxing problem for private firms in China is the discriminating rules that render their limited access to bank loans. Most private enterprises find it very difficult to obtain loans from state banks (detailed quantitative evidence to be given in the next chapter) due to very strict collateral requirements and other conditions, such as 'depositing part of their loans into non-interest-bearing accounts'.[21] State polices of financial credits are a good example of their changeability. The first wave of financial support to rural enterprises came in 1981, mainly for purchasing agricultural equipment, not for supporting private and family businesses. It is not clear, however, how these funds were used in reality, but it is reported that some were used for setting up new enterprises.[22] The supply of credit was tightened up for the first time during the period from 1981 to 1984. This had to be done since the central bank of China (People's Bank of China) discovered that in many areas the total amount of credits issued far exceeded what was available. In 1984, to slash the increasing gaps between fund availability and fund usage, the central banking system was launched, requiring that future credit-quota allotment be based on a particular bank's 1984 credit base. The policy caused a rush among local branches for increasing the total amount of loans by the end of 1984 in order to have a base for a bigger quota for 1985. Thanks to the shooting up of credits, the total number of private enterprises enjoyed a significant increase in 1984. However, credit control was applied soon afterwards (within just one year) in order to ease inflation and to cool down overheated investments. Such tightening was particularly painful for those who openly claimed themselves as private enterprises because the national bank commanded that all loans to private businesses be taken back despite the terms and no more loans be approved, resulting in tens of thousands of private firms going bankrupt.[23]

Entrepreneurial opportunities and strategies

What constitutes an opportunity for entrepreneurs? Schumpeter did not say very much about this question as he was focusing on entrepreneurial behaviours and their implications *after the opportunity had already been found*: providing new products

---

21 Ross Garnaut and Ligang Song, 'Correcting Constraints to Private Enterprise Development: Lessons from a Private Sector Survey', in *China's Economic Transformation: The Rise of the Private Economy*, pp. 228–229.

22 Zhang Houyi and Ming Lizhi, *Report on the Development of Private Enterprises in China*.

23 There is no reliable estimate of the number of bankrupt firms. My description is mainly based on the *Yearbook of Private Business in China*, 2000.

or services, discovering new geographical markets, introducing new raw materials, new methods of production, and new ways of organizing. We may induce from these functions that, for Schumpeter, entrepreneurial opportunities come from the lack of supply of a certain product or service, an unoccupied market in a particular geographical area, or unused materials, methods and ways of administration. But defining an opportunity as the absence of something else does not tell us very much about what it exactly is, as not everything absent necessarily has the potential of being recognized and exploited for developing a new business operation.

Following the Austrian approach, Kirzner sees an entrepreneurial opportunity 'as a result of the initially flawed plans',[24] that is, flawed plans made by other economic actors. To the entrepreneur, these flawed plans come as opportunities because profits could be made by correcting them. It is entrepreneurial to discover the flaws, to know how to correct them, and to be able to assemble sufficient resources for doing the correcting. Note that the flaws should not be simply understood as mistakes in the normal sense; they refer to the discrepancy between the expected market equilibrium and the actual economic situation emerging from individuals' economic actions. Kirzner thus emphasizes the exploring nature as a normal tendency inherent in all economic actions.

It is clear that, in the process of exploring, recognizing and exploiting, an entrepreneurial opportunity has a subjective side as well as an objective one. More recently, Scott Shane has defined an entrepreneurial opportunity as:

> a situation in which a person can create a new means-ends framework for recombining resources that the entrepreneur *believes* will yield a profit ... entrepreneurial opportunities are not necessarily profitable ... they should not be thought of as Ricardian, Schumpeterian or other kinds of rents.[25]

That is, entrepreneurial opportunity is a situation that prompts the formation of a subjective framework in the entrepreneur's mind that, once carried out, will yield a profit. In the meantime, Shane emphasizes that 'opportunities have an objective component that does not exist solely in the mind of the entrepreneur';[26] 'opportunities themselves lack agency' because they 'do not spontaneously result in exploitation. Rather, they are exploited only when a human being acts'.[27] Essentially, opportunities exist in the overall environment surrounding the entrepreneur, which contains other economic actors, the market, the state, and others, but they will not become true opportunities until the entrepreneur perceives them as such and then takes actions to exploit them. Therefore, entrepreneurial opportunities are dynamic processes rather than static conditions. It is thus also true that entrepreneurial opportunities do not necessarily or automatically imply successful entrepreneurial performance.

---

24 Israel Kirzner, 'Entrepreneurial Discovery and the Competitive Market Process: An Austrian Approach', *Journal of Economic Literature*, vol. XXXV (March 1997): 71.

25 Scott Shane, *A General Theory of Entrepreneurship, The Individual-Opportunity Nexus* (Edward Elgar, 2003), p. 18, emphasis original.

26 Ibid., p. 6.

27 Ibid., p. 7.

In the case of China, it is clear from the previous chapters that entrepreneurial opportunities come from the market as well as from changing institutional rules. Here, Shane's emphasis on the entrepreneur's exploitation as a condition for an opportunity-to-be to a realized opportunity is a valuable insight, because entrepreneurs in China must be imaginative in discovering or even fostering opportunities when the market or the institutional environment does not appear to be favourable.

Institutional discrimination: Strategy 1 – Using a legitimate identity

As presented before, the Chinese government has created many rules that either implicitly or explicitly discriminate against private businesses. If the entrepreneurs follow the rules, then they will have to quench their desire for getting out of poverty, realizing their potential, or enjoying the sense of achievement. Part of the competition in the world of business is to see who can better escape the constraints of rules. Following the rules is seen as a result of either bad luck or cowardice. As most of the discriminating rules are created based on private ownership, one obvious solution is to change the ownership. To an entrepreneur in China, a firm has two ownerships, one nominal and the other actual. The nominal ownership is registered at the Bureau of the Administration of Industries and Commerce. The actual ownership is the firm's true nature. A private firm can obtain a legitimate ownership once it is registered as, or becomes a part of, a public enterprise, either state-owned or collectively owned. This strategy is dubbed as 'red cap' or 'fake public' phenomenon in China.[28]

There are a variety of ways of putting on a 'red cap'. Perhaps the simplest is to submit a certain amount of extra fee to a local government as the payment for a public identity. The exact amount of the fee is a function of the firm's financial performance and the negotiation between the firm and local bureaucrats. Another method is to set up an actual private firm within a state or collective enterprise. Again, the private firm can negotiate a deal with the protecting firm to settle their financial relations. A more complicated way of operating a private in the name of a public business is to organize a joint-venture between the two so that they can exchange benefits.[29]

Obviously, this behaviour is cheating, but to many people in China, it is absolutely understandable and acceptable. Although no one has stood out to defend such cheating publicly, the fact that so many entrepreneurs and officials are involved

---

28 As the true ownership has been disguised, it is impossible to obtain a relatively accurate estimate of the scope of the 'red cap' phenomenon. According to Zhang Houyi (1999, p. 51), results from a sample survey of 178,000 collective enterprises, which was organized by the Bureau of the Administration of Industries and Commerce in 1995, revealed that 20.8 per cent of them were wearing a 'red cap', that is, more than 51 per cent of their assets were in the hand of some individual persons. It is very likely that the actual figure is much bigger and it varies from one place to another. For example, it is claimed that about 80 per cent of collective firms in Guangdong Province were private in 1999 (Li Zhenjie, 1999, p. 142). It is very difficult, if at all possible, to assess the reliability of these figures. In March 1998, the State Council issued a directive requiring private firms to take off their 'red cap' and show their true private ownership in November that year.

29 Joint-ventures can also be established between a private firm and a foreign firm from Hong Kong, Taiwan, or any other country, of course.

in it suggests that this tacit strategy is more than acceptable. Here are some possible excuses. For one thing, the rules are not fair in the first place. Given the significance of private firms' contributions, it is unfair to impose so many constraints on them simply because they are owned by individual persons. Also, the cheating has not really caused any damage to the public interest; although the State may have collected less tax and has been left in the dark, less tax is better than no tax at all. Still another excuse is that it is sometimes difficult to determine the true ownership of the firm even when the owners do not mind registering their firms as private. For example, what is the exact ownership of a joint-venture between some investors, a local government, and a small state-enterprise? In another situation, a private firm makes use of some resources of a local government or a state firm, and it is difficult to calculate how much the government or the state firm owes the private firm. These unclear relations have caused many confusions and disputes. Here, the point is that the 'red-cap' does not necessarily mean a fake identity.

A 'red cap' brings many benefits to private firms, their protecting enterprises, and the sponsoring local governments, although there is a risk of being discovered and then penalized. As indicated before, private enterprises have remained marginal or supplementary in China's national economy for a long time, even after their legitimate status was clearly established in the Constitution. Private ownership makes these firms vulnerable to a variety of discriminating treatments. Supervising agencies of local governments, such as taxation, technology and quality, hygiene, etc., will scrutinize private firms more carefully during inspections but will be lenient to state firms. For a long time, entrepreneurs of private firms were not allowed to join the CCP, and were consequently excluded from the circle of power. It was only until its sixteenth congress in 2002 that a clear policy was made for recruiting members from all economic sectors. After all, there has been a profound distrust of state policies, or more precisely, the stability of state policies. A 'red cap' can function as an insurance for not being cut off as 'the capitalist tail' in case the State someday wants to reverse its policies. This strategy works for local governments as well – political leaders of the areas with 'too many' private firms may be suspicious of encouraging the development of capitalism. By contrast, offering the 'red cap' to private firms can kill two birds with one stone. Politically, it is safe to allow more public (either state or collective) rather than private enterprises to grow. One only needs to recall the reverse of state ideologies and policies toward private enterprises during and after the political incidents in the spring and summer of 1989 to believe that these worries are warranted. Economically, local officials can bargain for a more favourable deal with private firms, thus driving up their local revenue and even their own personal income. For cases in which a private firm is registered in the name of a state or collective firm, the exchange between legitimacy and money is even more significant. Wearing the 'red cap', the private firm will have easier access to bank loans or land, enjoy a lower tax rate, have the privilege of doing imports and exports, use public resources and facilities, and escape from harassments by local officials. On the other hand, the public firm will obtain a considerable amount of payment from the private firm, which the former will most likely keep for its own use, sell off its products or turn its products saleable with the help of the private firm, and perhaps gain some employment opportunities in the private firm.

The main problem with such disguised relations is not that the relations are concealed, but that the exact economic obligations and responsibilities, usually defined in very unclear and ambivalent terms, are not clear even to the involved enterprises themselves. When the time comes that the relations are to be made open, either voluntarily or reluctantly, the ambiguities of the relations come to the surface and disputes follow.[30]

Institutional discrimination: Strategy 2 – Making an alliance with resourceful agents

Specialists on China have long identified local corporatism, or an alliance between entrepreneurs and local officials, as a working mechanism for explaining non-state firms' growth, especially in rural areas.[31] The alliances can be formed beyond local officials, of course, with any agent who has control of valuable information, power, or tangible materials. Recently, Krug and Mehta have emphasized the importance of such alliances in the Chinese entrepreneurship:

> The Western concept of entrepreneurship is focused on the ability of the individual to identify profitable opportunities (Kirzner, 1973; 1985). But, in China, the key factor in successful entrepreneurship is *the ability to form an alliance* with those economic agents who possess or control the financial assets, physical assets, or specific human capital needed for brokering market entry ...[32]

That is, for entrepreneurs in China, to identify an opportunity is only the first step, a task perhaps less demanding than forming an alliance to realize it. It is not surprising that often many entrepreneurs have identified the same opportunity at about the same time. But there is still quite a long way to go after the opportunity is identified. It is the ability to overcome the constraining rules with the help of allied agents that makes a winning entrepreneur stand out. As shown above, both general ideological principles and specific policies were not on the side of private entrepreneurs for many years in China. But the entrepreneurs knew that there were a vast number of opportunities and that the rules were not as strict as they sounded. To a large extent, how binding the rules were depends on the people who actually

---

30 Victor Nee and Sijin Su, 'Institutions, Social Ties and Commitment in China's Corporatist Transformation', pp. 111–134 in J. McMillan and B. Naughton (eds), *Reforming Asian Socialism: The Growth of Market Institutions* (Ann Arbor: University of Michigan Press, 1996). Li, Zhenjie, *Si Ying Qi Ye Tou Shi*.

31 J.C. Oi, 'Fiscal reform and the economic foundations of local state corporatism in China', *World Politics*, 45/1 (1992): 99–126. Nan Lin, 'Local Market Socialism: Local Corporatism in Action in Rural China', *Theory and Society*, 24 (1995): 301–354. Andrew Walder, 'Local Governments as Industrial Firms: An Organizational Analysis of China's Transitional Economy'. David Wank, *Commodifying Communism* (Cambridge University Press, 1999). Mike Peng and Y. Luo, 'Managerial Ties and Firm Performance in a Transition Economy: The Nature of a Macro-Micro Link', *Academy of Management Journal*, 43/3 (2000): 486–501.

32 Barbara Krug and Judith Mehta, 'Entrepreneurship by Alliance', in Barbara Krug (ed.), *China's Rational Entrepreneurs: The Development of the New Private Business Sector* (RoutledgeCurzon, 2004), p. 60, emphasis original.

used them, i.e., local officials or the agents in charge. Entrepreneurs, therefore, must compete on two fronts: establishing a favourable relationship with these resourceful agents on the one hand, and discovering and occupying a business opportunity in the market on the other. In many situations, the former is a pre-condition of the latter.

An alliance can be established in many ways. Some entrepreneurs were themselves local officials before starting their own businesses, so the connection was already there. What they needed to do was to carefully maintain the relationship so that it would not deteriorate due to the formal severance. Most of the time, the entrepreneur had to try very hard to keep his or her personal relations with the officials in various occasions of contact. But personal connections (or *guanxi*) were not always the key to establishing an alliance. This was especially true for the entrepreneurs who quickly became visible in the local economy. The economic resources that they had accumulated were so vital to the local economy that even local authorities had to show some respect. In this situation, the statuses of both sides of the alliance were roughly equal. The entrepreneur, by making significant contributions to the local government, such as donating to the construction of a public project, obtained information, favour, or other forms of support in exchange.

Institutional lacunae: Do what is not prohibited

Most entrepreneurs in China believe that rules are human inventions that are inherently changeable and imperfect, leaving opportunities for people who dare to make use of them. If permission must be obtained for doing a particular business, then in most cases there must be a way of obtaining that permission as long as you work hard enough. The permission can be rented, translated, borrowed, or purchased. The key is to find something that has not been explicitly or specifically prohibited in the official regulation. If one only wants to do what is permitted, then there will be very few opportunities. The chance of discovering an opportunity and acting upon it will increase significantly if one searches carefully between what has been doubtlessly stated as illegitimate and what is clearly permitted. For some critical issues, the entrepreneur may not find any clear policy or regulation; there is neither an explicit policy for encouraging a certain activity nor one prohibiting it. In such a situation, what is not illegitimate becomes legitimate. For example, the Chinese government has made it very difficult for private firms to acquire loans from state banks, but there are virtually no rules about how financial credits may be used informally. Consequently, personal and family savings, money borrowed from friends, colleagues, acquaintances and informal financial organizations such as rotating credit associations, even money borrowed from state enterprises all become important sources of start-up capitals for nascent entrepreneurs. A study based on a survey of private entrepreneurs in several provinces in China found that about 70 per cent of them engaged in some form of informal finance.[33] Obligations and mutual trusts based on family ties, friendships and shared identities functioned

---

33 Kellee Tsai, *Back-Alley Banking: Private Entrepreneurs in China* (Cornell University Press, 2004), p. 52.

as substitutes for formal administrative infrastructure.[34] Once the firm is up and running, the limited access to bank loans has forced a very high rate of re-investment in production among private firms, a major reason why the private sector as a whole has developed so fast.

Institutional flexibility and ambiguity: Bending the bars of the institutional cage

The Chinese style of transforming the socialist economy has followed an overall logic of introducing the market mechanisms into some industrial sectors or geographical areas while others remain under State plan and control. Flexibility of institutional rules has increased gradually to avoid unrecoverable disasters. Institutional ambiguity and inconsistency may come with flexibility, but State leaders believe that those problems will be sorted out eventually and will not entail too high a cost.

Perhaps a good example is the 'dual-track' price system. Introduced in 1984, the system allowed state enterprises to sell some of their resources (production materials such as steel and some products such as machines) to other firms at a market price. Therefore, many commodities had two prices: one assigned by the State and the other determined by the market, with the latter usually being much higher than the former, of course. Some private enterprises would have to pay the market price in order to have access to some valuable materials and products, while the more resourceful ones could pay less by yielding some of the difference between the two prices to the person in control of these resources. In such situations, competition was more about connections to powerful persons rather than better products and services. As institutional flexibility was not introduced systematically, it only generated opportunities for some entrepreneurs.

Obtaining a favourable ownership comes as another example. There are three types of private enterprises officially recognized in China: sole ownership, partnership, and limited liability companies. Accordingly, there have been three laws, respectively: *Law of Sole Ownership Firms*, *Law of Partnership Firms*, and *The Company Law*. Obviously, it is in the interests of entrepreneurs to register their firms as a 'limited liability company' because their personal wealth will not be affected in the case of bankruptcy and the firm appears more reliable to the public due to multiple ownerships. In theory, a firm's registration should represent its true ownership. The law requires that a firm can only register as a limited liability company when there are two or more investors. In reality, this is a constraint for a firm that actually has only one investor. To overcome the constraint, some entrepreneurs have 'created' the needed number of investors by simply inviting relatives and friends to join the team of investors. The entrepreneur and these nominal investors then reach a tacit agreement that the latter hold a certain number of shares of the company but they will not interfere with the company's management. These kind of shares are called '*gan gu*' (nominal shares) in China. The fact that researchers at the Chinese Academy of Social Sciences and in government agencies included a question about '*gan gu*' in

---

34 Mike W. Peng and P. Heath, 'The Growth of the Firm in Planned Economies in Transition: Institutions, Organizations, and Strategic Choices', *Academy of Management Review*, 21/2 (1996): 492–528.

the 2000 Sample Survey of Private Enterprises suggests that this has become popular strategy among private firms. As to what has happened to some firms wearing a 'red cap', the exchange of shares for the nominal status of an investor may collapse and disputes will arise.

Finally, there has been a controversy over whether private enterprises should be allowed to issue shares in the stock market. According to article 9(7) of the *Interim Regulation on Private Enterprises* (1988), the answer is negative. In reality, however, many entrepreneurs have managed to issue shares to the public. For example, a member of the National People's Political Consultation Assembly from Henan Province reported how he identified an institutional hole and thus jumped over the hurdle. When he attempted to issue stock shares in 1996, there were no clear laws or regulations that specified the qualifications of a private enterprise for issuing shares. After a careful reading of *The Company Law*, he came across a very useful piece of information – he could transform his company into a limited liability company and then apply for a stock listing, because limited liability companies were eligible to issue stock shares.[35] Although the bar for turning a company into a limited liability company was quite high – in general, the paid-up capital must be more than 300,000 yuan for most companies – the institutional problem was transformed into a financial one.[36] Since then, the rules have changed in favour of private firms since 1998, when private enterprises, under some strong conditions, of course, were allowed to issue stocks in Shanghai and Shenzhen. A more prominent example is Liu Yonghao's New Hope Group, who was listed on the Shanghai Stock Exchange in 1998.

Illegitimacy: Making it legitimate!

We have learnt that the success of a private business in China largely depends on the entrepreneur's ability to establish the business's legitimacy. For example, entrepreneurs, especially those who have attracted a lot of attention from the public and the government, cannot escape the issue of exploitation. It was still widely believed in the early stages of economic reform that exploitation was closely connected to private ownership. To many people in China, owners of private businesses would take away as much 'surplus value' as they could, and it is always unjust to do so. If the People's Republic was established to eliminate exploitation, how could it come back again? Indeed, for private business entrepreneurs, it is almost impossible to convince the public that what they have done is not exploitation, no matter how it is defined. Instead, what they have done is justify their exploitation of their employees by pointing out that the value produced by exploitation is much higher than its cost. In other words, the huge amount of tax paid, the new products and services provided, and the new jobs created all make private businesses deserve a legitimate status in the national economy, despite the possibility that, in the eyes of the public, they may have snatched away an unfair proportion of the value produced by their employees. In short, prosperity by exploitation is more legitimate than poverty for egalitarianism. The point is most explicitly articulated by Mr. Hu Deping, Vice President of the All-

35 Li Zhenjie, *Si Ying Qi Ye Tou Shi*, p. 117.
36 Jian Fu, 'Private Enterprises and the Law'.

China Business Federation, the national association of non-state enterprises. In a conference at the end of 1997 he made the following defending comments:

> I think we should acknowledge surplus values in private enterprises. Values are better produced than wasted, even though they are surplus values. As a nation with five thousand years of history, China deserves a much better economic situation than the current backwardness. China must produce surplus values by combining surplus labours, surplus time, surplus resources, and surplus capitals.[37]

The point should be clear: the legitimacy of private enterprises should rest on their contributions to China's economic development, not on their ownership. More generally, the legitimacy of all types of firm should be judged by what they have done to the national economy rather than by who owns them. Mr. Zhang Chunlai, an entrepreneur in the city of Tangshan, made an outcry when elaborating on his 'theory of wild chickens':

> Who are the minban (non-state) enterprises? They are those who do not rely on the State, do not occupy any critical industries of the national economy, but have to grow at the peripheries. By way of an analogy, they are like a flock of wild chickens searching for any eatables in deserted mountains. There are no roosts, no special feeds, let alone electronic bulbs. As long as the most necessary living conditions are available, such as sunlight, air and water, they will be capable of making a living … Excellent minban entrepreneurs are the strongest of surviving the 'wild environment'; therefore, they are more efficient in producing eggs. The smartest investment by the State is to adopt an easy-going policy, nursing a favourable, supporting and protecting environment. In return, we will let the State and the government pick up more eggs.[38]

It is clearly implied that state-owned enterprises (SOE) are the domestic chickens who have been raised in much better conditions but disappointingly have produced much fewer 'eggs'. It is therefore to the interest of the State to provide more support to the private sector.

Whilst arguments such as the above concentrate on the values produced by private enterprises, others have pursued the same goal by making the claim that these enterprises are not really private. For example, Mr Shi Shanlin, an entrepreneur who started a now large beverage company in Beijing, has tried to demonstrate that private businesses in China are private only in a very limited sense. He made the following calculation. Suppose that a private company has produced a total profit of 41 million yuan in the period of six years. There will be only 8.6 million left after tax and fees (21 million tax, 10 million tax for technology and research, and 2.4 million for administration fees). In addition, the company will also have to pay about 3 million as donations to public projects, including poverty relief, road construction, hospitals, schools, etc. As to the remaining 5.6 million, the owner of the company actually does not have much control, because according to China's law of taxation, half of it or 2.8 million must be reinvested in production, 1.12 million for employees' welfare, and only 1.68 million for bonuses. The owner cannot take away all that 1.68

---

37 Cited in Li Zhenjie, *Zhong Guo Si Ying Qi Ye Tou Shi*, p. 2.
38 *Zhong Guo Qi Ye Jia* (*The Chinese Entrepreneurs*), February 1998, no. 154, pp. 8–19.

million as his personal income, of course. At least 0.68 million will go to employees. Even if the owner can take the remaining 1 million as personal income, he has to pay an income tax of 0.4 million. In the end, what is left for the owner himself is only 0.6 million, a tiny proportion (0.015 per cent) of the total profit. In the end, Mr Shi concluded:

> Obviously, while a normal private enterprise produces enormous values for our society and submits a huge amount of tax, what is ultimately left for the owner as personal properties in the strict sense is very limited and negligible. Most private enterprises are private merely in the sense of allocating and using their resources. As a matter of fact, there are no significant differences between this kind of private ownership and public ownership.[39]

Concluding remarks

About two decades after its disappearance from China's economic landscape, entrepreneurship revived during the late 1970s. Initially an expedient measure for easing the problems of unemployment and poverty, releasing people's entrepreneurial energy soon proved to be a national economic policy that the Chinese State had to take very seriously. Soon after the emergence and initial success of non-state enterprises, the State became to realize that it was much more efficient to boost the economy by offering an institutional space than to control everything and every enterprise. It also came to the conclusion that letting people pursue a better material life could do a better job in enhancing the Party's political dominance than debating over the exact meaning of ideological principles. During the 1980s, both the State and the entrepreneurs in non-state sectors were in the process of learning new ideas and trying out new strategies, and they kept watching each other for signals suggesting the direction of the next move. It is in this interactive and negotiating process that the entrepreneurs and the Chinese State transformed each other. I shall come back to this dynamic in the final chapter.

For nearly two decades (the 1980s and the 1990s), most entrepreneurs in China found the overall institutional environment becoming more and more liberal but many institutional rules still unfair, constraining, discriminating, and even hostile. The rules of the game did have incentives and penalties. It was not very straightforward, however, to identify exactly what they were and how one could get the incentives whilst escaping the penalties. How would players play the game when they find the rules unfair? To stop playing is not an option, because that means giving up the hope of winning. The only choice is to play the game by playing at the rules. Wearing a 'red cap', becoming part of a state enterprise, blurring the line between 'collective' and 'private', establishing the legitimacy of private enterprises by highlighting their contributions rather than problems, etc., are all the strategies developed in the process of dealing with the imperfect rules. The dual tasks of filling up the gaps in the market and making use of the gaps in the rules have been accomplished in a single entrepreneurial process.

---

39 *Zhong Guo Qi Ye Jia* (*The Chinese Entrepreneurs*), April 1998, no. 156, pp. 8–20.

Chapter 5

The Entrepreneurial Process in China

Against the background laid out in the previous chapter, this chapter aims to offer a rather comprehensive and precise description of how entrepreneurs in China go through the steps of opening up a new business by analyzing the results of the Survey of Private Business Owners (SPBO).[1] First of all, who are these entrepreneurs? Do they share any demographic, social and economic characteristics? Why do they choose to start up their own business instead of working for the State or someone else? We know they have had a difficult time acquiring the necessary resources, but we need a clearer idea of how bad (or good) the situation is. When different options or strategies are available, how are the entrepreneurs distributed across them? We know entrepreneurs in China have constant interactions with local officials. It would be much more informative if we could measure the level of their political participation and relations with local authorities. These are all the questions I shall try to answer in this chapter.

The phrase 'entrepreneurial process' implies an orderly sequence of events. Entrepreneurship, by its very nature, defies such simplification.[2] It would not be entrepreneurial at all if one could become an entrepreneur by simply following a predetermined set of steps. A challenge to entrepreneurs everywhere is to decide what is the first thing to do and what to do next. This does not mean, however, there are no patterns emerging from the venture of starting up new businesses. Subject to administrative regulations, new economic organizations have to pass a series of bureaucratic procedures in order to be protected by the law. Technologically and organizationally, the entrepreneur may have to do one thing before moving on to another. In short, it is still sensible to talk about the entrepreneurial process in analytical terms if we keep in mind that it does not have to loyally represent every case in reality.

There exist different ways of specifying the sequential steps in the entrepreneurial process,[3] but I find the following ideal-type intuitively useful: the entrepreneurial process starts from the recognition of opportunities, then the entrepreneur (or a team of entrepreneurs) needs to evaluate the likelihood of success and failure, and then

---

1   The reader might want to go back to the section of 'Research Design' in Chapter 1 to recall what the survey is about. It is also helpful to consult the appendix.

2   Andrew Van de Ven, Douglas Polley, Raghu Garud, and Sankaran Venkataraman, *The Innovation Journey* (New York: Oxford University Press, 1999).

3   Paul Reynolds and Sammis White, *The Entrepreneurial Process: Economic Growth, Men, Women, and Minorities* (Westport, CN: Quorum Books, 1997). Martin Ruef, 'Origins of Organizations: The Entrepreneurial Process', *Entrepreneurship (Research in the Sociology of Work)*, 15 (2005): 63–100.

decides whether actions will be taken. If the answer is positive, then the entrepreneur needs to acquire the resources necessary for making the project successful and to put them together in order to get the business up and running. In each of these steps, the entrepreneur must offer some input, such as knowledge, advice, decision, social connections, etc., which matter significantly for the ultimate performance of the business. It is therefore crucial to follow an integrative conceptual framework so that different aspects of the entrepreneurial process are to be understood and analyzed as interrelated parts of a whole. Here I shall follow the conceptual scheme proposed by Scott Shane.[4]

Whilst the overall conceptual idea is clear, it is unrealistic to expect that the empirical investigation will match up. The difficulty stems from the fact that the data used here were not collected by following a coherent conceptual framework of the entrepreneurial process. Researchers responsible for the design of SPBO obviously had a plan of collecting information on as many important aspects of private businesses in China as they could. In particular, as we shall see later in this chapter, there are some quite specific questions about the entrepreneurs and their firms. It is disappointing to find no survey instruments, however, that solicit information about how the entrepreneurs identify opportunities. This is very likely because the researchers believe that the large number of different opportunities make it unfeasible to use a unified format in survey instruments. In addition, it is unrealistic to expect entrepreneurs to reveal all the thoughts behind their decisions in a highly structured survey; some decisions are perhaps just too sensitive to be told to a government-affiliated researcher.

The survey does have some merits, however. For example, it contains quite a number of useful questions about the entrepreneur's relations with governments and employees. On balance, the survey is by far the most comprehensive in covering the important aspects of the entrepreneurial process in China. I have no plan, however, to carry out a comprehensive analysis of the data themselves, and I have tried to keep the statistical presentation as easy to understand as possible.

A brief social-demographic profile

First of all, entrepreneurs in China are a group dominated by males: the percentage of female entrepreneurs has remained quite stable from 1992 to 2004, which has increased slightly from 10 per cent in 1992, 1994 and 1996 to 11 per cent in 1999 and 2001, and finally to 13.9 per cent in 2004.[5] Few researchers have conducted rigorously designed empirical investigations for comparing male and female entrepreneurs in China.[6] To systematically examine the role of gender in entrepreneurship would be the task of a separate project.

---

4   Scott Shane, *A General Theory of Entrepreneurship: The Individual-Opportunity Nexus* (Edward Elgar, 2003), pp. 250–251.

5   The percentage for 2004 comes from *Report of the Survey on Private Enterprises in China* (http://www.southcn.com/finance/gdmqgc/gdmqyyrl/200502030218.htm).

6   After interviewing 25 female business owners in the City of Chengdu and five others in Beijing, Maja Linnemann (1998) found it difficult to determine the gross effect of the

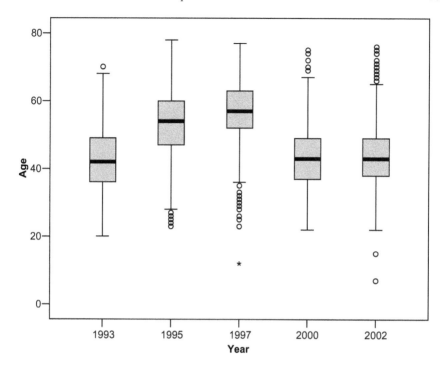

Figure 5.1 Age of private business owners in China, 1993 to 2002

The boxplots in Figure 5.1 show the age distributions of the surveyed private entrepreneurs from 1993 to 2002. The average age in 1993 is 42. Then it goes up quite dramatically to 54 in 1995 and to 57 in 1997, but it finally comes down to 43 at the beginning of this century.[7]

It is very unlikely that the fluctuation is a result of sampling variations; it is clear that entrepreneurs in the 1995 and 1997 were older than those in other years. This is so because, by the end of the last century, most of the entrepreneurs who started their businesses in the late 1970s or early 1980s had retired; most of those selected in the 2000 and 2002 surveys were likely to be a new generation of entrepreneurs. The outliers in the chart offer further support to such observation: nearly all the outliers in 1995 and 1997 are at the lower end, which could be the growing second

---

'pulling' and the 'pushing' factors: on the one hand, women were more likely to become self-employed because they were more vulnerable to redundancy, but on the other hand they were facing higher hurdles for entering into the business world due to their lower level of education and professional training, lack of experience, and limited networks. In a much larger but convenient sample, Shi Qingqi (2002) studied female entrepreneurs in eight provinces in China. As no male entrepreneurs were selected in the sample, the study was not designed to compare the female entrepreneurs with the males.

7　The average age from the most recent 2005 survey was 42.

generation, whilst the outliers in 2000 and 2002 are at the higher end, constituting much of the retiring first generation.

With their average age being in the 40s to the 50s, it is not surprising that about 90 per cent of the entrepreneurs are married. Another expected attribute consistent throughout the years is their ethnicity: about 95 per cent are Han (the major ethnic group in China).

Now let's take a look at the educational attainment of entrepreneurs in China (Figure 5.2).[8]

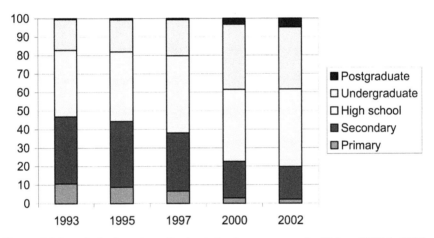

Figure 5.2 Level of education of private business owners in China, 1993 to 2002

The overall picture is quite clear: the educational level of private entrepreneurs in China has increased throughout the years: there are more and more university graduates and even postgraduates who have become entrepreneurs. More precisely, the percentage of the entrepreneurs with university degrees has jumped from 17.2 per cent in 1993 to 37.4 per cent in 2002. These percentages are substantially higher than the national average, which was only 2.4 per cent in 1994.[9] The rate of entrepreneurs with high school education has increased as well, but much more mildly. In contrast, the percentage of those with secondary school or less has gone down from 46.9 per cent to 19.8 per cent during the same period. Clearly, entrepreneurs are much more educated than ordinary people in China.

---

8 In the surveys, categories of educational levels remained the same until 2000 with the following nine categories: illiterate, primary school, secondary school, ordinary high school, vocational high school, specialist high school, specialist college, university undergraduate, and university postgraduate. In 2000, they were collapsed into five categories: primary, secondary, high school or equivalent, undergraduate, and postgraduate, which we shall use for making comparisons across the years.

9 Peng Xizhe, 'Education in China', pp. 115–133 in Peng Xizhe with Guo Zhigang (eds), *The Changing Population of China* (Blackwell, 2000).

To summarize, most entrepreneurs who set up an officially registered private business in China are males, in their 40s, and better educated.

Previous employment and motivation

What motivated some people in China to open up their own businesses? Did unemployment or any other economic difficulty push them into the commercial world? Or did they 'jump into the sea' voluntarily because they had the desire of achieving something? We have learnt that the institutional environment for entrepreneurship in China has become more and more friendly since the 1970s. Therefore, we should expect more and more entrepreneurs to have jumped into entrepreneurial ventures. Even so, starting up a new business is not an easy decision to make. To better understand the statistics to be presented below, it helps to say a few words about the employment context.

Recall that private businesses disappeared almost completely in the 1960s. When they first re-emerged at the end of the 1970s, the only legitimate form that they could take was individual business (*ge ti hu*) in the urban areas or household business in the rural areas. As the issue of employment is not really relevant for rural areas, here we focus on cities and towns. We can talk about two types of people in urban China: those employed by state or collective enterprises and those unemployed. The unemployed were pretty much pushed to become entrepreneurs as there were no other options. There was a risk of failure and loss, but fortunately the level of risk seemed to be very low: there was a huge demand for everyday products, appliances, and services and it did not demand much investment to set up an individual business.

To start a private business was a different story for those who had a job in state enterprises. Their work units (*dan wei*) administered almost every aspect of their life. It would be a much bigger decision to make for those whose work units were in a reasonably good condition, such as a state or collective enterprise, or a local governmental agency. These people had to make a bigger sacrifice if they wanted to 'jump into the sea': by voluntarily severing their administrative ties with their work units, they would not only lose a secure job but they would lose many benefits and protections as well, including housing, childcare, pension, administrative facilities (rubber stamps), etc. Either there must be something else more valuable than employment in a state enterprise or the potential entrepreneur did not lose the benefits after opening the new business. The point is, to understand why the survey respondents started their own businesses, we need to examine their previous employment then relate the employment status to the way in which they dealt with the relationship of their work units and to the motivations that eventually pushed them into the business world.

However, not every survey included a question about the entrepreneur's motivation to start a new business. Such a question was only asked in the first three surveys (1993, 1995, and 1997), and it is not clear why the principal investigators decided to exclude it from 2000. Furthermore, the listed motivations have changed slightly, making the results from the three surveys not completely comparable. In 1993, respondents were asked what was the most important reason for them wanting to open a business, and five choices were offered: (1) I could not keep a good relationship with the head of my original work unit; (2) my original work unit did not allow a full play of my skills; (3) I earned too little at my original work unit; (4) I had no secure job; (5) other. In 1995 and 1997, while the first four items were retained, very likely because the investigators discovered two new popular choices, the fifth residual item was replaced with the following: (5) I wanted to realize my own value; (6) I wanted to leave the rural area. The proportion for each motivation chosen as 'the most important' is shown in Table 5.1.

Table 5.1 The most important motivation for starting up own business, 1993, 1995, and 1997

Motivation	1993		1995		1997	
	%	95% CI	%	95% CI	%	95% CI
Poor relation with head of work unit	3.7	(2.7, 4.7)	2.2	(1.7, 2.7)	2.4	(1.7, 3.1)
No full play of skills	41.3	(38.7, 43.9)	13.6	(12.3, 14.9)	9.0	(7.7, 10.3)
Income too low	15.6	(13.7, 17.5)	5.9	(5.0, 6.8)	31.8	(29.7, 33.9)
Job not secure	21.8	(19.6, 24.0)	9.1	(8.0, 10.2)	4.7	(3.8, 5.6)
To realize own value	–		65.9	(64.2, 67.9)	48.6	(46.4, 50.8)
To leave rural area	–		3.2	(2.6, 3.8)	1.9	(1.3, 2.5)
Other	17.6	(15.6, 19.6)	–		–	
N	1407		2846		1929	

The reader may have already noticed that 'to realize my own value' stands out as the most important motivation in both 1995 and 1997. Similarly, 'there was no full play of my skills' was the most frequently reported motivation in 1993. Although different in wording, the two items share the dissatisfaction with the constraints experienced in the original work unit and the desire to realize one's potential. In other words, they are not mutually exclusive and therefore should have been combined in 1995 and 1997. The next strong motivation is to increase income, whose percentages curiously fluctuated during the years. Job insecurity was found to be the second most popular motivation in 1993 but lost its popularity in the following years. Finally, poor relations with the head of original work unit was a motivation only recognized by a very small minority of entrepreneurs in China. Overall, Chinese entrepreneurs did not claim that they set up their businesses for the sake of money in the mid 1990s. Rather, they reported that it was the sense of achievement that drove them to venture into a new business. The 2002 survey included the same question. Although the options offered were not exactly the same, the results remained the same: nearly 77 per cent of studied entrepreneurs stated that they opened their businesses to realize their own value, while the second important motivation (33 per cent) was to earn more money. In this sense, most entrepreneurs in China qualify for the Schumpeterian notion of entrepreneurs: they are entrepreneurs because they enjoy a feeling of control and accomplishment, not any particular result.

If the above observation is correct, then we will expect that those who set up their own business in order to realize their personal value would voluntarily leave their original work units. The 1993 and 1995 surveys questioned the respondents of the way they left their work units, including 'resigned', 'kept position without pay', 'left without notice', 'made redundant', 'retired', 'retired due to illness', 'fired', and 'unemployed'. The first three categories fall into the category of 'voluntary severance', while the following four 'involuntary severance'.[10] The effect of the way of leaving original work unit will be tested on two motivations: 'unable to have full play of my own capacity' (plus 'to realize own value' for 1995) versus 'earn too little in the original work unit'.[11] The results are organized in the following table.

Table 5.2 Entrepreneurial motivations and ways of leaving original work unit, 1993 and 1995

Way of leaving work	1993		1995	
	Earn too little	To realize own value	Earn too little	To realize own value
Involuntary	7.0%	8.6%	8.5%	8.8%
Voluntary	93.0%	91.4%	91.5%	91.2%
N	187	523	142	1438

The two rows of percentages in Table 5.2 show the relative popularity of each entrepreneurial motivation in 1993 and 1995, respectively. The last row shows the total number of entrepreneurs for each category. It is clear that the percentages of the ways of leaving original work unit remained nearly the same regardless of entrepreneurs' motivations – the vast majority of entrepreneurs (about 91 per cent) left their work voluntarily, providing no statistical evidence for any relationship between motivation and the way of leaving original work unit.[12]

---

10 Here, the category 'unemployed' is obviously irrelevant.

11 All other motivations, as they related neither to voluntary or involuntary severance, have been ignored.

12 A formal test was conducted by calculating the odds ratio between the two variables, which turns out to be 0.79 with a 95 per cent asymptotic CI (0.42, 1.50) for 1993 and 0.95 with a 95 per cent asymptotic CI (0.51, 1.77) for 1995. As both include 1, the relationship between the two variables is not statistically significant.

Starting up the business

Market entry

As mentioned before, the surveys on private entrepreneurs in China do not contain much information about how entrepreneurs discover and interpret opportunities. The most useful indicator available for analysis is their initial choice of the industry that they would like to enter. To some extent, the status of private businesses in China can be measured by the number of industries that the Chinese State allows them to enter. The number has been gradually increasing since the late 1970s, when only simple service businesses were permitted. Since then, private entrepreneurs have complained about being treated as 'secondary citizens' not being able to enter the markets dominated or even monopolized by state-owned enterprises. After years of campaigns and negotiations, at the Third Plenary Session of CCP's sixteenth Congress in October 2003, the Party finally and explicitly pledged to expand market entry for non-state sectors, allowing them to enter any industries as long as the entry is not against law. For the first time, the Party resolution stated that 'Non-state enterprises should enjoy a status equal to other types of enterprises in terms of investments, financing, taxation, land use, import and export, and other areas'.[13] If such policy has been fully implemented in practice, then we would expect a trend of diversification of industries among private enterprises in China.

It is impossible to test the above hypothesis, however, by analyzing the available survey data because the data were collected before the meeting.[14] Nevertheless, it is still worth looking at the distribution of private businesses across the industries. On the one hand, we can verify the clustering of private enterprises in non-state dominant industries. On the other hand, we may gain a glimpse of the change, if any, of industries among private firms across the years. As the categorization of the 1993 survey is not consistent with those in the following years, I shall start with the 1995 survey.

The reader can see the percentage of enterprises for each industry in the following table (Table 5.3). In each survey, respondents were asked to identify the major industry when they initially started their business and the major industry at the end of 1994, 1996, 1999, and 2001, respectively. As the responses to this question are highly consistent (not shown here), a weighted average is calculated.

The distribution of private enterprises in China across the industries has been extremely stable, and it clearly reflects the status of private enterprises in the market. From the time the business was firstly started (mostly in the late 1970s to the early 1980s) to the end of 2003, around 40 per cent of the businesses were in manufacturing and about 20 per cent in service and catering. With minor fluctuations, the percentage of private firms in construction and social service was around 6 per cent throughout

---

13 Xinhua News: http://news.xinhuanet.com/ziliao/2003-01/21/content_699208.htm.

14 The data from the 2005 survey were not available for public use yet at the time of writing. The report of this survey is published, and it contains the percentages of private enterprises across some but not all industries. The results are not used here, however, as the sum of the reported percentages for the selected industries exceeds 100 per cent.

the years. Agriculture came next, with about 4 per cent to 5 per cent. These were the markets initially open to the private sector. Transportation, real estate, science and technology each constituted about 2 per cent to 3 per cent, which have grown slightly due to gradually liberalization of state policies. The position of private firms is marginal in following areas that are dominated by state-owned enterprises: industries related to natural resources (mining, power, water), financial services, hygiene and sports, education and culture. Overall, the data show that even up to the beginning of the twenty-first century, firms in the private sector in China were highly clustered in a limited number of industries due to strict state control of market entry. Entrepreneurs who want to enter the restricted areas have to be very imaginative in discovering and making use of institutional holes. The case of Mou Qizhong, to be presented in Chapter 7, offers an illustrative although unusual example.

Table 5.3 Percentage of private enterprises in each industry, 1995 to 2002

Industry	Initial (average)	1995	1997	2000	2002
Agriculture	4.6	4.1	4.1	4.7	5.6
Mining	1.3	1.2	2.0	1.2	1.3
Manufacturing	39.3	40.4	42.3	39.8	38.3
Power	0.8	0.9	1.0	1.1	0.7
Construction	6.7	5.5	8.9	6.4	5.9
Geology and watering	0.1	0.0	0.1	0.0	0.1
Transportation	2.7	2.4	3.5	2.3	2.5
Service and catering	22.1	27.4	16.2	20.6	21.4
Finance and insurance	0.2	0.3	0.2	0.2	0.3
Real estate	1.9	0.9	1.4	3.2	3.8
Social service	6.5	7.2	5.8	6.2	5.6
Hygiene and sports	0.9	0.5	0.6	1.1	1.3
Education and culture	1.2	0.3	2.9	1.0	1.1
Science and technology	2.5	2.5	2.1	2.6	2.1
Others	9.2	6.5	9.0	9.6	9.9
N	11014	2787	1775	2798	3094

Start-up capital

Having decided on the market niche to enter, entrepreneurs in China would soon find it enormously difficult to prepare the initial capital for setting up a new business. The difficulty of obtaining financial support from state banks has been consistently found in all studies on private businesses in China.[15] In the 1997 and 2000 surveys, researchers in China asked private entrepreneurs to report the level of difficulty in

---

15 Various academic reports in the series of *Report of the Development of Private Enterprises in China* and *Almanac of Private Enterprises in China*.

acquiring bank loans. In 1997, 56.7 per cent said it was either extremely difficult or difficult. Surprisingly, despite increasingly stronger calls for better support for the private sector from the top, the percentage increased to 63.3 per cent in 2000. For both years, only about 13 per cent of private business owners agreed that it was easy or very easy to obtain bank loans. They were also asked to identify the key barriers that prevented them from accessing financial credits for the years 2000 and 2002. The majority (about 70 per cent for the two years) claimed that the conditions imposed by state banks were simply too restrictive and discriminating against private firms; compared with state or collective enterprises, they had to show much more convincing evidence of their capacity to pay the money back. About 18 per cent complained that even when they could get the loan, the interest rate was too high and the term too short.

If it is very difficult to obtain bank loans, what are the major sources of financial capital for private entrepreneurs in China? Let's take a look at how their start-up capital is composed. In 1993 and 1995, the surveys included a question that directly asked the entrepreneurs to choose the first three most important (out of the following ten) sources of their start-up capital: (1) inheritance, (2) savings from work or business, (3) capital gain from stocks and real estate, (4) overseas investment, (5) borrowing from relatives and friends, (6) bank loan, (7) loan from credit association, (8) borrowing from collective enterprise or community, (9) borrowing from other individuals, (10) others. Table 5.4 lists the percentages of entrepreneurs who identified a particular source of start-up capital for each year.

Table 5.4 First three most important sources of start-up capital, 1993 and 1995

Source	1st		2nd		3rd	
	1993	1995	1993	1995	1993	1995
Inheritance	7.9	6.2	2.4	3.0	4.5	3.1
Savings	46.2	56.3	22.8	20.7	13.9	13.9
Capital gain	12.2	0.5	14.9	1.2	9.8	1.7
Overseas	3.0	1.7	2.4	1.7	2.4	1.3
Friends and relatives	16.4	16.7	30.8	37.4	23.0	17.5
Bank	5.6	4.9	11.3	8.6	14.1	10.9
Credit association	5.2	6.6	7.5	11.0	10.5	11.9
Collective	1.0	1.6	2.2	3.3	3.6	6.9
Other people	1.4	4.8	4.7	12.1	16.6	31.8
Other	1.1	0.9	1.0	0.9	1.6	0.9
N	1421	2822	1053	2463	674	2037

Not surprisingly, without much access to loans by state banks, about half of private entrepreneurs in China had to resort to personal savings. Another major source of capital was actually personal savings as well, i.e., the savings of their friends and relatives – more than 16 per cent of private entrepreneurs identified it as the first important source. Put together, two-thirds of private entrepreneurs started their businesses with personal savings either of their own or of their extended families and friends. The 2002 survey included a similar question with somewhat different categories, but the results are almost the same: 72.6 per cent of the studied entrepreneurs reported that the major sources of start-up capital were savings either from a small business or salaries. The limited personal savings or profits determined that the initial size of a private enterprise in terms of capital could not be very large. Indeed, the medium of reported amount of registered capital ranges from 300 thousand yuan in 1992 to 2.5 million yuan in 2001.

The growth of registered capital during the years of the surveys reflects the effects of at least two factors: firstly and obviously, with very high re-investment ratio (to be reported more precisely later), the total amount of capital was on the rise. Secondly and more importantly, the way of collecting initial capital changed among private enterprises in China. Before, I have reported that private enterprises in China fall into three general categories: sole ownership, partnership, and limited liability companies, and more and more of them prefer the last type to the other two because they can protect their personal assets and collect capital from people beyond their family and friendship circles. Since the end of the last century, a growing number of private enterprises have started to adopt another type of ownership, shareholding a limited liability company. The change of the distribution of private enterprises across these ownerships is presented in Table 5.5.

Table 5.5 Ownerships of private enterprises in China, 1993–2002

Ownership	1993	1995	1997	2000	2002
Sole	63.6	57.3	38.3	39.0	28.7
Partnership	16.0	15.4	13.3	7.3	5.7
Limited liability	16.8	27.3	48.4	46.4	57.2
Shareholding	0.0	0.0	0.0	7.3	8.4
Other	3.6	0.0	0.0	0.0	0.0
N	1428	2847	805	2973	3180

The percentage of sole ownership firms declined from 63.6 per cent in 1993 to 28.7 per cent in 2002. Partnership firms also declined from 16 per cent to 5.7 per cent. In contrast, limited liability firms increased sharply from nearly 17 per cent to more than 57 per cent during the same period, and shareholding companies constituted 7 per cent to 8 per cent at the turn of the century. Although to go public is an effective way of gathering start-up capital, the rules of setting up a shareholding company are highly restrictive, putting off especially financially weak firms and those without a strong credit history.

Registration

When starting a private business, an important question that the entrepreneur has to think about carefully is what kind of firm to register at the Bureau of Administration of Commerce and Industry. In the previous chapter, I discussed the strategy of putting on a 'red cap' in order to avoid discrimination and harassment by local officials for ideological reasons and to benefit from favourable treatments. Now I provide a quantitative assessment of the use of this strategy. As the 1993 survey didn't touch on this issue, my analysis starts from the 1995 survey.

More precisely, my objective is to examine the relationship between the year of registration and the officially registered type of the firm. I expect that, as the overall institutional environment became more and more friendly to private firms, the proportion of these firms registered as 'state' or 'collective' should decline through the years. Therefore, I analyse the responses to two questions: one, the year in which a private enterprise was firstly registered, and two, the first official registration. According to Zhang Huoyi's analysis, the most meaningful way of recoding the year of registration consists of the following periods: before 1978, 1979 to 1986, 1987 to 1991, 1992 and after.[16] Further, since these two questions were repeatedly included in the 1995, 1997, 2000, and 2002 surveys, the cases have been merged together into a single data file so as to include the maximal number of years of initial registration.[17]

Table 5.6 Registrations of private enterprises in China by time period

Initial registration	Before 1978	1979–1986	1987–1991	1992 and after
State-owned	5.2	2.1	2.5	2.0
Urban collective	17.8	10.7	10.8	7.6
Rural collective	20.4	11.5	9.0	3.8
Cooperative	2.1	2.4	2.7	1.7
Shareholding	3.9	3.7	5.4	17.8
Overseas	0.5	0.4	1.2	1.7
Private	13.4	21.4	37.7	55.1
Individual (*ge ti hu*)	35.7	47.0	30.2	10.0
Other	1.0	0.7	0.6	0.3
N	397	3111	2687	4620

Officially, these enterprises should all be registered as either 'private enterprise' or 'individual business' (*ge ti hu*). Nevertheless, as shown in Table 5.6, before

---

16 Zhang Huoyi, 'The Upsurge of An Alternative Force', pp. 3–59 in Zhang and Ming (eds), *Report of the Development of Private Enterprises in China (1978–1998)*.

17 Obviously, this assumes that the number of enterprises participating in two or more surveys is ignorable.

1978 less than half (49.1 per cent) of them were registered as such. Since 1979, the percentage increased to about 65 per cent. In other words, since the launch of economic reforms, a bit more than one-third of private enterprises have been registered other than 'private' or 'individual'. Whether this can be extended to the whole private sector is a difficult question to answer because the definition of private enterprise has been changing and ambiguous, the sample did not strictly follow a probability sampling procedure, and there may exist many private enterprises that were registered in other titles.

That said, the results do make sense if analyzed against the background of China's institutional change. First and overall, the percentage of private enterprises who honestly reported their private nature has steadily increased during the reform period in a more friendlier institutional environment. The proportion of *ge ti hu* has declined because many of them have expanded their businesses and the ban on the number of employees has been lifted, so more and more have turned themselves into private enterprises with more than eight employees. The reverse is true for those wearing a 'red cap': the percentage of private enterprises registered as 'collective', either rural or urban, has decreased from 38.2 per cent before 1978 to nearly 20 per cent in 1991, and even more dramatically down to 11.4 per cent since 1992, the year Deng Xiaoping called for more liberal economic policies in his South China tour. The percentage of shareholding companies also jumped to 17.8 per cent from previously 3 per cent to 5 per cent due to his encouragement. With the growth of this type of companies, the distinction between 'private' and 'public' becomes more and more quantitative rather than qualitative – we have to ask 'how private' an enterprise is, not 'whether' it is private. These companies, the private ones, and *ge ti hu* all together constituted about 83 per cent of all surveyed private enterprises at the beginning of this century, indicating that those still wearing a 'red cap' counted only 13 per cent.

Recruitment of employees

Unlike state-owned enterprises, who enjoyed (or suffered from) a stable supply of employees by the state, most of whom were fresh graduates from schools or universities, private enterprises do not have an institutionalized source of employees. In some situations, however, that could be an advantage – private firms do not have to accept anybody assigned by local officials or state bureaucrats. Where do they find their employees (ordinary workers, technicians, and managers)? To answer this question, it helps to have a sense of the total number of employees in a private enterprise when it was first registered. As very likely the number will change through time, I present the change with the time period in which the private enterprise was initially registered (Table 5.7).[18] Note that, since the total number of employees varies greatly, ranging from less than ten to several thousand, it has been recoded in several categories.

---

18 Again, the data sets have been merged to produce the results.

Table 5.7 Change in the number of employees at initial registration among private enterprises in China

Number of employees	Before 1978	1979–1986	1987–1991	1992 and after
8 or less	22.4	30.2	29.8	27.6
9 to 50	45.5	48.3	53.2	51.1
51 to 100	17.7	12.4	10.4	12.1
101 to 300	10.8	7.2	5.2	7.2
301 to 500	1.7	0.9	0.8	1.2
501 to 1000	0.7	0.7	0.4	0.6
1001 and above	1.2	0.3	0.1	0.2
N	407	3607	3501	4740

It turns out that in terms of the total number of employees, the size of private enterprises has changed very moderately. The percentages for each category remain remarkably stable throughout the years. The percentages of firms with eight or fewer employees stay in the 20s while those with nine to 50 fall into range from 45 per cent to 53 per cent. Altogether, the percentage of private enterprises with fewer than 50 employees has increased from nearly 68 per cent prior to 1978 to more than 78 per cent since 1992, a small jump of 10 per cent for more than two decades. What is surprising are the percentages of firms with 50 or more employees, which have declined during that period, although the absolute numbers have increased due to the increase of the total number of firms. The private sector in China has been persistently dominated by small firms with fewer than 50 employees. In the meantime, although the percentage of very large firms (more than one thousand employees) is tiny, their absolute number has grown dramatically. Here, the absolute number matters because it is these large firms that have driven the development of many industries.

Now let's find out where private enterprises find these employees. Unfortunately, the data for analyzing this issue are not satisfactory. The question 'Please tick the most important source of managers, technicians, and workers in your enterprise' was included only in the 1993, 1995, and 1997 questionnaires. In addition, the question used in 1995 contained 'Recruited from the labour market', an option that obscures the true source of the employees but nonetheless about 45 per cent of studied private business owners ticked. As that is not comparable with the results from the 1993 and 1997 surveys, I have to ignore it (Table 5.8).

The results clearly suggest that private enterprises in China recruit their managers, technicians and workers from different organizations. Although the percentages have declined from 1993 to 1997, state and collective enterprises provided most of the managers and technicians for the private firms – in 1993 nearly 54 per cent private firms hired managers and 57 per cent hired technicians from them, which came down from nearly 48 per cent to 40 per cent, respectively, in 1997. In contrast, for both years, only about 17 per cent of private enterprises hired ordinary workers from state or collective firms. The major sources for workers were surplus labours from rural areas and the unemployed in urban areas, who supplied labour for more than 70 per cent of private firms. A notable trend is that graduates from schools constituted an increasing portion of managers and technicians in the private sector, both percentages were more than doubled from 1993 to 1997. The same is true for 'other private firms' as well, although at a smaller rate.

Table 5.8 Most important sources of employees for private enterprises in China, 1993 and 1997

Source	Managers		Technicians		Workers	
	1993	1997	1993	1997	1993	1997
State-owned enterprises	36.2	27.8	38.8	24.2	9.7	9.2
Collective enterprises	17.7	19.0	18.0	16.3	7.8	8.0
Graduates	3.7	9.3	8.0	16.8	6.8	5.1
Other private firms	8.0	12.4	7.4	15.3	2.9	4.0
Unemployed	13.5	8.5	10.0	6.7	28.9	19.0
Peasants	18.1	21.3	14.4	18.5	41.9	53.1
Other	2.8	1.7	3.4	2.1	2.1	1.6
N	1346	1512	1045	1460	1406	1594

Overall, the above figures support institutional as well as human capital explanations for the growth of private enterprises in China. The success of economic reforms in rural areas, led by the household responsibility system, has forced millions of farmers into a huge and cheap labour supply. On the other hand, reforms in the state and collective sectors have made their managers and technicians find offers by the private entrepreneurs too attractive to refuse.

Styles and strategies of management

The family business

It is reported that about 65 per cent to 80 per cent of all businesses in the world are run by families, which is still believed 'the most conservative estimate'.[19] The study

---

19 Kelin E. Gersick, et al. (eds), *Generation to Generation: Life Cycles of the Family Business* (Boston, Mass: Harvard Business School Press, 1997), p. 2. Based on Chau ('Approaches to Succession in Eastern Asian Business Organizations', *Family Business Review*, 4/2 (1991): 161–189), they pointed out that China was an exception. However, Chau only studied overseas Chinese family businesses, without looking at private firms in the mainland at all.

of family business has grown into a major field in economics and business history,[20] and a comprehensive study of family businesses in China is obviously beyond the scope of this section. Here I only hope to examine family business briefly as a part of the whole entrepreneurial process in China.

As we discovered before, about two-thirds of private enterprises in China started with personal savings and money borrowed from relatives and friends. Usually, the entrepreneur holds the largest proportion (often more than half) of the enterprise's total assets. Although a growing number of firms have turned themselves into limited liability companies, this is more a strategy of protecting their personal wealth than a way of diversifying the ownership structure. It is estimated that one in seven such limited liability companies actually have only one dominant investor.[21] As a consequence, most private firms are in the hands of the entrepreneur and his or her family members. For the management structure, this means that managers in the key positions, such as chief financial officer and director of personnel, most likely have very close family connections with the entrepreneur. For the jobs that demand professional training and experience but are less critical than finance and personnel, such as engineering and marketing, private business owners would like to offer them to managers from outside the family. It is not surprising that the CEO is usually the chairman of board of directors as well. The 2000 and 2002 surveys included the question 'Are you the chief executive officer or head of the enterprise as well?', and for both years around 96 per cent of the entrepreneurs gave a positive answer. While the first generation of entrepreneurs are now approaching retirement, they have started to hand the business down to their trusted sons (very few daughters).[22] For the criticism that such an arrangement may put limitations on the company's economic performance, entrepreneurs in the mainland would react by citing the successful stories of many business giants in Hong Kong, Taiwan, and other overseas Chinese firms.

Under such management structure, it is expected that the entrepreneur, perhaps with his or her closest family members and friends as members of 'board of directors' or 'key managers', will make all important decisions. There seems to be some changes, however, during the years of the surveys, as shown in Figure 5.3.

---

20 There have been quite a number of studies on family business by scholars in China, for example, Li Xinchun, 'Family Institutions and Enterprise Management in China' ('zhong guo jia zu zhi du yu qi ye zhu zhi'), *Quarterly Journal of Social Science in China* (Hong Kong, Spring, 1998); Chu Xiaoping, 'A Study of Family Business: A Topic of Modern Significance' ('jia zhu qi ye yan jiu: yi ge ju you xian dai yi yi de hua ti'), *Social Science in China* (*zhong guo she hui ke xue*, No. 5, 2000); Yao Xiantao and Wang Lianjuan, *The Current Situation, Problems and Strategies of Family Businesses in China* (*zhong guo jia zhu qi ye xian zhuang wen ti yu dui ci*, Beijing: Enterprise Management Publishing House, 2002).

21 'A Report of Private Enterprises in China, 2002', *China Business Times* (26 February 2003).

22 Gan De'an, et al., *A Study of Family Business in China* (*zhong guo jia zu qi ye yan jiu*, Beijing: China Social Sciences Publishing House, 2002, p. 179).

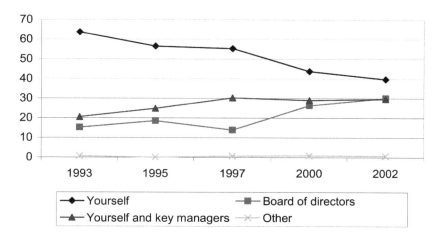

Figure 5.3 Makers of most important decisions in private enterprises in China, 1993 to 2002

At first appearance, among the three listed decision makers, the percentage of entrepreneurs who made decisions all on their own decreased from about 64 per cent in 1993 to 40 per cent in 2002, while the percentage for the entrepreneurs and key managers increased from about 20 per cent to 30 per cent. It is very likely that, in the latter situation, it is still the entrepreneur who has the final say, although more and more entrepreneurs would like to listen to their managers. It is also very likely that the key managers, or at least some of them, have some kinship relations with the entrepreneurs. We cannot verify these speculations, however.

During the same period, the percentages of private firms in which the board of directors made most important decisions climbed up from 15 per cent to 50 per cent. But, again, there are two questions that cannot be answered by the survey results. First, how many members did not have family relations with the entrepreneur? Second, how much power did the members without family connections with the entrepreneur have? In the 1997 and 2002 surveys, entrepreneurs were asked whether they thought that the enterprise must be directly managed by themselves or their family members, or it should be managed by some other more capable persons (implying no family connections). The results are almost the same for the two years: about 38 per cent agreed with the former statement and the other 62 per cent thought it would be fine to let others run their firms. How true this is in reality remains an issue to be investigated in future research. All in all, the available results do not provide much convincing evidence that private firms in China have transformed themselves from family businesses into companies responsible to public shareholders.

Constraints on daily operations

Drawing on interviews and media reports, Susan Young studied 'material constraints' on private businesses in China, including supplies, wholesale goods, utilities, business premises, and so on.[23] Here I verify and quantify her findings with the results from SPBO.

Nevertheless, compared with the entrepreneur's personal background and other subjects, the information about actual business activities such as purchases and sales collected in the surveys is sketchy. First of all, the investigators stopped collecting such information after 1997. Second, given the large number of industries and products covered by private enterprises, it is understandably difficult to pin down the exact suppliers and clients. We can only know that from 1993 to 1997 about 38 per cent to 42 per cent of private firms still relied on the state-owned enterprises for purchasing raw materials or wholesale goods. Similarly, for about one-third private enterprises, the most important clients were state-owned firms. Nearly half private firms in 1995 and 1997 sold their products directly to consumers, a big jump from only 31 per cent in 1993. It is widely believed in China that in these private-public transactions, the private firm often had to offer some kickbacks to the state firm in order to either purchase valuable raw materials or sell their products, but it is difficult to know how exactly prevalent these practices are. It seems that the private sector has become less dependent on the state sector with the increasing importance of market in private firms' business transactions. For example, thanks to the liberation of many material markets, the percentage of private firms relying on state-controlled markets declined sharply from 45 per cent in 1993 to 17 per cent in 1995 and 21 per cent in 1997. In the meantime, exchanges of raw materials and goods among private firms themselves increased greatly from only a little more than 7 per cent (1993) to 42 per cent (1995) and 34 per cent (1997).

Table 5.9 Levels of difficulty in obtaining basic business conditions, 1993 to 2000

		Not difficult	Somewhat difficult	Very difficult	N
Raw materials	1993	67.5	28.2	4.3	1137
	1995	72.1	25.0	3.0	2652
	2000	79.2	17.1	3.7	2370
Water and power	1993	81.5	14.6	3.9	1128
	1995	74.7	19.9	5.4	2583
	2000	79.9	16.0	4.1	2464
Space for business premises	1993	81.5	14.6	3.9	1126
	1995	45.7	30.5	23.8	1208
	2000	59.1	26.7	14.2	2623
Marketing and sales	1993	63.7	33.7	2.6	1083
	1995	54.0	42.3	3.7	2648
	2000	49.9	41.4	8.7	2377

23 See Chapter 4 of *Private Business and Economic Reform in China* (M.E. Sharpe, 1995).

How business owners perceived these constraints was an important question for the surveys. In 1993, 1995 and 2000, private business owners were asked to rate the level of difficulty for obtaining raw materials, water and power, space for business premises, and sales, and three categories were offered: not difficult, somewhat difficult, and very difficult. I have summarized the responses in Table 5.9.

According to these results, the situation was not as bad as reported in Young's study. For purchasing raw materials, more than two-thirds of private entrepreneurs did not find it difficult at all in 1993, which climbed to nearly 80 per cent in 2000. The percentage of entrepreneurs finding it not difficult to obtain water and power remained stable at about 75 per cent to 80 per cent during those years. There were more complaints about obtaining space for business premises: the percentage having no difficulty in getting space dropped most sharply from 81.5 per cent in 1993 to 45.7 per cent in 1995, but it bounced back to 59.1 per cent in 2000. The declining satisfaction in getting space may very likely come from the increasing number of private enterprises.

The next question is, for those who did face a series of constraints, whom did they go to for help? The 1995 and 1997 surveys tended to answer this question by asking the respondents to identify the most helpful organization or person when they had difficulties in accomplishing some managerial tasks. Here I focus on four of them: lack of financial credits, difficulty in marking and sales, lack of technology, and difficulty in expanding business. The ten listed helpers can be put into three groups: the official helpers (the government and trade unions), the informal helpers (relatives and friends), and the media. China specialists have debated over whether the role of *guanxi* (personal connections) has declined with the development of China's economic reform.[24] Again, the survey results (Table 5.10) may shed some light on this issue.[25]

First of all, government and banks clearly played an important role in resolving the five listed difficulties: about 40 per cent to 50 per cent private entrepreneurs would seek help from them for financial credits, space for businesses, water and power. In contrast, for sales and technology, most private firms (56 per cent to 61 per cent) tended to resolve the difficulty by themselves, either through market mechanisms or by negotiations with relevant parties, which were the second most important sources of help (more than one-third have identified them) for obtaining space, water, and

---

24 Douglas Guthrie and Amy Hanser have argued that the importance of *guanxi* has declined, while Yanjie Bian and Mayfair Yang have argued for the opposite. For details, see relevant chapters in Thomas Gold, Doug Guthrie, and David Wank (eds), *Social Connections in China: Institutions, Culture, and the Changing Nature of Guanxi* (Cambridge University Press, 2002), and Mayfair Yang, 'The Resilience of Guanxi and Its New Deployment: A Critique of Some New Guanxi Scholarship', *The China Quarterly*, 170 (2002): 459–476.

25 Unfortunately, the questions used in the two surveys are not exactly the same. In the 1995 survey, one difficulty was 'preparing for expanding business scope', which was listed separately and more specifically as difficulties in obtaining 'space' and 'water and power' in the 1997 survey. Also, the 1995 survey listed 'searching for new markets or change products' as an option, which was replaced by 'negotiations among ourselves' in 1997. As most financial institutions are under the State's control and very few respondents chose them as a helper, as a source of help they were merged with 'government'.

power. Note that trade unions were not popular at all among private entrepreneurs, even including the most important organization for private enterprises, *gong shang lian*, a quasi-government agency as a liaison between the state and private business owners.

Table 5.10 Most helpful organization or person when facing difficulty for private entrepreneurs in China, 1995 and 1997

	Finance		Sales		Technology		Expansion	Space	Water and power
	1995	1997	1995	1997	1995	1997	1995	1997	1997
Government or banks	34.3	55.7	3.8	1.6	12.3	5.0	58.8	45.0	46.5
Association of private businesses	1.7	1.4	0.7	2.1	1.8	8.3	1.7	3.0	1.9
Trade unions	7.9	3.4	2.9	5.4	11.2	8.7	7.4	6.4	3.0
Other private firms	6.6	1.1	8.6	7.3	18.4	1.6	4.7	1.5	0.4
Relatives	13.9	9.5	0.8	2.2	3.8	13.3	1.9	1.4	0.8
Friends	25.6	8.9	13.5	11.3	28.8	5.1	10.0	5.4	4.7
Powerful persons	3.2	0.4	3.0	4.5	12.5	0.2	4.0	3.6	3.7
Court or media	0.2	0.3	0.2	4.2	0.3	1.3	0.3	0.4	1.2
New market or product	6.6	0.0	66.6	0.0	10.8	0.0	11.2	0.0	0.0
Negotiations	0.0	19.3	0.0	61.4	0.0	56.3	0.0	33.2	37.7
N	2692	1896	2459	1750	2220	1709	2503	1759	1718

For *guanxi*, firstly we need to specify who and what we are talking about: in 1995 and 1997, relatives were very important in having access to technology but not so important in financial matters, and their role in sales was marginal. The effect of friends declined, particularly in finance and technology. Overall, the results lend some support to the 'declining' thesis. These observations, I should add, are highly suggestive because of the different categories used in the two surveys.

Competing strategies

With the dramatic increase of private enterprises[26] and the liberalization of state policies, market competition has been increasingly fierce for all type of businesses. It is thus reasonable to expect that more and more private entrepreneurs would report their feelings of increased competitions in the surveys. Our analysis, however, has to be confined to the 1997 and 2000 surveys as the surveys in other years did not include any questions on competition. The results are almost the same: for both years, more than half of private entrepreneurs (56 per cent for 1997 and 54 per cent for 2000) felt they were facing very fierce competition, and 40 per cent felt they were facing fierce competition. The limited time span therefore does not allow the emergence of a trend.

Nor can we learn very much about their competing strategies from the survey results. Researchers in China asked their entrepreneur respondents to choose three from the listed nine strategies and rank them by importance. Again, the results for 1997 and 2000 turn out to be highly similar: the most important strategy that came to the entrepreneurs' mind was to improve the quality of their product, with about 47 per cent of them choosing it as the first important thing they had to do. Reducing costs came as the second most important strategy, with improving after-sale service following as the third. These are clearly very rough descriptions of business strategies, demanding further and more refined analysis.

Settling business disputes

How to compete is one thing, the fairness of competition is another. In the eyes of private business owners in China, a series of factors make competition in the market unfair, such as the 'red cap' phenomenon and other hidden business relations, the lack of or the ambiguity of state regulations, and various discriminating policies or practices created by local authorities. The number of disputes between private enterprises and local governments and among private enterprises themselves can be taken as an indicator of the institutionalization of market competitions in China.

From 1995 to 2002 SPBO included three questions on disputes where private enterprises were involved: who they had disputes with, how the disputes were resolved, and whether they were satisfied with the solutions. A major problem with these questions is the assumption that the surveyed enterprises must have had some disputes before. Without a filtering question that firstly checks whether a surveyed private firm did have any disputes before, it is impossible to estimate the scope of various disputes in the private sector, let alone the change of the scope through time. In addition, the question designed for the 2002 survey is so incomparable with those for the previous years that the following table (Table 5.11) contains results only for 1995, 1997, and 2000. Fortunately, the results still offer some interesting information on this aspect of the entrepreneurial process.

It is clear that the most frequently reported complaints were about the clients – about 61 per cent in 1995, then down to 55 per cent in 1997 and 2000. The percentage

---

26 Please refer to Tables 1.1 and 1.2 in Chapter 1 for details.

of complaints about their suppliers, in contrast, was only around 17 per cent for the three years. This is understandable because China in the 1990s was (and still is) a buyer's market, making the seller constantly in a disadvantageous position, chasing after the buyer for payment. The reader must have noted that the relative frequencies of disputes with government were quite low, only about 9 per cent, which is at odds with the widely reported complaints and protests by private entrepreneurs about the ruthless charges imposed by local authorities. One possible explanation is that although entrepreneurs complain about those charges, it is not in their interests to dispute with the authorities.

Table 5.11 Disputes reported by private enterprises in China, 1995, 1997, and 2000

		1995	1997	2000
Dispute with	Supplier	17.6	18.7	16.7
	Client	60.8	55.1	55.0
	Customers	13.0	10.6	13.5
	Government	8.6	9.7	9.5
	Local residents	–	5.9	2.8
	Other	–	–	2.4
	N	2296	1693	2572
Way of resolving	Ignore	1.8	1.0	1.2
	Negotiate	79.7	76.7	79.4
	Report to authority	3.1	7.1	4.0
	Bring to court	9.2	8.3	11.6
	Mediate via personal connections	6.2	6.3	3.5
	Other	–	0.6	0.4
	N	2323	1774	2695
Satisfaction with result	Very unsatisfied	5.1	3.3	4.6
	Unsatisfied	24.0	16.6	14.7
	Hard to say	–	44.1	46.1
	Satisfied	66.3	33.7	30.9
	Very satisfied	4.6	2.4	3.8
	N	2304	1750	2681

Being involved in disputes, most owners of private business in China (nearly 80 per cent) tended to negotiate with their clients or suppliers, not to resort to legal procedures. This is very likely so because of their lack of trust in China's legal system. It is interesting to note that the percentages of private firms resolving disputes via personal mediations were surprisingly very low as well, from only a little more than 6 per cent in 1995 and 1997 to 3.5 per cent in 2000.[27]

It is difficult to compare the results about entrepreneurs' satisfaction in solutions to disputes, because the 1995 survey did not contain the category of 'Hard to say', which however had the largest reporting frequencies in the other two years. Perhaps we can only say that, at least in the late 1990s, about two-thirds of private businessmen were not really happy with the solutions.

Relations with employees

China's huge population makes the nation 'a labour surplus economy *par excellence*'.[28] Consequently, the labour market is always that of the employers, making employees, especially the migrant workers from poor rural areas, vulnerable to poor welfare and working conditions. It was not until very recently that researchers both within and outside China started to pay attention to the unsatisfactory, sometimes even appalling, conditions under which employees were working in private firms. To my knowledge, little research has been done on the employment relations within private enterprises in China in general and on disputes between employers and employees in particular. As shown in the previous section, researchers organizing SPBO did not list the disputes between private business owners and their employees as one of the disputes, assuming that this kind of dispute were not a serious problem. But, according to a recent report by Xia Xiaolin, the number of employment disputes in China has increased at an annual rate of more than 30 per cent.[29]

The controversial nature of employment disputes makes it nearly impossible to produce a relatively accurate estimate of their scale. Scattered academic and journalist reports published in China, however, have suggested that there are three major problems. The first is related to remuneration. In China, vast variations in economic development across different areas makes it nonsensical to keep a national minimum wage. Rather, each provincial government determines a minimum wage in its own jurisdiction. We do not know the number of private firms that offer employees a wage below the minimum level. The most recent report on private firms has found that the average employee salary was lower than that in state and collective enterprises and declined from 2002 to 2004,[30] which is surprising because it is usually expected that salaries at private firms should be higher than those in other types of firms due to poor job security and welfare. The second, and more widely experienced, problem, according to Xia's report, is delay and deduction of

---

27 This finding can also be taken as a supporting evidence for the decline of the importance of guanxi.

28 J. Knight and L. Song, 'Towards a labour market in China', *Oxford Review of Economic Policy*, 11 (1995): 97–117.

29 Xia Xiaolin, 'Si Ying Bu Men: Lao Zi Guan Xi He Xie Tiao Ji Zhi' ('The Private Sector: Employment Relations and Mechanisms of Mediation'), *Guan Li Shi Jie* (*The World of Management*), 6 (2004), accessed at http://theory.people.com.cn/GB/40555/3833168.html#.

30 *A Report of Private Enterprises in China*, 2005. According to SSPE, the medium of an employee's annual salary increased from 5,000 yuan (about $600) in 1995 and 1997 to 7,000 yuan (about $840) in 2000 and 8,000 yuan (about $950) in 2002.

pay. Finally, some private business owners have extended working hours without extra pay.

The second employment relation problem is poor welfare coverage. In China, employees in state-owned firms enjoy a comprehensive welfare coverage of nearly every aspect of their life. Although the situation has been deteriorating since the Chinese State tried to relinquish some of its responsibilities for employees in order to improve the state sector's economic performance, these employees still have pensions and medical insurance. The situation in the collective sector varies with each enterprise's economic performance, but as most of them are linked with state-sponsored industries, the overall welfare conditions are better than those in private firms. More specific information for 1994, 1996, 1999 and 2001 in the private sector is shown in Figure 5.4.[31]

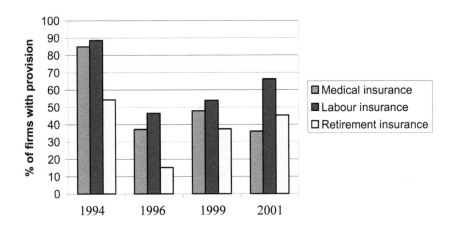

Figure 5.4 Selected welfare provisions by private enterprises in China, 1994, 1996, 1999, and 2001

While the percentage of private firms offering labour insurance and retirement insurance increased in the second half of the twentieth century, that for medical insurance surprisingly declined. These numbers are still much smaller than those in the state and collective sectors; only the percentage of labour insurance in 2001 was more than 50 per cent. Results from the most recent survey show that, in 2004, only one-third of private firms offered medical insurance to employees, and the corresponding percentages for retirement insurance and unemployment insurance

---

31 I have excluded the results for 1993 and 1995 because, unlike those used in the following years, the questions used in those two years did not include the option of 'no coverage at all', rendering the results quite suspicious. Meanwhile, questions about life insurance, retirement insurance, and housing were designed only in selected years, which are not used here either in order to make comparisons across years.

were 8.7 per cent and 16.6 per cent, respectively.[32] From these results we cannot tell, however, who the recipients of welfare coverage were – private entrepreneurs were only asked to report what kinds of welfare they provided to employees, not how many employees received them and who they were. It may well be the case that welfare has been offered only to the most important employees, such as managers, chief engineers, and marketing executives. Further studies are needed on this issue.

For now, we can have an idea of the situation by looking at the turnover rate in private enterprises, here measured as the percentage of the number of employees voluntarily leaving the enterprise of the total number of employees in a particular year. The underlying logic runs like this: although there are a number of reasons for employees to leave a private firm, absence of welfare or poor welfare coverage should be a crucial cause, and as the percentages of firms with provisions of labour insurance and retirement insurance were growing from 1994 to 2001, we should expect the turnover rate at least not to go up (that is, either going down or stable) during the same period. The hypothesis is confirmed by the stability of the turnover rates: 5.58 per cent in 1996 and 4.94 per cent in 1999,[33] and the difference is not statistically significant.

A third important aspect of employment relations within private firms in China is the institutionalization of the relationship. Drawing on available data, I discuss this issue from two perspectives. The first is the extent to which employment relationship is institutionally settled. Whilst state-owned enterprises have always been criticized for their bureaucratic procedures and administrative inefficiency, complaints to the opposite exist about private firms, that is, the lack of clear procedures, policies, and rules. We have learnt that private entrepreneurs follow rules only when they have to, but their disrespect for formal and written contracts means that employee welfare will be at their employers' mercy. This did not come as an important issue for researchers in China until 1997, and the question disappeared in the 2002 survey. Even the results for 1997 and 2000 look questionable: in 1997, the percentages of private firms having written rules for employment, labour contract, and salary were 27.4 per cent, 32.4 per cent, and 24.8 per cent, respectively, which then all had a big jump in 2000 to 66.6 per cent, 78.0 per cent, and 56.9 per cent. At least, this is at odds with Xia's finding in Zhejiang, the province with the most developed private sector in China, where only 40 per cent of private firms sign labour contracts with employees.

We end this section by examining a second aspect of the institutional relationship of employment – the role of labour union. China's first *Law of Labour Unions* was passed in 1950. It then was systematically revised in 1992, with further amendments in 2001. Curiously, it contains specific articles about labour union in all types of companies, but not for private enterprises. Nevertheless, that does not seem to have prevented the Law from promoting the establishment of labour unions in private businesses: the survey results show that the percentage of private firms with a labour union increased rapidly from only 8 per cent in 1993 to 12.7 per cent in 1995, 34.4 per

---

32 *A Report of Private Enterprises in China, 2005.*

33 Surveys in other years did not include the number of employees who voluntarily left the company.

cent in 2000, and finally to 49.7 per cent in 2002.[34] While this is encouraging, there is a more important question: given the existence of a labour union in a private firm, is it of any help to protect employee welfare? To acquire a relatively sophisticated answer to this question, I have constructed the following statistical model on the data collected in the 2002 survey:

$$\ln(\frac{p}{1-p}) = X\beta$$

Its specific objective is to single out the effect of labour union on the provision of labour insurance for employees in private firms. As the dependent variable, provision of labour insurance, has only two values (yes or no), a binary logistic regression is needed, with p representing the probability of offering labour insurance. X is the matrix of five explanatory variables, including two variables about the business owner's political status (membership of the CCP, member of the People's Congress), two variables about the business's economic performance (size of profit and number of employees), and finally the owner's education level, simplified to whether or not the owner has a university degree. Relevant information is presented below.

Table 5.12 A binary logistic regression modelling the effect of labour unions on employee welfare, 2002

Independent variables	Values	Adjusted odds ratio	95% C.I.
CCP membership	Yes	1.1	(0.9, 1.4)
People's representative	Yes	1.2	(0.9, 1.5)
After tax profit	≤ 10K	1.0	
	10 to 50K	0.8	(0.5, 1.2)
	51 to 200K	1.1	(0.8, 1.5)
	200K to 1 million	1.1	(0.8, 1.4)
	Above 1 million	1.1	(0.8, 1.4)
Employee size	≤ 8	1.0	
	9 to 60	0.2	(0.1, 0.5)
	61 to 500	0.7	(0.4, 1.5)
	501 to 1000	1.3	(0.7, 2.7)
	≥ 1001	1.5	(0.7, 3.4)
Level of education	≤ High school	1.0	
	≥ University	0.9	(0.8, 1.1)
Labour union	Yes	1.8	(1.5, 2.2)

---

34 No data for 1996 as the 1997 survey excluded the question on labour union.

It turns out that labour union is the only explanatory variable that is statistically significant (i.e., whose 95 per cent confidence interval does not include 1). The adjusted odds ratio is 1.8, with a 95 per cent confidence interval (1.5, 2.2).[35] Substantively, this means that private enterprises with a labour union would be 50 per cent to 120 per cent more likely to provide labour insurance to employees than those without a labour union. A labour union does seem to help. This finding, however, should be taken with caution as the survey was conducted by interviewing the business owners, not their employees; therefore, the provision of welfare and the establishment of labour union may have been over-reported in order to appear politically correct.

Political relations and participations

Politics is an inherent part of the Chinese entrepreneurial process because entrepreneurship has grown out of the ruling political party's struggle for survival, and because entrepreneurs will be economically more competitive if they enjoy better political relations. Recall that one of the two important missions of double entrepreneurship is to establish, nurture, and develop favourable relations with political authorities so that entrepreneurs can put themselves in a better position in exploiting institutional holes. In this section I describe the entrepreneur-state relationship with some quantitative information. The plan is to start with political participation by private entrepreneurs, then to examine their relations with local authorities, and finally to analyze whether the level of political participation has any effect on their relations with authorities.

Political participation

In its Constitution, the Chinese Communist Party (CCP) declares itself as the pioneering team of the proletariat, of which private entrepreneurs are obviously not a part. The political chaos and economic stagnation caused by the Cultural Revolution made the CCP realize that blind ideological commitment would compromise its political power. Since then, it has increased its political suppleness by allowing some of its members to become originally the opponent of the proletariat, i.e., the capitalists. This is why there were some private business owners who were at the same time members of the CCP. During the 1990s, the percentage of CCP members among private business owners steadily increased from 13 per cent to 20 per cent. In July 2001, while celebrating the CCP's eightieth birthday, General Secretary Jiang Zemin called for the Party to accept anybody who can represent the interest of the population's majority, advanced technology and culture, including private entrepreneurs. Although his speech has entailed some debates within the Party due to concerns over the Party's identity and the employment problems discussed before,

---

35 For readers who would like to keep away from statistics, an odds ratio measures the strength of the association between two categorical variables. The further away it is from 1, the stronger the relationship is. An adjusted odds ratio is the odds ratio after taking into account of the effects of other variables.

the new policy has pushed CCP membership in the private sector to 30 per cent in 2002 and 34 per cent in 2004. That is, in today's China, one in three private business owners are Communists! The Party hopes that the increased intake from the private sector will create a symbiotic situation, in which the State gains tighter control of the fastest growing part of the economy while private entrepreneurs enjoy better treatment by the government. Survey results also show that in 2002 about 27 per cent of private firms had a CCP committee. Further studies are needed, however, to learn who the committee members are and what they actually do.

Joining the CCP is a first step of winning political protection and establishing a good relationship with authorities. With the CCP membership, some more capable private entrepreneurs have advanced their political participation by managing to become members of the People's Congress and the People's Assembly of Political Consultation. The former is politically more powerful than the latter, and it is more difficult to join. The year 2000 witnessed the highest rates of private business members in both organizations, with 27.5 per cent of Congress members and 54.7 per cent of Assembly members from the private sector, but then the percentages went down to 17.4 per cent and 35.1 per cent, respectively, in 2002.[36] Some highly successful private entrepreneurs have become members of the National Congress or the National Assembly. While it is hard to tell what exactly they could do at the top of the political infrastructure, the State has earned the credit of being politically liberal and the entrepreneurs have enhanced their reputation, visibility in the public, and perhaps social capital.

Their political participation cannot represent that of 'politically ordinary' ones, of course. To get a better idea of how 'an average entrepreneur' has participated in politics, survey researchers in China asked private entrepreneurs to assess their level of political participation by putting themselves in a scale of 1 to 10 (with 1 being the highest). The mean score changed from 4.6 in 1993 to a bit more than 5 in the following years, suggesting that most private entrepreneurs did not think that they were politically more involved than other citizens. Furthermore, as the differences between these scores are not statistically significant, there is no evidence for any increase or decrease through the years.

Relations with local authorities

The question is: is CCP membership, or membership of the People's Congress or the Consultative Assembly, of any help for establishing and running a private business? It implies the following causal relationship: political membership improves business performance. In many cases, however, the causality may run in the opposite direction: the owners of better performing businesses will enjoy a better chance of joining the political organizations. SPBO is a cross-sectional survey, so interviews were not conducted on the same entrepreneurs repeatedly over time, nor has the survey included any questions that indicate the temporal sequence of the entrepreneur's political membership and business development. It is thus not feasible to test the direction of causal relationship with the collected data.

36 These include members at all levels (national, provincial, regional and county).

We can explore this issue, however, by analyzing the association between political membership and each of the following two factors: the evaluation of governmental support to business and the amount of money extracted by local authorities. First, private entrepreneurs were asked to assess the supportiveness of some government agencies in the 1993 and 1995 surveys. Here, it is sufficient to focus on the 1995 survey, in which ten government agencies were listed for evaluation. Their support in the eyes of private entrepreneurs was classified into three levels: supportive, indifferent, and not supportive. In Table 5.13 I report the distribution of the private entrepreneurs who expressed their views for each particular agency as well as a measurement of the association between the evaluation and political memberships.

Table 5.13 Reported supportiveness of government agencies and their association with political memberships, 1994

	Percentage			Somer's d		
	Supportive	**Indifferent**	**Not supportive**	**CCP**	**PC**	**PAPC**
Local govnt	72.0	25.7	2.2	0.08***	0.13***	0.13***
Police	46.9	48.1	5.0	0.10***	0.06**	0.02
Environment	30.4	62.3	7.4	0.10***	0.06*	0.02
Quality inspt	44.4	52.2	3.4	0.10***	0.01	0.03
Taxation	63.7	32.5	3.8	0.07***	−0.03	−0.01
Price control	33.5	62.1	4.4	0.04	0.01	0.04*
Hygiene	32.1	63.0	4.9	0.05*	0.03	0.06**
Customs	29.9	61.5	8.5	0.06	0.16***	0.15***
Administration	77.2	20.7	2.1	0.04*	−0.02	0.01
Measurement	36.9	59.4	3.7	0.10***	0.08**	0.06**

Notes: ***= p < 0.001, **= p < 0.05, *=p < 0.1.

Overall, private entrepreneurs' view of government agencies were quite positive in 1995; those holding a negative opinion constituted only less than 10 per cent for all agencies. Local government and the Administration of Industries and Commerce scored the best, with more than 70 per cent entrepreneurs thinking they were supportive. The least supportive agencies seemed to be those in charge of the environment and customs. Assuming we do not have to worry about the effect of social desirability on the scores, we can say that private entrepreneurs were generally satisfied with governmental service, although their feeling for particular agencies varied greatly. We should also keep in mind that this is only a one-sided story by the entrepreneurs; we need a story by governmental agencies in future studies.

Numbers in the last three columns are the values of *Somer's d*, a statistic that measures the strength of association between two categorical variables, with one believed to be the cause of the other. It is used here because the associations are directed from the column variables to the row variables. Here I am interested in how membership in CCP, People's Congress, and People's Assembly of Political Consultative have an effect on the entrepreneur's evaluations of government agencies, not the reverse. Statistically speaking, CCP membership is significantly associated with positive evaluations of most of the agencies, expect for 'Price control' and 'Customs'. Although the relationship is not very strong (0.1 or lower), being a member of the CCP did connect to a better experience with government agencies. Memberships in the Congress and the Assembly did not have such a wide range of effect, but they did have relatively stronger relationships with positive reports of local governments, customs, and measurement agencies, which are of high statistical significance as well. Three scores were negative, suggesting that a Congress or Assembly membership was associated with negative views of the agencies, but they are not statistically significant. The big picture is that participation in these political organizations was associated with a positive view of the government.

We now turn to the financial aspect of the entrepreneur-government relationship. Several studies of private enterprises in China have long reported the costs for cultivating good relations with local governments. Many officials relentlessly seek to rent out their power, and private firms have been their most vulnerable prey. In exchange for administrative facilitation and protection, involuntary donations and locally imposed fees have become a major source of local revenues not only for public projects but for increasing local officials' personal incomes as well.[37] For example, from 1985 to 1988 there were about 43 types of administration fees and charges that private enterprises were asked to pay.[38] And the average amount of fees and charges per private firm went up from about 22,000 yuan in 1992 to 35,000 yuan in 1994, and to 39,000 yuan in 1996.[39] The Chinese government has launched several waves of campaigns to curb 'three indiscriminating collections of money' (*san luan*) – fines, fees, and charges, but the effectiveness of these campaigns remains unclear. Again, we can advance our knowledge of this issue, albeit to a limited extent, by analyzing the SPBO data. First of all, the indiscriminate charges were indeed a problem for private entrepreneurs in the mid 1990s:[40] in both 1995 and 1997 the foremost serious social problem they recognized was the exchange between power and money, and the second was the fees, fines, and charges.

---

37 Liu, Yia-Ling, 'Reform From Below: The Private Economy and Local Politics in the Rural Industrialization of Wenzhou', *The China Quarterly*, 130 (1992): 293–316.

38 Willy Kraus, *Private Business in China: Revival between Ideology and Pragmatism* (Hurst & Company, 1991), pp. 157–159.

39 Zhang and Ming (eds), *Report of Private Enterprises in China* (1999), p. 140.

40 Only the 1995 and 1997 surveys included a question about the most serious social problems in the mind of entrepreneurs. They were asked to identify one problem in 1995 but the 1997 survey asked them to identify two. It is difficult to tell whether the exclusion of this question in the following surveys indicates the fading importance of this issue or if there was any other consideration.

We can have a better idea of the effects of these fees and charges imposed by examining their shares in the total amount of profits earned in each particular year (Figure 5.5).[41]

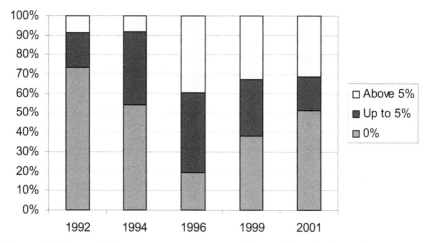

Figure 5.5 Fees and charges as percentages of annual profit for private enterprises in China, 1992 to 2001

In Figure 5.5, the overall pattern is that the burden was becoming heavier up to 1996, after which the situation somewhat improved but remained quite serious. More precisely, in 1992, more than 73 per cent of private firms didn't pay any imposed fees and charges at all, but that shrank to 54 per cent in 1994 mainly due to the increase of the number of firms who had to take up to 5 per cent of their annual profit for those kinds of payments. The worst year was 1996, in which only about 20 per cent of private firms didn't pay anything, 40 per cent paid up to 5 per cent of their total profit, and about another 40 per cent paid more than 5 per cent of profit for the fees and charges. Although the percentages of firms not paying bounced back to 38 per cent in 1999 and 51 per cent in 2001, the percentage of firms paying above 5 per cent remained at about 31 per cent. That is, even at the beginning of this century, for nearly one in three private enterprises, 5 per cent or more of their annual profit was taken away by local officials.

Obviously, among the private firms, some did not pay at all, while others had no choice but to pay a lot more. How could we explain such a difference? To make a comprehensive answer to this question across all surveys, we need theoretically informed statistical models, a task that cannot be done in this section. What we can

---

41 This is done by assuming that (1) every enterprise made a profit rather than a loss and (2) the amount of charges paid was less than the profit. Therefore, both negative values (loss) and proportions equal to or larger than one (charges exceed profit) have been treated as missing. The number of such cases varies during the years, but they do not constitute more than 1 per cent of the sample size.

do here is to test whether membership of political organizations make a difference to the relative burden of the imposed fees and charges. The test is conducted by calculating the *Somer's d* for the 1995, 1997 and 2000 surveys,[42] with the percentage of fees and charges as the dependent variable and the membership of each political organization as the independent variable. The results are shown in Table 5.14.

Table 5.14 Relationship between political memberships and level of fees and charges paid by private entrepreneurs, 1994, 1996, and 1999

	1994		1996		1999	
	Somer's d	p-value	Somer's d	p-value	Somer's d	p-value
CCP	0.01	0.80	0.05	0.26	0.01	0.74
PC	0.05	0.11	0.04	0.47	0.14	0.00
PAPC	0.07	0.00	0.10	0.01	0.11	0.00

We can see that CCP membership does not have any effect on the level of fees and charged paid – the values of *Somer's d* are very small and not statistically significant. People's Congress membership has a significant effect in 1999 only. Interestingly, Political Assembly membership was statistically significant through the years, and its association with the relative burden of fees and charges increased as well. This is so very likely because Political Assembly is an organization especially targeting the non-CCP members – the so-called 'united front' under the leadership of the CCP. Membership of the Assembly indicates recognition of the private entrepreneur's economic success and the CCP's willingness to establish a good relationship. It is very likely that the fees and charges are part of the membership, and making the payment is an important gesture by the private entrepreneur of acquiring or maintaining the membership.

Public relations

Finally, we take a look at the way in which private entrepreneurs handle their relations with the general public. This is an important step of the entrepreneurial process in China because the relations make a big difference to private firms' survival and performance.

Like the Communist Party, ordinary people have held ambivalent attitudes towards private entrepreneurs. Whilst admiring them and wishing to be one of them, fellow citizens often question the legitimacy of the enormous amount of money earned by the entrepreneurs. The logic of their suspicion is that one simply cannot make a huge profit in a short period of time without some wrongdoings; either the entrepreneurs have something to hide, or they have bribed local officials, or

---

42 The instruments used in the 1993 and 2002 surveys do not allow such computation.

they have broken the law or any other state regulations. Media coverage of some private entrepreneurs found guilty of breaking law or state regulations has reinforced such impression, and people do not seem very much concerned with whether these intensively covered cases by the media can represent the whole private sector. Many urban residents are still reluctant to work for private firms unless they have no other choice, another reason why most employees at private firms are from rural areas or redundant employees from the state and collective firms. Those who voluntarily work for a private employer are usually attracted by a bigger salary or a promise of quick promotion, and some of them plan to set up their own firms after gaining some work experience in a private firm. In this social atmosphere, carefully managing a peaceful relationship with the public has been a great challenge for private entrepreneurs in China. They have to be careful not to live too showy a way of life in order to not arouse resentment from others.

Let's analyze the survey data to learn where private entrepreneurs themselves think they are in the class structure of the Chinese society. Same as measuring self-reported political participation, the entrepreneurs were asked to put themselves in a ladder of ten steps (1 being the highest) in terms of income and social reputation. To make the results more meaningful, I have recoded the scales to represent three classes: the higher class (1 to 3), the middle class (4 to 7), and the lower class (8 to 10). Results are summarized in Table 5.15.

Table 5.15 Self-assessed positions in income and social reputation by private entrepreneurs in China, 1993 to 2002

	1993		1995		1997		1999		2002	
	Income	**SR**	**Income**	**SR**	**Income**	**SR**	**Income**	**SR**	**Income**	**SR**
Higher	29.3	43.6	25.0	38.1	24.9	34.8	24.9	37.0	27.5	43.4
Middle	64.8	49.5	67.2	54.3	68.9	57.5	67.9	56.0	64.8	49.4
Lower	5.9	6.9	7.8	7.6	6.2	7.6	7.1	7.0	7.7	7.3
N	1435	1435	2859	2859	1900	1896	2970	2972	3224	3224

The first striking feature of the results is the obvious structural stability. Respectively for income and social reputation, the percentages of private entrepreneurs in each class have remained nearly the same for the ten years from 1993 to 2002.[43] For example, in terms of self-assessed position in the income hierarchy, about 25 per cent to 29 per cent put themselves in the higher class, another 65 per cent to 69 per cent in the middle class, and finally about 7 per cent in the lower class. This is somewhat surprising given the remarkable growth of private enterprises. On the other hand, it may not be so surprising if we put the results in the context described at the beginning of this section – private entrepreneurs have tried to downplay

---

43 Note that answers to these questions were made in the year which each survey was conducted, not referring to the year previous to the survey year.

their economic privileges in front of others. Even after taking into account the high likelihood that they under-reported their personal incomes in the surveys, the medium of self-reported annual income increased from 20,000 yuan before 1997 to 30,000 yuan in 2000 and 50,000 yuan in 2002. Clearly, the increase was truthfully reflected in the entrepreneurs' self-identified position of class.

Also striking is the finding that, compared with their positions in the income class, more private entrepreneurs identified themselves as members of the higher class of social reputation: whilst the percentages of higher class for income are in the range of 25 per cent to 29 per cent, those for social reputation are from 35 per cent to 43 per cent. In addition, the scores for income and social reputation are highly correlated,[44] meaning that those who thought they were in the higher class of income tended to think they were in the higher class of social reputation as well.

All these lead to an interesting observation: private entrepreneurs in China tend to report that their social status is higher than their economic status. It will be even more interesting to learn what the general public think about the social status of private entrepreneurs in future research.

Perhaps private entrepreneurs' self-reported high social status is partly purported by the financial contributions they made to public welfare. Either to maintain a good relationship with local authorities by taking their call for donations, or to smother resentments from their fellow residents, more and more private entrepreneurs have shown their generosity to the public. For example, the percentage of entrepreneurs having donated to social welfare increased from 63 per cent in 1993 to about 85 per cent in 1995 and 1997, and finally to about 90 per cent at the turn of the century. In the meantime, the medium amount of contribution experienced a much bigger jump, from only 3,000 yuan in 1993 to around 10,000 in the mid 1990s and to 32,000 in 2000, and finally to 48,000 in 2002. If these figures are reliable, then we have a puzzle for future research: why did most of them not put themselves in the higher class of income given that they have donated more and more money to society?

Concluding remarks

Scott Shane has offered perhaps the first conceptual framework for studying the entrepreneurial process as a whole.[45] The framework aims to explain the emergence and performance of entrepreneurship by examining the interaction between individual entrepreneurs and opportunities. Therefore, the existence of opportunity is a precondition of entrepreneurship. Opportunities come from a variety of sources: technological innovations, change of demographic compositions, social and regulatory changes, etc. The true first step of the entrepreneurial process is to discover opportunity; entrepreneurs must have the capacity of recognizing the opportunity and have the access to necessary information for evaluating the potential risks and benefits. Both individual attributes of the entrepreneur and contextual

---

44 The *Pearson's R* between the score of income and the score of social reputation for 1993 and 1995 is about 0.56, then it goes up to 0.60 in 1997 but comes back to 0.54 in 2000 and 0.57 in 2002. All are statistically significant at the 0.001 level.

45 Scott Shane, *A General Theory of Entrepreneurship*.

factors in the environment will influence the likelihood of making the decision to open a new business. Once the decision is made, the entrepreneur must acquire and mobilize necessary resources and put them together in an organized structure. Depending on the nature of a particular resource, the entrepreneur adopts different strategies for overcoming real or perceived difficulties. Managerial responsibilities gain an increasing weight at the later stage of the entrepreneurial process when the entrepreneur is designing organizational structures, dealing with administrative procedures, and handling relations in and outside the new organization.

China has, since the end of the 1970s, been full of opportunities for entrepreneurs. In the market, shortage is opportunity. Once the demand for quantity is satisfied, there is a new demand for quality. The size of the population is huge, people's life expectancy is rising, and they are craving a better material life. All institutional rules, ideological, political, economic, regulatory, and cultural, are changing. Not all these changes are welcomed by the entrepreneur, but they have opened up the door for exploration and exploitation. It will not be too big an exaggeration to say that no other country has offered so many opportunities for entrepreneurs.

The abundance of opportunities means that, except for a few exceptions, it should not be very difficult to recognize them. What especially makes one an entrepreneur in China is one's imagination and the capacity to mobilize resources and deal with institutional constraints. In this chapter we have learnt that most entrepreneurs in China are well-educated and middle-aged men with a very strong desire to have their own businesses, either to make money or to realize their personal worth, or both.

In acquiring resources and setting up their new organizations, entrepreneurs in China have employed a variety of strategies, which perhaps can be generalized into two categories. The first is to maximize the use of 'informal resources': money and information collected from family members, relatives and friends, and employees hired through social ties. The second general strategy is to make use of institutional holes: renting a title of state enterprise, gaining legitimacy by making a connection with local governments and state enterprises, manipulating administrative procedures, joining political organizations, and consolidating the ideological legitimacy of private firms with their economic contributions. Some of these strategies have lost their popularity with the increasing institutionalization of the market, a point I shall return to in the last chapter.

I have described some important aspects of the entrepreneurial process in China by teasing out useful information from the survey results. But they cannot tell very much about how the entrepreneurs discover, manipulate, and make use of opportunities, nor can they show how the entrepreneurs react to difficulties and problems. Those are the topics for the case studies in the following three chapters.

Chapter 6

The Entrepreneur, the Bureaucrats, and the Journalists: Huo Hongmin and the Huaqi Group

I hope the reader now has a general idea of entrepreneurship in China – who the entrepreneurs are and how they get their businesses up and running. The idea may still be general because the descriptions and analyses are about private entrepreneurs as a whole, so the idiosyncrasies of each of them have been lost in the historical narratives and statistics. In each of the following three chapters I shall analyze a particular case that will not only supplement previous analyses with stories but also bring to light some of the issues that could not be seriously addressed before, for example, the role of the media. These cases will also illustrate a variety of ways in which double entrepreneurship exploits institutional holes and the prices they may have to pay for doing so. These case studies are meant to highlight that uncertainties in institutional changes have introduced both opportunities and risks, both financially and politically, for private entrepreneurs in China. To obtain simultaneous profitability and legitimacy is a distinctive feature of entrepreneurship in China.

The first entrepreneur, to be analyzed in this chapter, is Mrs. Huo Hongmin, who started a soft-drink company in the city of Tianjin, one of the three metropolitan areas under the direct control of the central government at that time,[1] and built it into a business group highly visible in the market. While trying to depict a rounded picture, I shall pay special attention to the incident in which Huo was struggling to survive confrontation with state bureaucrats. Here are the questions that I would like to answer: why did such incident happen in the first place? What role did each party involved – the entrepreneur, the bureaucrat, and the media – play? What can we learn from this incident about entrepreneurship and its institutional environment in China? The incident will show just how precarious the relationship between entrepreneurs and bureaucrats is. As a consequence, the journalists, or the media in general, have emerged as a new form of influence. Sources for this case study come from interview records, company archives, and newspaper reports.

---

1 The other two cities were Beijing and Shanghai. On 14 March 1997, Chongqing became the fourth one.

The initial success

Hawthorn is a kind of fruit with a large output in Northern China. Although it is claimed to contain many healthy elements, very few people would eat it directly due to its extremely sour taste. A string of hawthorn with a sugar coating has been a traditional children's snack, but such consumption would not make a large sale. How to make use of the large supply while keeping people's appetite at the same time was a difficult question for the food industry in Northern China. In 1988 scientists at a food research institute in Tianjin discovered a solution to the problem: producing a nectar with hawthorn as the main ingredient. The dramatic increase in the number of companies with the required production capacity – from about a dozen in 1991 to several hundred in 1996 across China – indicates that it must not be difficult technology to follow.

It was in one of the dozen companies that Huo Hongmin was working as a sales representative. The fast sale of this not yet popularly known soft drink made her realize that this was an emerging opportunity. Rather than making profit for her employer, she was determined to set up her own company. Although she never directly spoke about her motivation of starting up the business, later she suggested that, besides making a bigger income, she had a very strong sense of taking control and outperforming others.

It was hard to turn the desire into reality, however. Financially, she was not ready to set up a company. To overcome the financial constraint, she rented a restaurant with all her assets as the deposit. After half a year's hard work, her savings increased to more than 70,000 yuan, and the idea of running her own company became achievable. She clearly realized that the money was nothing if the business was to be set up in the metropolitan areas of Tianjin.[2] Rather, she had to find a place where people 'would see 70,000 as some money and thus like to do business with me'.[3] Fortunately, there were several towns in the outskirts of the city that were desperately in need of external financial investments. Which one should she pick up for setting up her business? It was at this point of decision-making that social connections came into play: her elder brother introduced her to one of his friends at the town of Dazhong, who happened to be an entrepreneur as well and was very enthusiastic in giving her a hand to set up a factory. This social tie then brought Huo into the acquaintance of some leaders of the town who were happy to do business with her. With her personal savings and the earnings of her husband, who was a restaurant manager and later became the chief executive of production, she bought some deserted machines and equipments from a beverage factory and employed 27 workers.

---

2   It may sound ironic to the readers not familiar with China's administrative structure, but it is true that metropolitan cities in China actually contain urban as well as surrounding rural areas. The urban areas are usually called 'districts' (*qu*) while the rural areas 'counties' (*xian*). Each county then administers a certain number of towns and each town a certain number of villages.

3   Unless otherwise indicated, direct quotations in this chapter are taken from records of face-to-face interviews or company archives.

The business was registered as a town-and-village enterprise (TVE) at the beginning of 1991. In 1995, Huo Hongmin was honoured as one of the 'Exemplary TVE Entrepreneurs' by both municipal and national governments. If by definition a TVE should be owned and managed by a local government, then clearly this was not the true nature of this business. To some extent, it was a joint venture between Huo and the town of Dazhong: she agreed to invest her money in the factory and manage its daily operations, while the town would supply the land and other business premises. In reality, however, Huo took control of the business from the very beginning; the town government had little involvement in the management of the business, and it is not clear how much the town got back from providing the land and facilities. Nominally, each of the two sides owned 50 per cent of the business, although a formal contract was not put in writing until as late as the mid 1990s.

The two sides were clearly not bothered by the firm's ambiguous identity because it was a good deal for both of them. The town was successful in attracting external investment without any monetary input and could reap some dividends once the business started to make a profit. Indeed, the firm was one of the top tax payers in the county. As she later admitted, Huo was an even bigger beneficiary, having successfully established a company with a very limited amount of money and enjoying the status of a town-and-village enterprise:

> It [the enterprise] has brought me many benefits. For example, at that time banks didn't offer any loan to the private sector. At the very least I got money from banks.[4] Second, private firms were not allowed to set up joint ventures with foreign companies, but mine was a collective, so I could set up a joint venture [with a foreign company]. Next, private firms do not enjoy tax deductions, while, as a collective, my firm got a lot of deductions! Therefore, although it sounds like I gave away 50 per cent of ownership, I have benefited far more than that. In a word, talking about ownership, my firm was private at its very beginning. After making a large amount of money, it turned into a collective. Later, I turned part of it into a joint venture with a Chinese-American businessman. At the end of 1995, I set up another joint venture with an Italian wine company. All the other parts of my company are collective.

Note that although the firm's asset is hybrid, it is not ambiguous.[5] It is hybrid because it has both public and private investments. Hybridity does not necessarily mean ambiguity as long as the line between the private and the public is clearly drawn, and it is to the interest of the parties involved to draw a clear line so that dividends can be made without dispute. Ambiguous hybridity only occurs when the asset owners were not aware of the consequences of the ambiguity or when they had no other choice but to get locked into the pursuit of short-term profits. Furthermore, it is hard to conclude from this case that the hybrid form of assets is a result of market

---

4   To support the development of TVE, the Bank of China reserved a large sum of money in 1991 as guaranteed credits. As long as one can prove the collective nature of a firm with a letter from local government, a state bank will offer the credits.

5   David Stark and his colleagues have made some excellent analyses of hybrid property relations in Hungary, but they seem to suggest that hybrid properties will necessarily be ambiguous. See Stark (1996), Stark and Bruszt (1998), Stark and Vedres (2006).

mechanisms.[6] It is true that Huo searched for opportunities in remote areas of Tianjin because of the fierceness of competition in the metropolitan areas. Nevertheless, the hybrid asset relationship eventually came into existence because both sides could benefit from preferential state policies for the collective sector. In essence, this is an example of making use of institutional holes with the supplementary help of social connections.

The notion of double entrepreneurship can also find a good illustration in Huo's experience. In setting up her business, both financial as well as political concerns had a significant weight in making the decision of how the business should be set up. She confessed that what people thought about the nature of her company was, in her mind, a serious issue:

> From the bottom of my heart I would like my firm to be collective, not private [when it firstly started]. Why? Because policies have changed. Today, you can hear a lot of talk of how private enterprises should be encouraged to develop, but at that time, things were different. You would even fall into the contempt of local workers simply by being private. Anyone could bully you. Local governments did not dare to support you. A county magistrate once said, 'Is her firm collective or private? If private, don't ask me to go there'. Why did he say so? Because he was afraid of being suspected of receiving bribes. People would ask why you support a private firm if you have not taken bribes. Ideologically, many local leaders would be unwilling to get themselves involved in private businesses.

Entrepreneurship in China, especially in the early stages of the economic reform, had to be a double mission because the market mechanisms and government interventions were intermingled in the entrepreneurial process. Managing a good relationship with the officials, or more generally, nurturing and maintaining a relatively predictable and favourable political environment, is definitely no less challenging than managing the business itself. On the other hand, Hou's confession suggests that the officials also need to maintain a balance – they need to show a studied support of private businesses, that is, demonstrating that they have been following the Party's overall policy of supporting the private sector without being trapped into any relations with a private firm that may jeopardize their political careers.

Eventually, the business was set up without much trouble. In May 1991, the first batch of Huaqi[7] Nectar was dispatched to Beijing. Mrs. Huo wanted her products to be of a high profile, targeting luxury hotels, restaurants, and supermarkets, although their production equipment and sales facilities were not high profile by any standard. With manual tricycles, she and her first team of sales staff brought the bottles from one door to another in that year's hot summer, repeating the same set of words in an attempt to convince those in charge of purchasing soft-drinks. Unfortunately, hard labour does not necessarily guarantee business breakthrough. By the end of the year

---

6   Victor Nee (1992) defined 'a hybrid organizational form' as 'the marketized redistributive firm' or 'marketized firm', which represents 'an intermediate property form shaped by new pressures for efficiency and flexibility in rapidly changing environments in which market forces incrementally replace the state redistributive mechanism'.

7   Literally, *huaqi* means 'flag of China'.

most of the bottles had to be brought back to the factory at Dazhong. And the reasons were obvious. The business clearly suffered from 'the liability of newness': nobody had ever heard of their products. Why would people spend their money on a drink without seeing any evidence of its reliability? Even when a new product's quality is truly outstanding, an initial wave of consumption is necessary for triggering the following purchase. For Huaqi Nectar, however, there were no advertisements, no media coverage, and no reports of assessment issued by any authoritative body.

After learning hard lessons, Huo revealed her entrepreneurship by taking two courses of actions. Firstly, to increase the credibility and public awareness of the product, she invited several prominent food and beverage scientists from the National Academy of Science and other research institutions to make a scientific assessment of Huaqi Nectar. After finding that the evaluations were quite positive, she organized a large press conference in the People's Congress Hall, which secured the product's visibility in the market. Secondly, she needed someone who could establish a sales network in the capital. Soon, Mr. Zhang Chunlin, a local resident of Beijing with an experience of managing a wholesale food store, was invited to join the company as the chief executive for sales. A team of sales representatives was then organized in Beijing and Tianjin, respectively, and each showed an excellent sales record to the company.

These strategies seem to have worked. By the end of 1992, that is, in just one and half years, the total value of products was claimed to have reached 120 million yuan. In the next year, the total income from sales was reported to have exceeded 6 million yuan. With most of the initial earnings reinvested into production and sales, the business soon expanded to several other major cities in China, including Xian, Baotou, Shijiazhuang, Wuhan, Changsha, Shanghai, and Guangzhou. The total number of employees grew above 1,500. The company then made an application to be recognized as a business group with six sub-companies, which was promptly approved by the municipal government of Tianjin. This was more than a matter of registration, because a business had to demonstrate some strong financial figures to qualify. To the general public, at least, the title 'business group' suggests strong financial power, high credibility, and trustworthiness.

Being asked how she came across the idea of turning her company into a business group, Huo immediately thought of the movement of cutting ponytails in the Capitalist Revolution in the early 1910s. To her, just as cutting off one's ponytail was a sign of making a complete severance with the dying feudalist empire in the revolutionary years, building up a business group was another wind that had swept through China in the early 1990s. The wind became especially strong when local officials saw it as a political matter. Huo explained that entrepreneurs had few choices but to comply. Reflecting on the swift progress, she said:

> In fact, at that time I had no idea what a business group would look like. None of us did. We did not know what an investment company was either. They [local officials] suggested that since my company had grown so quickly, we should establish a business group. That was the environment at that time. Every big company was doing that. Among the several firms with the highest profits, you've got the highest sales income. Alright, turn yours into a group. It was assigned from the top. For example, the Baodi County needed to fulfill its

quota of three business groups. Then they talked to the three biggest enterprises, who then became business groups. They called this institutional reform, like a wind. Entrepreneurs didn't do it voluntarily; they were induced.

At the back of many local officials' minds is a presumption that everything is under their administration, so they have every right to intervene into internal matters of a business. In theory, business owners may not have to follow suit, but in reality, they would soon feel the pressure simply too strong to resist, because there must be some point at which the business falls into the hands of the local authorities. Clearly, it is not wise to resist. A smart strategy is to accept 'the assignment from the top' and then figure out how to make use of it. As we shall see in the following two cases, this is not always true, especially for the entrepreneurs who can display a certain level of independence with the backup of their financial power, but it is a high risk game to play, even for the most successful entrepreneurs. For the vast majority of private entrepreneurs, a passive but exploitative approach to dealing with government interventions is the best strategy. In the end, many entrepreneurs may not find the interventions so disrupting. To Huo, it was a fantastic deal:

> Well, we do get some benefits by becoming a group. First, it sounds very powerful. A group, not a single firm! Second, we've got some further deductions in tax rates, or we are allowed to turn in our tax far later than it is required. Simply think about how much interest you would have lost if you had to pay millions of money three months or even half a year ago. Third, we now have the right of doing direct exports. Fourth, we can use our money in whatever way we like. Some business groups have even set up their own financial companies.

This explains why government interventions can always find their market – they are not without some attractions. Political leaders in China, no matter at what level, have learnt that ruthless imposition of a policy will not work; in order to put a policy into practice, both pushing as well as pulling are needed.

It is important to note that, to a large extent, the considerations of local leaders such as town or village party secretaries are often very different from those of the bureaucrats who are in charge of a particular aspect of private business. Unlike party secretaries and governors, most bureaucrats do not have a strong sense of political career and therefore have no interest in creating a politically collegial relationship. In the minds of the bureaucrats is another balance to strike: maximizing financial extractions from private businesses without going as far as risking their professional careers. We shall see how this is so in the following analysis of the confrontation between some bureaucrats and Huo.

The confrontation

What went wrong?

In November 1992, when Huo Hongmin and her employees were busy increasing production capacity and market share, they received a letter from the National Bureau of Technology Inspection (NBTI). According to the letter, assessment results of hawthorn nectars on the mark in the year's fourth quarter showed that Huaqi's products had failed to meet the standards in two aspects. First, the volume was labelled 245ml on the bottles, but the examiners discovered that the actual volume was no more than 235ml. The 10ml discrepancy far exceeded the acceptable variation of 2 per cent of the labelled volume, or 4.9ml. Second, NBTI found elements of artificial pigment in Huaqi Nectar, which should have been printed as one of the components in the label. The letter also said that Huaqi could file a complaint within 15 days if they wanted to challenge the results.

Initially, these allegations did not appear to be very serious. It would not cost Huaqi very much to either increase the actual volume or to reduce the printed volume. Nor would it be a big problem to simply include artificial pigment on the label, an element commonly used in soft drinks.

Huo, however, found these claims unfounded and did not want to keep quiet. Accompanied by her assistants, she went to the headquarters of NBTI in Beijing in an attempt to defend their honesty to the customers. In the end, they did not get what they wanted from the bureaucrats. No specific information is available as to why they failed; Huo only made a brief comment, 'We had no idea or experience of how to deal with government agencies, which ultimately led to the later more complex situation'.

But she simply could not accept the results. With no hope of arguing with those at NBTI, she instructed her secretaries to write several letters and circulated them to local officials of Tinajin, arguing that the problems found by NBTI were all beyond the control of Huaqi. These arguments deserve careful analysis as they illustrate how the entrepreneur can deal with the rules imposed by state agencies. First of all, Huaqi pointed out that 'there have been no national standards of production for hawthorn nectar'. As 'every company follows its own standards', 'substantial discrepancies of production standards exist across the industry'. With no national standards, it is therefore pointless to talk about complying with them. Whilst these points may be valid, the reader may have noted that what NBTI wanted was not *compliance* with national standards but the *consistency* of the actual volume with the volume printed on the label.

The second argument Huaqi made was that the instability of gross volume should be attributed to the thickness of bottle glass. More specifically, although the acceptable variation to NBTI was ±2 per cent, or 5ml, according to Beijing Glass Factory of No. 5 and No. 6, the two major suppliers of bottles to Huaqi, the acceptable variation should be in the range of 3.3 per cent to 4.1 per cent, or 8 to 10ml. Hou seemed to have forgotten that it was NBTI, not the bottle factories, who had the authority to determine what variation was acceptable. An additional challenging point was that it was Huaqi, not the bottle makers, who had the responsibility of ensuring that the variation of bottle volume falls into the specified range.

At the end of a letter to local officials, Huo claimed that:

Despite the above two objective matters, we have taken the following managerial measures after receiving the letter: (1) we examined the 10,000 boxes of bottles in our stocks but found no problems about their volume; (2) we have changed the labelled volume from

245ml to 240ml; (3) to select bottles more carefully, we have put tighter quality control in our production process.

These are clear concessions to NBTI's allegations, although the tone was still defensive. Thereafter, Huo won some sympathy from local officials at Tianjin, but none of them expressed any support, at least not publicly. All believed that the problem was resolved after Huaqi made those adjustments. But it soon turned out that it was only the beginning of an even worse confrontation.

On 11 January 1993, *Xiao Fei Zhi Nan* (*Guide to Consumption*), a magazine under the administration of Ministry of Light Industries (MLI), sent the following letter to Huaqi:

> In issue No. 3 (1993) of *Guide to Consumption* by Ministry of Light Industries, the results of quality assessment of hawthorn beverages (both juice and nectar), which was organized by National Bureau of Technology Inspection, will be fully published. It is shown that every indicator of Ugly Baby[8] and Huaqi Nectar made by your company is up to standard, and they have both been honoured 'Excellent Products'.
>
> In order to make these results as well-known as possible to businesses and customers, and to promote marketing, results of scientific assessment need to be visualized and presented in such a way that qualified products can leave a deep impression in the customer's mind. Besides making a full publication of assessment results, we shall reserve some pages for colourful or black-and-white advertisements for all qualified products, honouring them 'National Excellent Products'. Advertisements by *Guide to Consumption* are creative in words, innovative in design, and impressive in print. We hope that every enterprise will not miss this opportunity and will actively participate.

Then the letter ended with a list of prices for posting an advertisement in *Guide to Consumption*, followed by contact details.

What is most striking in this letter is the obviously contradictory claim to what was said in the letter of NBTI to Huaqi about two months previously. There should be no doubt that the two letters were referring to the same results, because there were no other results. Huo Hongmin believed that *Guide to Consumption* must have made a mistake in stating that Huaqi nectars had passed the assessment. As she and her senior managers had never heard of this magazine before, and given the letter's commercial nature, they decided to ignore it, an action that triggered the following series of confrontational interactions between the entrepreneur and state officials.

About two months later, that is, in early March 1993, NBTI published their assessment results of nectars, in which Huaqi was listed 'not up to standards' for the two reasons mentioned before. Note that, at this moment, Huaqi had already changed their labels and reported the adjustments to NBTI.

One month later, two other investigations were conducted on the quality of nectars in the market. The first was by NBTI's Beijing branch, whose results showed that Huaqi Nectar was a product excellent in every aspect concerned. In the meantime, China's National Association for the Protection of Customers organized their own investigation. Again, Huaqi Nectar was published as 'A Trustworthy Product' with

---

8   Huaqi's hawthorn nectar for children.

no complaints. Receiving all this good news, Huo thought that the dispute with NBTI was definitely over.

An official at NBTI, however, approached Huaqi again. This time, it was in an attempt to do Huaqi a favour by offering a piece of information: to help promote market shares of some of the best nectars, NBTI was planning to organize a press conference. In retrospect, the most important part of the message was that the press conference would actually be organized by *Guide to Consumption* and its related advertising company. But the official only mentioned that there would be a registration fee of 8,000 yuan. Again, Huo and her senior managers did not pay serious heed to the message, because they thought that their products' reputation had been redeemed by the two most recent assessments, therefore, it would not be necessary for them to spend the money on another press conference.

As scheduled, the conference was held on 16 April, which Huo Hongmin later called 'Huaqi's Waterloo Day'. She was shocked when she saw Huaqi Nectar being listed at the top of products of poor quality in a press release published by the conference. The press release, nevertheless, did not specify the terms in which the product was not up to standard and when the assessment was conducted. If it referred to the results of last November, then it was actually correct. More importantly, it did not mention that Huaqi had changed the information on the labels and already regained its reputation as an excellent product in two recent assessments.

From then onwards, things went terribly wrong for Huaqi. Following the conference, Huaqi's alleged failure became the headline in some local newspapers. Worse, Huaqi's competitors seemed to have been waiting for this opportunity – some printed and circulated fliers to wholesalers, retailers and customers, highlighting or even exaggerating what was claimed in the press release; others spread rumours, such as 'Huaqi will go bankrupt, and the boss is going abroad with a huge amount of cash'. Ignorant of the fact that Huaqi had made improvements and was just recently honoured as an excellent product, many retailers and wholesalers were in a rush to return Huaqi Nectars and ask for refunds.

On 2 June, Huaqi received another official letter from NBTI, which simply stated that their nectars had now been verified to be up to the standards due to the improvements they had made. No other organizations were informed of this letter's content. And it was too late; the damage was already done. It is hard to give an accurate estimate of how much Huaqi had lost since the 'Waterloo Day'. Huo claimed that within the two months after the 16 April press conference, her company had lost about 80 million yuan, hence the eye-catching title of a journalist's report: 'Losing Eighty Million by Not Giving Away Eight Thousand: Who Created the Huaqi Tragedy?', published on 25 June in *Zhong Hua Gong Shang Shi Bao* (*China Business Times*). As we shall see, the media played an increasingly important role in the rest of the incident.

The entrepreneur, the bureaucrats, and the journalists

That report was one of the first newspaper articles that brought the confrontation between the entrepreneur and the bureaucrats into the public domain. In the meantime, it created another confrontation between two groups of newspapers, one on the side of Huaqi, and the other on the side of the bureaucrats who claimed to represent the interest of the customers. On Huaqi's side were *China Business Times*, a newspaper usually speaking in the interests of the non-state sectors, and *Beijing Youth Daily* (*Beijing Qing Nian Bao*), one of the most outspoken newspapers in China. On the side of *Guide to Consumption* and NBTI were *Consumption Times* (*Xiao Fei Shi Bao*) and *Guide to Shopping* (*Gou Wu Dao Bao*). During the two months from mid June to mid August of 1993, many other newspapers either reprinted the reports in those four newspapers or expressed their own but relatively mild views. The following analysis will concentrate on the coverage by the four newspapers on the front line.

First of all, it is important to learn how the journalists became involved in the dispute. On 15 June, Huo and her chief executive of marketing, Mr. Zhang Chunlin, paid a visit to NBTI's Division of Quality Inspection to complain about their heavy loss due to the 16 April press conference. Ms. Gu Yumei, the deputy editor of *Guide to Consumption*, who was also in charge of the magazine's advertising business, was invited to attend the meeting as well. Although we don't know exactly what was said in their conversations, the meeting obviously did not produce anything that could make Huo and Zhang happy. Another round of talks between the two executives and Gu was arranged that evening in a hotel.

It was in that meeting that the journalists started their direct involvement in the incident. How Zhang Chunlin came to know the journalist for *The People's Daily* is not important here. What is important is that he told the journalist what happened at NBTI during the day and that he was scheduled to meet Gu again that evening. The journalist was shocked by what Zhang told him and decided to join them in order to witness the confrontation. What he heard at the meeting later became the major source of his report.

As the CCP's Party newspaper, *The People's Daily* has an authoritative voice, representing the policies from the very top of the Chinese State. If a report in support of Huaqi's point of view could be printed in this newspaper, then it would indicate strong support from an authority above NBTI. Curiously, the report, which was clearly sympathetic to Huaqi's difficult situation, was not published in *The People's Daily*, but in *China Business Times*. It provided the raw material for a series of arguments and counter-arguments in the following months. The dispute became so fierce that on 20 August both Huaqi and *Guide to Consumption* were given the chance of publishing their own version of the 15 June meeting at the hotel.

My purpose here is not to assess the reliability of these reports to judge who told the truth. More relevant, and important, to my research is to learn how the entrepreneur and the bureaucrats interacted with each other in the media. Therefore, the statements published in the newspapers become the key documents for my analysis, and it is necessary to reproduce and analyze the 'facts' reported by each side.

At their meeting with two division heads of NBTI from 9:40 to 11:15a.m. on 15 June, Huo and Zhang learnt that at the root of the whole trouble was the fact that they failed to make everyone happy by giving away enough money. One of the heads said: 'You are not actually in a trouble. You just have not taken care of your public relations well, so you have offended many people. They all hate you!'

Then Huo asked him who was offended.

The answer was, 'Some related agencies at the national government, including our division, agencies at Tianjin, the media, and some businesses, they all hate you badly!'

'What for?', asked Huo.

For not giving away money: 'A big business group like yours', a head of division reminded her, 'making so much money each year, simply has not done a good job on *public relations*! Did you really give away a million yuan in last year's sales promotion?'.

'We did', said Huo, also pointing out that the results were in fact reported on a programme by China Central Television (CCTV).

In the rest of the conversation, a head revealed their connection to the magazine. That is, the 16 April press conference was sponsored by NBTI and organized by *Guide to Consumption*, and every participating company paid the 8,000 yuan conference fee.

At this moment, Gu Yumei came in. Zhang and Huo then turned to her, asking why their products were listed as 'not up to standards' even after they made the adjustments and the products were reassessed as 'excellent' later. To their surprise, Gu was not actually concerned about this matter, because it would be all too easy for her to turn around the current situation:

> Don't worry. This time I ruined your 'Huaqi Nectar', but I could help you build it up again. You just need to pay some money. You have made so much money each year. It's time for you to spend, and this is the right time! I can call back all the news reporters at the conference. They are all my close friends, and those at radio and TV stations are all my relatives. As long as you show the money, I can organize [another conference] for you, and I guarantee there will be no problem at all. In the past, we ruined Jinglan Mattress and Heilongjiang's milk powder, but I helped pick all of them up. Now they are all very hot in the market. In those days, Jinglan was so hot, just because of several springs I ruined them!

Now the bureaucrat's logic of extracting money from entrepreneurs cannot be clearer: once an entrepreneur becomes successful in starting up a business, some of the profits will have to be given away to please all of the people who are able to do something about the new business, especially those in powerful positions. And there are only two options for the entrepreneur: either paying off the extraction so as to keep the business, or facing the consequence of going out of business. Obviously, neither was acceptable to Huo, who talked about the thought of giving up:

> From the very beginning we have put quality as our top priority. We have put the best equipment, the best hawthorn, and the best water into our nectar, but simply because of this reason our sales have come to a halt. There has been a huge overstock, and the employees are in very bad mood. I don't want to carry on anymore. I simply cannot work like this! I have survived so many fierce competitions, but I have to quit because of this incident!

Gu did not seem to realize how far she had gone because she was carrying on further. To her, Huo Hongmin's emotional comments came as an opportunity to increase her leverage of controlling the business. Here is the offer she made:

> Oh, no, don't quit! Last year I ruined a milk powder factory in Heilongjiang for a small problem. Then the old Head kneeled on the floor begging me, saying 'You don't have to have mercy on me, but please have mercy on all the employees. They cannot make a living now'. Hearing those words, my heart became softened, so I went there with several journalists to help them get a better reputation back. With our help, their sales are very hot now. It's fine, Chief Huo. Don't give up. Let me have a share [of your business], and let's join forces. I have money, but I don't know where to invest. You take care of production and I will be in charge of sales and advertising. Now I want to step in an industry, and let's do it together.

It is very likely that she was exaggerating her power in order to extract as much as she could from Huaqi, but what she said showed just how she had abused her power. By now, it should be clear that the reason she seemed to be able to do whatever she liked to a private firm was because of her affiliation with a government agency, namely, NBTI.

To gather some evidence for this, the journalist asked Gu whether she collected any money from the 16 April press conference. She confessed that:

> This time we asked every participating company to pay 8,000 at maximum, 4,000 at minimum. Actually, we didn't make much money, only 15,000 after some hard work. Then we gave 5,000 to NBTI, and it's not easy to deal with them. [In the end] we only got 10,000, but it was not our main objective to make money.

Note that Gu's magazine had no administrative relationship with NBTI. Rather, it was a part of MLI. So the question is: why did she give away some money to NBTI rather than MLI? We can get the answer from what she said below:

> In the past we published inspection results for MLI, but now the Ministry has been turned into a trade association.[9] Who can our magazine rely on? Who else can we rely on if not NBTI? We can publish inspection results for them and in the meantime make some advertisements.

These words have revealed the murky nature of the magazine. As a part of MLI, *Guide to Consumption* was not supposed to act on behalf of a government agency anymore after MLI was transformed into a civil organization. It actually became a commercial organization with an objective of making profits from publishing the magazine and the accompanied advertisements. What is intriguing about the business is what it published in the magazine, namely, assessment results authorized by a government agency. Had NBTI published the results on its own rather than through the magazine, neither NBTI nor the magazine could have made any money, and it would be hard to imagine how Gu could wield so much power over entrepreneurs. As

---

9   It means that the Ministry was not a government agency anymore.

one reader pointed out in *Beijing Youth Daily*, 'with the sacred sword commissioned by government agencies, she could readily become the master of business'.[10]

Gu denied the above allegations. In her version of the whole incident, she defended herself with the following statements:

1. We invited Ugly Baby to attend the conference, which was one of Huaqi's products and found up to the standards, but the invitation was returned to us. Huaqi Nectar was not up to the standards, so it is not relevant at all to talk about paying the 8,000 registration fee. Although Huaqi Nectar was found to be up to the standards later, it was in May and June, that is, after the 16 April press conference.
2. The 16 April press conference was organized at the request of customers and businesses. We only made about 14,000, or 10 per cent of the total income, which is completely in line with state regulations on advertising charges.
3. The truth is that, seeing Huo being so worried, I comforted her by telling her the following: 'Don't worry. Such things have happened before in the light industries. Some products did not pass the assessment, so their reputations were ruined. They immediately improved themselves, however. Then they came to us again, and their sales picked up after showing the improvements in news conferences.'

Then I told her two examples ... After they made improvements, we either helped them invite reporters to come back to their factories, or to hold a press conference to let customers know the situation as soon as possible ...

Here is a proof in writing from a deputy-director of the mattress company:

It has nothing to do with Ms. Gu that we had a quality problem and had our reputation damaged. It was Ms. Gu and some other people who helped us promote our sales up. We have been very grateful for their work.

As of the old Head kneeling on the floor, this is what I said:

At that moment the old Head was far more worried than you are. He grasped my hands, almost kneeling on the floor, asking us to go to their factory immediately to help them make their adjustments and improvements known to the public.

At the end of her statement, Gu claimed that Huo and the journalists on Huo's side had infringed upon her personal reputation; she would consider filing a lawsuit if the situation was not improved to her satisfaction.

The first point in Gu's statement regards the letter that *Guide to Consumption* sent to Huaqi, in which both Ugly Baby and Huaqi Nectar were clearly listed as good products. This contradicts to the results published by NBTI, according to which only Ugly Baby passed. It was not until 27 August that a deputy editor of *Guide to Consumption* provided an explanation for the inconsistency, published in *Voice of Civil Administration* (*Min Zheng Zhi Sheng*), a newspaper not widely known to the general public. According to this explanation, it was the staff member who prepared the letter who was to blame, because the staff member made two typographical errors. First, the staff member put down 'Ugly Baby, Huaqi Nectar' – two products, which should have been 'Ugly Baby by Huaqi Nectar' – only one product. The second, and more serious, error is that the staff wrote on a piece of paper with a pre-printed date '11 January', while in fact the letter was not sent out until 15 February.

---

10 See the comments made by Liang You on 7 August 1993.

This is critical because the journalist for *The People's Daily* connected this letter to the publication of the assessment results, implying that NBTI deliberately failed Huaqi Nectar after waiting for several days without receiving the registration fee from Huaqi. It is now very difficult, if at all possible, to verify what really happened, but it is absolutely clear that *Guide to Consumption* failed to inform Huaqi of the mistakes and its relationship with NBTI.

Nor could the other two points in the statement help Gu keep clear of the suspicion of abusing her power, buttressed by her relationship with NBTI. Because she was working with NBTI, she must have known that it was in early April, that is, before the April 16 press conference, that the Beijing branch of NBTI approved the improvements made by Huaqi and actually listed Huaqi Nectar as an excellent product.

Also, what matters is not how much Gu and her magazine made from organizing the conference but whether they were supposed to make any profits from such activities in the first place. That they did make profits was a clear indication that NBTI, as a government agency, was involved in commercial activities. Even Gu's own version of what she said about the ruined factories failed to conceal the fact that she was in a powerful position of shaping the fate of a business. Had she not been so powerful, why would the old Head have come to her for help? In claiming that her ultimate intention was to help Huaqi rebuild its reputation, she actually admitted her capacity to manipulate a firm's future, something an ordinary magazine editor would not be able to do.

After the publication of their statements, the battle between the two sides became even more fierce in the mass media. Huaqi organized two press conferences, one on 29 June in Beijing and the other on 6 July in Tianjin, registering serious complaints about *Guide to Consumption*. Then Gu Yumei accused Huaqi of manipulating and abusing the media. In the meantime, the journalists on each side launched a series of attacks on the other. While Huaqi did not seem to have any connection with its supporting journalists, *Guide to Consumption* and its supporting journalists were clearly connected by their administrative affiliations to the National Association of Light Industries (the former MLI). While Huo and the journalists on her side portrayed Gu as a high-handed bureaucrat abusing her illegitimate power, those on the side of Gu made every effort to set up an image of Huo as a selfish business woman who cheated her customers without any remorse:

- As we have already known, in the assessment carried out in the fourth quarter of 1992, the quantity of Huaqi Nectar was at least 5ml less than the minimum level. To show that this is nothing for a bottle of drink, Mr. Zhang Chunlin, the vice president of Huaqi, complained about the thickness of bottles and translated 5ml into 'about 10 drops'. We did a translation too, but with a different equation: Huaqi made 2.4 million yuan from the consumers' pocket, which is the product of 5ml multiplied by the number of bottles of Huaqi Nectar sold last year. If we make the calculation based on the difference between the quantity claimed by Huaqi and the quantity found in the assessment, then Huaqi has stolen nearly 4.8 million yuan from its customers.

- After Huaqi changed its labels from 245ml to 240ml, it has never lowered the price.
- Since Huaqi was not qualified when the 16 April conference was held, there is no connection between the 8,000 yuan conference fee and Huaqi's loss.
- Given its production value was 1.2 billion a year, it is impossible for Huaqi to lose 80 million yuan in two months. Huaqi and its journalists have made up the news.
- After Huaqi claimed that its production was suspended between 20 May and 30 June due to the 16 April conference, some customers have found Huaqi Nectar [in the market] dated 28 May and 13 June. This is another lie.
- Huaqi invited some journalists to set Ms. Gu up, because they didn't tell her in advance what the conversation would be about.
- Huaqi's credibility was poor because they cheated customers in their 1 Million Award sales promotion and because they violated their contracts with hawthorn farmers.[11]

Unlike those on the side of Huaqi, the two journalists defending Gu went further to make some personal attacks on Huo, elevating the whole confrontation into an matter of some political significance:

- Mrs. Huo, how could you lose your face by telling these big lies! … It is not really true that Huaqi wanted to attack *Guide to Consumption* and Ms. Gu alone. What the managers of Huaqi really want is to do whatever they like by destroying the authority of our national technology supervision agencies … The development of Huaqi, however, cannot be separated from our motherland, from Party policies, and from the contributions made by the workers at Huaqi. People in the socialist China would not tolerate turning truths into lies and manipulating the media with the money in your hands.[12]
- The real target of Huaqi was actually NBTI, not *Guide to Consumption*. Ms. Gu and *Guide to Consumption* were the victims of the news manipulated by Huaqi. How horrible the power of money! So horrible that it drives its possessors to abandon their moral values, to attack government agencies, and even to damage an institution.[13]

These are serious allegations. Huo Hongmin thus decided to file a lawsuit against Mr. Zhang Donghan, the journalist who wrote the first article damaging her personal

---

11 Huaqi announced a one million yuan award in a sales promotion. Later, however, several customers complained that the company tried to find various excuses for not paying the award. In another dispute, many farmers in Hebei province filed a lawsuit against Huaqi, claiming that Huaqi broke the contract by refusing to purchase their hawthorn because the company got a better deal somewhere else. Whether these allegations are true is beyond the discussion of this chapter.

12 Zhang Donghan, 'Hua Qi Chou Wen' ('The Huaqi Scandal'), *Gou Wu Dao Bao* (*Guide to Shopping*), 5 August 1993.

13 Li Zhiping, He Hu, and Du Shumin, 'It's Time to End the "Huaqi Farce"' (Hua Qi Nao Ju Gai Shou Chang Le),' *Consumption Times* (*Xiao Fei Shi Bao*), 31 July 1993.

image and reputation. On 16 May 1994, Mr. Zhang made an apology to Huo in a local court in Beijing, admitting the inappropriateness of his claims. In return, Huo agreed to withdraw the case against him.

A lose-lose ending

Curiously, there were few reports in the media about how the general public reacted to the row, particularly to the newspaper reports, perhaps because it was very difficult to find out who 'the public' was and what was really in their mind. The dozen wholesalers and some 20 customers that I interviewed informally during and after the incident told me that they were simply confused. Few had strong opinions of which side was wrong, and most of them suspected that there must be something wrong on each side. The comments by a resident in Beijing (male, about 50 years old) perhaps can tell us why the whole incident ended in a lose-lose situation:

> How could the government have made such a fuss if everything were alright [within Huaqi]? Of course, it was not right for the officials to try to make money out of this, but it was Huaqi's fault to cheat we customers from the very beginning ... Don't trust the newspapers – they [the journalists] wanted stories like this, so they could sell their newspapers. In the end, it's all about money!

That is the last thing NBTI would want to hear. Still, as a national government agency, NBTI would want to set up and maintain an image of fairness and impartiality; staying clear of commercial interests is the bottom line NBTI would want to keep.

But the media, more precisely the journalists, became increasingly influential in affecting to NBTI's image. On 25 June 1993, the Quality Monitoring Division of NBTI sent an official letter to news agencies, requesting that nothing be published about the Huaqi incident without its permission, and their objective was 'to integrate and protect the interests of our country, businesses, and customers'. Its authority was bluntly challenged again as no one seemed to have listened. About a week later, on 2 July, the spokesman of NBTI announced that in the future, NBTI would not publish any results of assessment through a news agency and no fees would be collected. He also added that it was *Guide to Consumption* that should be responsible for all the troubles during the whole incident.

It seemed that the whole affair would drag on endlessly without an intervention from someone at the top of the government. Following an order from the very top, the State Council's Ministry of Supervision and Investigation (MSI, *jian cha bu*) conducted their own investigation. I learnt from Huaqi that overall, MSI's final report – circulated only to Huaqi and some other related agencies – was basically on the company's side. The report acknowledged that Huaqi suffered some financial loss, but their figure was only 20 million rather than 80 million, implying that the journalist for *The People's Daily* and Huaqi were exaggerating the amount of loss. In the meantime, MSI criticised the officials at NBTI for their inappropriate involvement in the 16 April press conference. In particular, it pointed out some financial frauds committed by Gu Yumei and requested that further investigations be made. Finally,

SMI made a suggestion to the media that they should publish more positive reports about Huaqi.

For Huo Hongmin, there is a bitter lesson to learn: an entrepreneur in China should never let the customers believe that she only cares about money. Although she won the case against Zhang Donghan, she knew that winning the case was only the first step toward winning back her customers. To do so, she needed to make a symbolic move of much more significance. After several months of preparation, she decided to donate 500,000 yuan towards giving the Tiananmen Tower a facelift. In China, few things could be more symbolic than the Tiananmen Tower. And 500,000 yuan was just a fraction of Huaqi's annual advertising budget, but what Huaqi earned was far beyond the effect of an advertisement: nearly 100 journalists and 50 officials from the municipal governments of Tianjin and Beijing attended the donation ceremony, showcased at the top of the Tiananmen Tower. Most of the guests also enjoyed the banquet in a luxurious restaurant that followed the ceremony.

Another lesson Huo learnt is that she simply cannot escape politics. In the summer of 1997, i.e., four years after the incident, I asked her to reflect on the difficult experience. Here is what came to her mind:

> That is the way things go in China. Many things are political. People think keeping a political position is the most important thing, because you can get money from your political position … I don't think we can escape politics. I am not good at playing political games, and haven't paid much attention to it. Consequently, I suffered from my ignorance. I was not politically mature in the '93 incident. I failed to establish some political connections and to cultivate relations with politicians. Otherwise, everything would have been just fine.

Concluding observations

This is a case of double entrepreneurship under institutional constraints. Although it can by no means verify the validity of the general model proposed in the introductory chapter, I hope it has illustrated the institutional conditions and processes through which the entrepreneur, the officials, the journalists, and to a limited extent, the general public interact with one another.

To summarize, we can use the analytical scheme of legitimacy and profitability specified in Chapter 1 to represent the experience of Huaqi in Figure 6.1.

Several phases can be detected in Figure 6.1 throughout the development of Huaqi. At its entrance to the hawthorn nectar market, the enterprise did not experience any serious problems of legitimacy and profitability. Although it was difficult in the first few months to make a breakthrough, Huo Hongmin's entrepreneurship quickly brought her company out of the initial stagnation. A thriving period soon followed. The early success was partly on account of a favourable relationship with the local government, which was established based on Huo's social capital as well as to both sides' satisfaction with the arrangement of joint venture. In theoretical terms, the initial thriving can be understood as successful exploitation of an institutional hole by setting up a nominal collective enterprise under an actual but concealed private ownership.

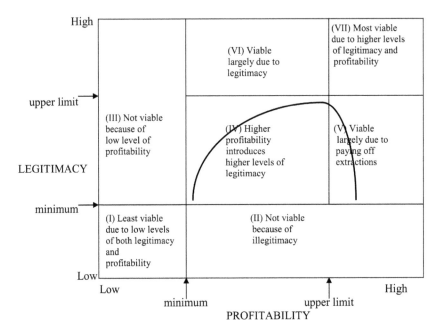

Figure 6.1 Legitimacy and profitability in the experience of Huaqi

With the growth of its profit, Huaqi became increasingly visibile in the mass media and in the eyes of the government and the public. Nevertheless, institutions regulating the relations between business, the media, and government agencies have fallen behind the growth of private enterprises. And this is the institutional source of Huaqi's confrontation with NBTI and *Guide to Consumption*, which eventually brought a major downturn to Huaqi's economic performance. Of course, not all bureaucrats are like those in NBTI and Gu Yumei, and not all private entrepreneurs would have behaved in the same way as Huo Hongmin, but what has happened to many entrepreneurs tells us that the incident is by no means rare in China's private sector.

All the vicissitudes were possible simply because of one consequence of the economic reforms: local officials and state bureaucrats have become active participants in business life in China. Their political power could lend heavy leverage to promoting local economies, but it could also spoil an entrepreneurial enterprise if their main objective was to extract rents from successful business. This is why Huaqi lost hope of getting any help from state officials in fighting for its legitimacy. The only people who could offer help to Huaqi turned out to be newspaper journalists. But just like the bureaucrats, some journalists may have their own interests in getting involved in commercial activities, so some became Huaqi's friends while others became its opponents. In the end, Huaqi had to help itself out of the trouble by making a case to the very top Chinese authority. The case was not processed in a transparent manner – it is not clear how Huaqi successfully drew the attention from a top leader to its letters of complaint. No matter how it happened, the way in which the incident was ended clearly shows that the Chinese State is still able to quickly respond to a particular incident in order to maintain order in an unstable institutional environment. Thanks to the profits accumulated before, Huaqi was able to keep its viability by buying out its legitimacy and reputation with a large donation to the government.

Many entrepreneurs in China would not be surprised by Huo Hongmin's experience. Although the local contexts of their own stories might be different, many entrepreneurs have followed the overall pattern of growing from an early success to a relatively visible business in the local market, then dealing with difficult relations with officials and bureaucrats – with the entrepreneur not always being innocent – and finally becoming 'politically mature'.

Entrepreneurs in China can learn at least two lessons from this path of business development. First, two things could significantly promote or damage an entrepreneurial business: the changes of institutional rules and the state officials' power of making use of the rules. Entrepreneurs in China have a lot of experience in dealing with changing rules, but they usually do not have a good sense of local officials' power until they have an experience similar to what Huo went through. As long as China's institutional structure allows state bureaucrats and local officials to make a living by misusing or abusing the power in their hands, sooner or later some private entrepreneurs will find themselves in a position similar to Huo's. A major challenge to China's economic development is therefore an institutional one: how to keep the bureaucrats and officials at bay while in the meantime ensuring they enjoy working as bureaucrats and officials.

A second and related lesson for private entrepreneurs in China is that they must keep the legitimacy of their business firmly in mind, because this is a double-edged sword for themselves and for state officials. Legitimacy is the field of their interactions or even the battleground in which they fight against each other. Both sides could make claims on the legitimacy (or illegitimacy) of the other side's words and behaviours, drawing on a variety of institutional sources, such as being loyalty to Party ideologies, protecting the national economy, keeping the interests of customers intact, and so on. For the entrepreneurs, justifying the legitimacy of their businesses is not necessarily a burdensome task that they can only hope to passively deal with. As we shall see in the following two case studies, it should also become one of the best survival strategies for private entrepreneurs, because the bureaucrats and officials are also exposed to political and moral principles. Indeed, Huo did not do a good job of defending her company's legitimacy. She was not good at arguing in political and moral terms. The two entrepreneurs we shall meet in the next two chapters are much better at this.

Chapter 7

The Limits on Playing Institutional Holes: Mou Qizhong and the Nande Group[1]

In this chapter, we shall learn about a second entrepreneur's case – Mr. Mou Qizhong, the founder and chief executive of the Nande Group. Mou's extraordinary ventures will give the reader a good idea of how far an entrepreneur can go in playing with rules and profits. It thus directly bears upon a central argument of this book, that is, how rules and their structural features become resources and motivating factors for entrepreneurial ventures largely depends on the ways in which entrepreneurs make use of the rules. In the meantime, entrepreneurial strategies, ideas, and behaviours have to be legitimate enough so as not to incur an unbearable cost to the whole entrepreneurial enterprise.

If Huo Hongmin is one of the many entrepreneurs in China who have benefited from unstable and ambiguous state policies but then suffered from a legitimacy crisis in dealing with state bureaucrats, then Mou Qizhong is one of the few who would see dealing with state policies and bureaucrats as an essential part of the entrepreneurial process. Although he did not use the term, to Mou, making use of institutional holes is not only a business strategy but the core idea of a new philosophy as well as a new promising industry. And he took venturous actions to put his firm into the leading role of that industry. Unlike Huo, who had little idea of the relationship between legitimacy and profitability until her company's sales suffered a big downturn and had no one else but some journalists to help her, Mou put the task of legitimizing his enterprise at the very top of his agenda throughout his entrepreneurial career. He wrote essays, delivered speeches, held interviews with journalists, all addressing not merely his own firm but China's economic development as a whole and even the global economic situation. After discovering the trick of creating business opportunities by connecting institutionally segregated economic players, he reflected on the experience and went one step further to wrap up ideas with novel expressions and theories. He is an entrepreneur not only in the sense of venturing on new businesses but more importantly in analyzing and then making use of the institutional relations between the different parties involved in business transactions.

---

1   Unless otherwise specified, this case study draws heavily on the interviews I conducted at Nande, a collection of Mou's speeches and writings printed by Nande, and some other company documents. I am aware of some books about Mou published in China, such as a biography of Mou Qizhong by Yuan Guanghou, *Shang Hai Ju Zi Mou Qizhong* (*Mou Qizhong: A Business Giant*, Beijing: Zu Jia Chu Ban She, 1994). Due to their literary nature, I have kept the use of these books to the minimum.

He pushed his ideas and theories to the point where his businesses became a potential threat to the interests of the Chinese State.

To a large extent, Huaqi and Nande have followed a similar trajectory, although Nande's experience has been much more dramatic. That is, at the beginning, they worked very hard, carefully minding every aspect of their business. After a breakthrough, the business grew at an exponential rate, and the entrepreneur became ignorant of the institutional constraints that they had to put up with until they suffered a serious blow. The case of Nande is more dramatic because Mou ended up in jail whilst Mrs. Huo survived a tragic incident.

Figure 7.1 shows what Nande's life course would look like in the two dimensional scheme of legitimacy and profitability.

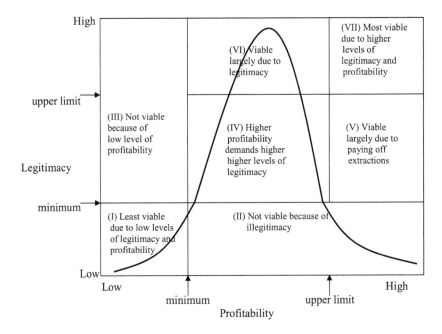

Figure 7.1 Legitimacy and profitability in the life course of Nande

The first striking feature of Nande's development trajectory is that, compared with that of Huaqi (see Figure 6.1 in the previous chapter), it runs into more areas in the chart and changes more abruptly. I shall present the details in the rest of this chapter, but here it is necessary to sketch out the big picture. At the very beginning, Mou's business was neither legitimate nor profitable. Local officials prohibited him from doing 'capitalist' businesses, and he barely survived political confrontations and business stagnations. Two incidents, however, saved him from desperation. First, he discovered the trick of cross-trading in a simple transaction. Second, in the increasingly liberal context of China's economic transition in the early 1980s, some state officials and journalists helped him legitimatize his business ventures.

The effect of institutional holes manifests itself most clearly in this period. Later, he expanded his business enormously by making use of his established reputation and financial credits. The successful transactions led him to believe that there were so many opportunities in the changing economies of China and other parts of the world that institutional constraints could never be too suppressing to overcome – either he could always find an institutional hole or some social connections would come and help. When he pushed his strategies to the point where his businesses entered into the politically sensitive zones, the viability of his enterprise dropped sharply as he could no longer handle the balance between legitimacy and profitability. Desperate efforts to get out of the troubles led him to encroach upon the even more profitable, but highly illegitimate territories, which eventually landed him in jail.

A businessman with a political ambition

Mou was nine years old when the People's Republic was established in 1949. Like most others growing up with the new Republic, Mou spent his best years (from the age of 26 to 38) in the disastrous Cultural Revolution. Unlike most of the youths in those years, whose main concern was to survive each political movement, he and several of his best friends organized a study group of Marxism and Leninism. The works of Marx, Engels and Lenin were the source of inspiration for making sense of China's chaotic situation – killings in armed fights between contentious sects of Red Guards (middle school students claiming loyalty to Mao Zedong), broken families as a result of political conflicts, and an economy at the edge of collapse. How could such a massive movement encouraged by the great Chairman Mao end up in a regression rather than a revolution? A fervent admirer of Mao, Mou was terribly confused by what was happening around him. 'Is such a "revolution" what we really wanted?', Mou asked. 'Why was Chairman Mao persistently in favour of it? What would happen to China if these fights continue endlessly?'

After mulling over the Communist classics and reflecting on the events in the second half of the 1970s, Mou and his friends believed that Mao made two blunders during his later life. First, Mao should not have taken class struggle as the guiding theme for understanding the history of every country. In China's socialist period, class struggle must come to an end; otherwise, it would cause serious damages to the socialist mission. Second, Mao deviated from one of the basic principles of Marxism: that it is material interests, not ideological principles, that ultimately direct people's behaviours. That was not an easy experience for these young men. 'I extremely admired Chairman Mao', confessed Mou while telling the story of this study group. 'When I discovered that he violated Marxist principles but still insisted on his erroneous decisions, the godly glamour around his head waned away from my heart. It was a great torture for me.'

What they talked and wrote about was reported to the police. On 24 August 1975, all eight members of the group were arrested and put into prison. Four years later, for some unknown reason, their case was brought to the attention of some top CCP leaders. 1979 was the year in which Hu Yaobang, then the General Secretary of the CCP, started to liberalize China's political and economic policies. Thousands categorized as 'anti-revolutionary activists', 'capitalists', or 'five bad elements' were released from political camps, with their reputations redeemed and personal assets returned. Following Hu's general instruction, the CCP also dispatched a small group of delegates to Sichuan at the end of 1979, who released Mou and other political activists.

After several years of political ordeal, Mou decided to make some direct contributions to China's economic development by engaging himself in commercial activities. He came to believe that only a market economy could help China grow into a strong nation, and he found a supporting argument in *The Communist Manifesto*: '[t]he cheap prices of its [the capitalist's] commodities are the heavy artillery with which it [the capitalist] batters down all Chinese walls'.[2] In February 1980, at the age of 40, Mou Qizhong quit his job as an ordinary worker in a small state-owned enterprise in Sichuan Province to start his own business. At that time it was a rare and extraordinary move, so rare and extraordinary that the head of his factory did not really know how to handle his resignation. Although the national government had already issued a mandate for encouraging the growth of individual businesses, the policy was targeting those unemployed, particularly the youths who returned to cities from rural areas, in order to ease the unemployment crisis. But Mou was not one of them: he was not a returning youth and he was employed by state enterprise. The head could not find a written policy according to which he could make a decision of granting Mou's request or not. Rather than waiting for an official permission, Mou went ahead and set up a trading firm.

Even more extraordinary was his claim from the outset that making money was not the ultimate purpose of his business. Inspired by Deng Xiaoping's vision of economic reform and pragmatism, Mou's ambition was to become a pioneer of China's economic revival. He took his business as a case of experimenting Deng's ideas so that China's economic development could benefit from his experience. Regardless of whether the Party would acknowledge his contributions or whether his business could truly represent the Party's economic policies, he was however persistent in viewing both his fortunes and misfortunes as signals of the overall situation of the economic reforms. He believed that his enterprise and China's economic development were so tightly connected that 'the problems that Nande is facing will certainly appear in several years' time in China's macro economy'. From the very beginning, Mou's entrepreneurial adventure was bound to be a double mission of making his business profitable and demonstrating the business's legitimacy in the light of state policies.

Making profits from the disunion of others

Officially still an employee of a state enterprise, Mou could not obtain the official permission from local authorities to start a business. To overcome the constraint, he adopted a strategy similar to Huo's: disguising the firm's true nature by registering

---

2   Robert C. Tucker (ed.), *The Marx-Engels Reader*, 2nd edition (New York & London: W.W. Norton & Company, 1978), p. 477.

his trading service company in the name of his mother. Ironically, the local authority would not help a middle-aged man open a trading firm but would register the firm in the name of an old lady. It was nearly two years later at end of 1982 that Mou and his three partners (including his wife and his wife's sister) could register their firm in their own names. During Nande's 20-year life course, Mou and his associates accomplished, or attempted to accomplish, many business deals. Below I shall present four of them to illustrate how he made use of institutional holes by combining available resources separately located in different institutional domains.

The rattan chairs deal

One of the local products that made Mou's hometown, Wanxian, famous was hand-made rattan chairs. Not part of the State's planned economy, the production of the chairs was carried out in families rather than in state enterprises, and no government agent would purchase the chairs; they would have to go to the market. The market, however, was confined to the surrounding areas. Individual families did not have the necessary resources for selling the chairs to places outside of the city, and there was no enterprise who could organize sales of the chairs on a large scale. A wonderful product needed a market. Mou recognized that this could be an excellent opportunity.

But it was not clear how to turn the opportunity into real profit. Initially, he planned to sell the chairs in Chongqing, the biggest city in Sichuan and the closest to his hometown. It soon became clear, however, that he was simply unable to do the business. Local chair makers would not put their chairs in his hands without any payment; all he had was 300 yuan, which was only enough for a trip to Chongqing. In addition, having no past experience, no social connections, and no bank credits, Mou could not convince anybody in Chongqing to make payment upfront to allow him to purchase the chairs and ship the chairs to the big city. He got stuck in between the sellers and the buyers.

Unexpectedly, things turned in his favour on his way back home. While worrying about what he could do on the ship from Chongqing to Wanxian, he overheard something that put him into great excitement: also on board was a sales manager from Henan Province who had just sold a large amount of pears in Sichuan, and on his way back to Henan he would like to buy something special from Sichuan. Mou Qizhong thought that this was the opportunity he must seize.

He immediately realized, however, that he was facing a dilemma. On the one hand, he must convince the sales manager that Wanxian's rattan chairs were the special products to buy. He talked to the manager for several hours, explaining why the chairs were too good to miss. He did a very good job of marketing, and the manager decided to purchase some chairs. On the other hand, however, Mou must stop the manager from going to Wanxian to purchase the chairs on his own; otherwise, he would only do the manager a favour by passing the information to him but lose the opportunity to make money. What Mou had to achieve was to make the manager entrust him as the middleman for purchasing the chairs. To make that happen, Mou started to exaggerate the security situation in his hometown after talking about the chairs, warning the manager that it would not be safe for him as a stranger to go there. Eventually, the manager agreed to let Mou work as his agent and went back to Chongqing straightaway.

Soon after the trip, Mou received 6,400 yuan from the Henan manager, enough to make his business take off. Now Mou became an indispensable tradesman welcomed by the chair makers. Not having had a big buyer for a long time, they happily allowed Mou to pay only 30 per cent of the total payment on the delivery of chairs, which left Mou enough money for expanding his business. Clearly, trust was critical in the transaction – the manager was taking a big risk of easily losing that 6,400 yuan, not a small amount in those years, if Mou did not send the chairs to him. Figure 7.2 below gives a simple illustration of their relations.

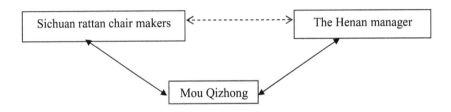

Figure 7.2 Trading rattan chairs

The dotted line in the chart indicates an unrealized transaction between the chair makers and the manager. Instead, the transaction was made through Mou, who occupied a structurally advantageous position in the middle. This is a real life illustration of Burt's idea of structural holes. Obviously, it also serves a case of institutional holes as the chair makers and the managers were not actually segregated by market procedures or the lack of communications but more fundamentally by China's overall institutional structure.

The desk clocks deal

In the early 1980s an ingenious desk clock of the brand '555' was in great demand in Shanghai. Due to limited manufacturing capacity, the municipal government only granted newly married couples the privilege of purchasing one such clock. In contrast to the previous transaction, in which a demand side was needed for a large supply of a good product, this time an increasing supply was wanted under the pressure of an enormous demand. In the rattan chairs deal, Mou's main objective was to find a buyer, but now he had to find a manufacturer, which was more demanding because in those years production was more heavily controlled than sales in China's economy. Nevertheless, his entrepreneurial strategy remained the same: keeping the demand side and the supply side isolated from each other so that he could show each side the value of his role.

Again, it was hard to turn an idea into reality. Mou simply did not know any other manufacturer of the '555' clocks. In the end, knowing that he would be able to find one, he decided to turn a factory into a clock manufacturer. The factory he discovered was Jiangling Machinery Factory near Chongqing. It was one of the many military factories, previously part of China's People's Liberation Army, that were now ordered to turn themselves into manufacturers of civil products. The transformation was difficult for Jiangling as the demand by the State for their products suddenly stopped and the executives had no experience of dealing with the commercial market. But they had what Mou wanted – the capacity to produce the '555' clock.

Desperately looking for a way to survive, and under Mou's drumming up, Jiangling signed a contract with him, by which the factory would produce a certain number of '555' clocks – at that time people in China had little or no sense of copyright – while Mou would be responsible for sales. Next, he found a wholesaler for the clocks in Shangahi, Songjiang Trading Company, which was the easier part of the whole process because of the shortage. What he had to do was to sign a contract with Songjiang, ensuring that it would pay for the clocks when they arrived in Shanghai. Now the chain of transactions was complete (Figure 7.3).

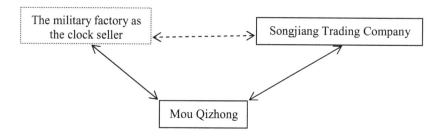

Figure 7.3 Trading desk clocks

The structural relations between the three parties may look similar to those in the previous deal, but there are two important differences. First, Mou did not find the supplier. In a sense, he made one by turning Jiangling into the manufacturer and original seller (its textbox has been made with dotted rather than solid lines to indicate this). The second difference between this deal and the previous one is that Mou found it more difficult to keep his role indispensable. Again, the difficulty was to show evidence of purchasing power and to finish a transaction to each side simultaneously without leaving the two sides a chance of making the deal directly on their own.

By taking advantage of two conditions, Mou successfully solved the problem. First, timing was a key. Once Jiangling finished the production of about 10,000 '555' clocks, Mou brought them to Chongqing's train station to be shipped to Shanghai. When the train was ready to leave, the station issued a shipping record to Mou. As it was Mou's name on the record, it became a proof that it was Mou rather than Jiangling who owned the clocks. It would take several days for the train to arrive at Shanghai, but it took only several hours for Mou to get there by air. Upon arriving, he then showed the shipping record to Songjiang as a proof that the clocks were already on their way to Shanghai. Now Songjiang had no reason to disbelieve Mou and thus issued a bank draft to him, which he immediately brought back to his bank at Wanxian. Speed was critical because he had to put enough money into his bank account to pay Jiangling.

And it was here that the second condition came in his favour – at that time there was a rule that a state enterprise was not allowed to accept payment directly from a client but had to go through each side's local bank to receive the payment. According to the contract between Mou's firm and Jiangling, the latter could make a request for payment after giving the clocks to Mou. The longer the time it took for Jiangling's request to reach Mou's bank, the more time Mou would have for making the money ready. To make the whole process as long as possible, Mou purposefully shipped the clocks on a Tuesday, because Jiangling closed on Wednesday,[3] giving him one more day to collect the money from Songjiang. Before the request reached Wanxian, Mou had already deposited enough money in his account.

Mou learnt a simple, but useful, trick from these deals: in China's fast developing economy, it would soon be the buyers' market. The days of products like the '555' clocks were numbered as there was a huge army of manufacturers who did not know what to make and where to sell. Therefore, once the buyer was found, it would be only a matter of time to complete the deal. The next deal was an excellent application of this logic.

The Russian aircraft deal

Mou's strategy for making profits from the disunion of others found a brilliant application in trading Russian aircraft with Chinese consumer goods. He believed that the industries of China and Russia were extremely complementary to each other and would generate numerous opportunities for entrepreneurs like himself. In 1988, he learned that, to expand its business, Sichuan Airlines was planning to purchase airplanes. Nevertheless, its officials did not have the privilege of purchasing planes from overseas, nor did they know where to find an ideal manufacturer. To purchase airplanes from overseas also demanded a large amount of hard currency. The Russians had aircraft for sale but they didn't know who would buy. On the other hand, they were in great shortage of daily appliances, which were overstocked in many Chinese factories. It became clear to Mou that it would be an excellent business opportunity if he could make a connection with each of the two sides.

Some retired state officials and army generals became Mou's consultants as their club sometimes organized gatherings in Nande's building. They had long experience of dealing with the Russians in the 1950s and 1960s. According to their advice, despite high oil consumption and excessive noise, Russian airplanes cost far less than others and were very reliable. In contrast, American airplanes were of higher quality and carrying capabilities but cost two-thirds to three-quarters more. After

---

3   In those years employees at state enterprises could have only one day off during a week, and it was not necessarily a Saturday or a Sunday.

searching for more than a year Mou and his advisors found that the Soviet TU-154 planes, overstocked in Russia, would be good carriers for Sichuan Airlines.

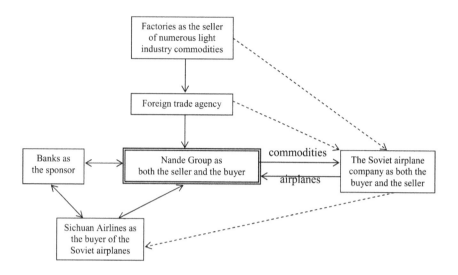

Figure 7.4 Trading airplanes with the Russians

Six institutionally separated business parties were involved in this project, and Mou's firm was squarely in the position of an institutional hole (Figure 7.4):

1. A Russian aircraft company as the seller of airplanes and the buyer of light industry commodities
2. Sichuan Airlines as the buyer of the airplanes
3. Hundreds of factories in China as the sellers of light industry commodities
4. A foreign trade agency representing the Chinese factories
5. Chinese banks as financial sponsors of all the transactions
6. Mou's Nande Group as the broker amid all these parties.

Note that the solid arrows in Figure 7.4 refer to directly connected relations and dotted ones refer to potential but unrealized relations. Mou's plan was to barter four Russian-made airplanes for hundreds of train cars fully loaded with daily appliances manufactured by Chinese workers. Although Russian airplane manufacturers agreed to exchange planes for light industrial commodities, they didn't possess the organizational capabilities of doing business with hundreds of Chinese factories. Nominally as the plane buyer and seller of daily appliances, Nande was indispensable to all of them.

Personal connections and official relations helped Mou establish trust with the Russians. He then constructed, in a few months, a large warehouse of sample commodities to convince the Russians that he did have what they wanted. The real buyer of the planes, Sichuan Airlines, had no access to the Russian airplane manufacturers, nor could they find a solution for solving their financial difficulties.

According to government regulations, to purchase airplanes from another country, a Chinese company must have the privileges of conducting aviation business and international trading, which the Nande Group, as a private enterprise, did not have. Sichuan Airlines could purchase foreign airplanes, but it had to be authorized by the National Aviation Bureau (NAB). Mou persuaded the president of Sichuan Airlines to apply for NAB's permission. The application was turned down, however, because the NAB saw Sichuan Airlines as a potential competitor for industrial monopoly. Mou and Sichuan Airlines then turned to the Government of Sichuan Province and the National Commission of Economic Planning (NCEP) for help. In May 1990, NCEP finally approved Sichuan Airline's application. Nande then commissioned the China Company of Import and Export of Machineries to take care of the administrative procedures for purchasing the airplanes.

But that was not enough. Still, Mou could not sell appliances directly to the Russians without the privilege of conducting foreign trade, nor was he capable of collecting products from hundreds of factories. Mou and his colleagues soon discovered that, to promote exports, the Ministry of Foreign Trade had recently endorsed a new institutional rule, the 'entrusted agency system', according to which companies with no foreign trade privileges could pay 1 per cent to 3 per cent of earnings as a commission fee to those who did enjoy such privileges and would like to help them export products. The problem of foreign trade license was then solved by employing a foreign trade agent in Beijing.

Another problem was setting up a chain of mutual responsibilities among the organizations involved. By a contract between the Nande Group, Sichuan Airlines, and several state banks, Mou leased the planes to Sichuan Airlines for five years. In the meantime, Sichuan Airlines promised to pay the capital and the interest, on the basis of which the banks agreed to put the same amount of money for purchasing the planes into Nande's bank account. The banks were willing to do so for several reasons. Firstly, they and Sichuan Airlines were all under the direct control of the national government; therefore, the deal was virtually a government-to-government transaction. Secondly, Mou allowed them to take the planes as security once they arrived at Sichuan. Finally, the banks simply could not resist the attraction of the generous interest rate that Mou agreed to pay. The agreement between the banks and Mou became a proof of Mou's financial capability for purchasing light industry commodities from factories. The factories obviously could not bypass Nande since most of them had no foreign trade privileges or connections to the Russians.

On 18 November 1991, the first Russian airplane landed at Chengdu Airport (the capital of Sichuan). The other three followed in February, April, and August 1992. In the meantime, Nande shipped more than 1,000 carriages of goods to Russia, collected from more than 300 factories in China. With this deal completed, his firm came to the peak of its history. As Mou said, 'the aircraft trade earned us the status of a large enterprise'. The money earned from it not only significantly increased the firm's economic strength but more importantly laid a solid foundation for its future acquisitions of financial credits and business opportunities. What Nande benefited most from the deal, however, was the sudden and positive visibility in China's economic platform – Mou was overwhelmed by the requests from journalists for visits and interviews, an invisible but valuable asset.

Theorizing entrepreneurial strategies

The success of exchanging Russian aircraft with Chinese goods made Mou believe that 'The only thing we cannot do in this world is that which we haven't thought of', the motto every visitor would see immediately in the lobby of Nande's headquarters in Beijing. After that deal, Mou and his associates initiated some more adventurous projects. But before introducing the later developments, to better understand his entrepreneurial strategies and behaviours, we need to learn the core ideas of his entrepreneurial strategies and philosophies.

It is nothing unusual for an entrepreneur to reflect on the experience of failure or success in an attempt to learn some lessons. What distinguishes Mou from other entrepreneurs in China is his persistent effort in putting his business in the context of China's overall economic reform and comparing it with the most successful companies in the world. He would not be happy if people attributed his success simply to sharp recognition of the opportunity or smart connections to the agencies involved. He seemed to be obsessed with discovering a more fundamental source for his success by linking his business to general human history and the world economy. During the four or five years after the Russian aircraft deal, he spent a lot of time mulling over the theoretical significance of his business strategies. Although he made some unfounded claims or promises in popularizing his ideas, such as that Nande would become one of the largest companies in the world by the year 2000 and his ideas would deserve the Nobel prize, and so on, there are a few thought-provoking points in his reflections, from which we can see how his entrepreneurial strategies illustrate the notions of 'institutional holes' and 'double entrepreneurship'.

Copying the Marxist and Maoist model of dividing human history into several evolutionary phases, Mou thinks that there have been three civilizations. The first is the agricultural civilization, in which the dominant mode of production is the exploitation of slaves by their masters and the exploitation of peasants by landlords. The second civilization is the industrial civilization, in which the financial capital dominates and exploits the labour. Today, we are in the transition from the industrial civilization to the third and new one – the wisdom civilization, in which the power of production shall be represented by the amount of wisdom and the dominant mode of production will be a system of cooperative intellectual labour. The new civilization is far more advanced than the previous ones because it is wisdom, ideas, and other intelligent forms of capital that determine the ultimate uses and values of material and financial capitals.

Corresponding to the wisdom civilization comes 'the fourth industry', following agriculture as the first, manufacturing the second, and service the third. Its distinguishing feature and function is to combine the available but isolated resources in the other industries. As Mou explains:

> We move across many different domains, putting some of the smartest people in each
> domain together in an organized way. The process of organizing the most active elements

of production in every domain and putting them into operation constitutes the entire content of our fourth industry ... The operation has to go back to the original first, second, and third industries.[4] One of the most important principles in the operation of businesses in the fourth industry is that we buy various production elements from the first, the second, and the third industries, then after recombining them in a synthetic way we sell them back to the original industries. As the operating agent of the synthetic recombination, we take all the risks in the whole process.[5]

The fourth industry is therefore the antithesis of the third. Whilst the advantage of the third industry lies in its economic efficiency due to division of labour and specialization, what makes the fourth industry surpass the third is its power of synthesizing. On 5 January 1996, Mou claimed with great pride that:

> the biggest contribution made by Nande is our critique of Adam Smith ... Division of labour does bring efficiency, but such theory is obsolete ... because it runs into contradiction with the globalization of market, modern transportation and communications. What Nande has done, and will continue to do, is recombine segmented production elements, which will be the essential hallmark of the post-industrial era.[6]

In its extreme forms, specialization causes segmentation among elements of production, leaving producers ignorant of how to connect their products with those in other industries. In other words, specialization institutionalizes the isolation of producers in different domains. The three business deals presented in the previous section are vivid illustrations of segmentation, both geographical and institutional: the rattan chair makers and the Henan sales manager, people in Shanghai looking for '555' desk clocks and the military factory in Sichuan, hundreds of daily appliance manufacturers in China and the aircraft maker in Russia.

In Mou's view, the large number of state-owned enterprises in the first three industries in China, albeit having fallen behind those in the West, have already produced an enormous amount of resources and wealth. Consequently, the value one could add on top of these resources and wealth would be extremely marginal by setting up another similar enterprise. As a result of institutional segmentation under the old system of socialist planned economy, the assets accumulated within state enterprises have not been utilized to develop their full potential. With the introduction of market mechanisms under Deng Xiaoping's leadership, the most efficient way of producing added values is to make profitable connections among the enterprises located in different geographical and institutional sites.

---

4   Mou Qizhong, *Le Guan De Zhong Guo Jing Ji* (*An Optimistic View of China's Economy*, Land Research Institute, 1997), p. 84. I have no plan to make direct comments on his ideas and theories. I present them in this chapter for illustrating and explaining his entrepreneurial strategies.

5   Ibid., p. 65. Mou established The University of the Fourth Industry, which, however, ceased to exist soon afterwards. He made the quoted comments in his lecture at the University in November, 1994.

6   *Nande Shijie* (*The Land's View*, Nande's internal newsletter), No. 238, 22 January 1996.

Mou has illustrated his idea by using the metaphor of boiling water. Water will not boil at 99°C. The last 1°C increase is therefore critical for making all the previous heating worthwhile. Resources in state-owned enterprises are like the water at 99°C while strategic combination is the last 1°C. This is his 'One-Degree Theory', which was once heatedly discussed not only within Nande but also in some popular newspapers. According to this theory, the mission of Mou's business ventures is not to produce any particular product or service, but to make connections of available but segmented resources. Mou claimed that by discovering the fourth industry and 'One-Degree Theory', Nande became the pioneer of the most advanced mode of production in the world.

Combination and recombination require synthetic thinking, which Mou believes the Chinese people are especially good at. Drawing on the works of some prominent scholars of Chinese philosophy and culture, Mou thinks that the West is the master of analyzing while the East of synthesizing. Accordingly, the coming wisdom civilization and the era of the fourth industry will be the golden days of China. 'It is hopeless to establish in China an industrial civilization similar to that in the West', he claimed, 'because the era of financial capital has come to an end' and 'its grave digger – the wisdom capital – has already stood in front of its door'. Therefore, 'we should no longer aim to produce property from the nature; rather, we should firstly discover marketable elements in production and then recombine them in the best way by following the principles of market economy'.[7]

Entering into the dangerous zone

These ideas have lent great support for Mou's craving for building up a business empire at an exponential speed. Obviously, it is much faster and more efficient to organize a recombination of ready-made resources than to manufacture tangible products. The Russian aircraft deal has proved that his strategy and philosophy are not just maniac illusions; rather, they can work wonderfully in reality. Increasing with the soar of his firm's profits was Mou's self-efficacy and ambition. He believed that he had accumulated enough 'invisible assets' for faster business expansion. These 'invisible assets' almost exclusively came from the media coverage of his projects and from his activities of propagating his own ideas. Unlike Huo and many other entrepreneurs in China, who would spend their time taking care of their hard products and would keep journalists at a distance, unless they had no other choice, Mou was a self-made business celebrity, never becoming tired of delivering speeches, talking to journalists, organizing press conferences, writing essays, and proposing attractive business deals on his business tours.

His logic was that these activities would increase his 'invisible assets' – reputation, popularity, and credibility, which then would put him in an advantageous position for acquiring tangible assets – financial credits, land, employees, raw materials, and so on. The accumulated tangible assets in turn would become credits for earning further more 'invisible assets', thus forming a self-reinforcing circle of progression toward

---

7 Mou, *Le Guan De Zhong Guo Jing Ji*, 'Preface'.

his ultimate goal of making Nande one of the world's top ten companies in less than ten years. That is to say, given that the total asset of the tenth largest company in the world in 1995 was about 23 billion US dollars and that Nande's total asset in the same year was 2 billion yuan (around 0.24 billion US dollars), disregarding factors including inflation and exchange rates, the total asset of Land would have to increase by nearly 100 times by 2005.

Mou did not think that the target was too far-fetched. He could build an empire through 'steady tillering', or expansion through the progressive establishment of subsidiaries. The idea runs as follows. Nande provides the start-up capital to anyone who has a very smart idea for a project. If the project fails, Nande would take the loss. If it succeeds, Nande will own 49 per cent of the new company and the person who initiated the project will own the other 51 per cent. The first company as an experiment of this model was Jiulong Casting Group, started by Mr. Tian Song in early 1995. The sponsor-subsidiary relationship did not sustain for long, however. When Mou Qizhong asked Tian Song to sell out Jiulong because Mou urgently needed cash, Tian refused, arguing that he was the actual owner of the company.

At the core of this and other forthcoming troubles for Mou is that his success and visibility in the media prevented him from realizing two critical conditions for his logic to work smoothly. On the one hand, his 'invisible assets' were built on his visible assets – financial gains from business transactions. Nevertheless, he came to despise all material and financial assets after the Russian aircraft deal and to believe that he could easily acquire financial credits from state banks. As we shall see later, such a way of thinking eventually landed him in jail. On the other hand, the media played a critical role in the formation of his 'invisible assets', which may not always stand on his side. Mou believed, however, that he could always work the media for his own interests. His ignorance of these conditions, purported by his initial success and his own theories, eventually led his enterprise to a fast track of collapse. Here I shall briefly introduce some of the major deals that dragged his business into a downward spiral.

After the Russian aircraft deal, Mou started to look for a business that could make an even more amazing connection between two separated parties. What is bigger than an airplane? A satellite. Following his logic of starting with the buyer, Mou and his assistants were looking for customers of satellite services – television stations. In China, television watching is one of the most popular leisure activities, with millions of people sitting in front of the television after the evening meal, and what has been shown on television usually becomes a frequent topic in daily conversations. Since 1990, many provinces have set up a television station, offering special programmes to their own viewers.

Although there was a market, Mou was institutionally banned from accessing it. As satellite service was closely connected with information control, only a few television stations under the direct control of the national government had the privilege of renting satellite service. Nor could he copy his strategy used in the Russian aircraft deal by employing a company with the required privilege – national television stations were not allowed to transfer their privilege to any other businesses. For the demand side, although Mou knew some Russian companies could provide the service, he had not found anyone who could offer a good deal. All suggested that this was not a feasible project; one of his assistant even thought it was just a joke.

Believing in his motto, Mou did not want to give up. Now that he already had thought through the whole plan, nothing would prevent him from carrying it out. With the help of some Russian engineers, he firstly found a company with a desirable communication satellite in Russia. He and his assistants, however, had to find the customers for it outside mainland China. A small group was dispatched to Southeast Asia to find a company who would rent the satellite service. Eventually, a company in Taiwan agreed to pay for the service. Nevertheless, Nande could not purchase the satellite service from its Russian partner and then resell it to the Taiwanese company, because the Chinese government prohibited all native firms buying or renting from any satellite service.

Mou sidestepped this institutional hurdle by registering a commercial satellite company in the US that, as an American firm, did not have to be constrained by Chinese regulations. In the end, the satellite was launched from Russia on 20 January 1994. The launch, however, was the only thing to celebrate. A senior executive of Nande confessed that they were actually planning to purchase the whole satellite, but they found it difficult even to rent it. To rent the satellite, they had to put down about 7 million US dollars and Mou had to borrow another 10 million US dollars from a company in the city of Wuxi in Jiangsu province.

If everything went well, they would have made tens of millions of dollars. Nevertheless, in that year China's national government was in the process of tightening up financial credits under the premiership of Zhu Rongji. Soon the company in Wuxi requested that their shares be returned. With no other choice, Mou had to sell off the service at a much lower price in order to survive the financial turbulence.

Another big deal was the Manzhouli Development Project. Located at the Russia–China border, Manzhouli is a small city under the administration of Mongolia Autonomous District. With an increasing number of business transactions across the border, the city seemed to have a promising future of developing into an international centre of commerce. Its conditions for investment in the early 1990s were less than satisfactory, however; there were no trains, motorways, airports, or long distance telephone services. But Mou spotted a great business opportunity in Manzhouli, proclaiming that Nande would turn it into 'the Northern Shenzhen'.[8] The project started in May 1993, and Nande claimed that it had successfully obtained a loan of 220 million yuan from state banks. At the same time, Russian authorities agreed to lease a piece of land of 1.5 square kilometres on the Russian side for Nande to develop as a special economic zone. Mou's ultimate goal was to take over Russia's market of light industry products through combining highly affordable land and raw materials on the Russian side with low-cost labour and manufacturing power on the Chinese side. In the meantime, since the products to be made would carry the label 'Made in Russia', exportation of the products would not be limited by the quota imposed by the US government.

---

8   Shenzhen was a small town right opposite Hong Kong, which has developed into a prosperous city, well known for its fast economic development with Deng Xiaoping's persistent support.

Wonderful as it might sound, the project experienced very difficult conditions from the outset. Soon after it started, the state banks made an urgent request that the loans be returned, partly because China's central bank was in a process of tightening financial credits and partly because some people started to question the credibility of Mou's business, which we shall discuss in detail in the next section. With the bulk of start-up capital withdrawn, Mou could not put the project in operation until the summer of 1996, when Nande invested more than 50 million yuan in the construction of a new part of motorway at the border. It took quite some time for investments to have decent returns. Many of Mou's debtors – he also borrowed a lot of money from other companies – could not wait. By 1998, it was clear that Mou and his Nande Group could no longer hold on to this project. In a press conference on 26 September 1998, Mou told the media that the land that he rented in Manzhouli had already been taken back by the Chinese State, and he did not give any explanation.

We end this section with Mou's most politically sensitive plan: the 765 project. According to Mou, its claimed goal was to turn those half-dead state-owned enterprises into thriving businesses and the way of achieving that goal was to follow his idea of 'private management of state-owned enterprises'. In a nutshell, he should be given the opportunity to take charge of those state assets and to bring them to stock markets in western countries. Again, there was a connection to make. The non-performing state enterprises were on one side, and on the other side was the huge amount of financial credit in economically advanced countries, perhaps up to several hundreds of billions in US dollars, that were looking for profitable investment opportunities.

The first step of Mou's plan was to set up many financial institutions in the West, the US in particular, to absorb as much as 'wasted' financial capital as possible. He believed that this was feasible because a trick of operating a bank was to show only a small amount of money as proof of repaying power to attract a large amount of investment. More precisely, he only needed a million dollars to be able to attract a billion. As most of these financial institutions were to be established in the US, they would be foreign companies in China and, therefore, would not be constrained by China's government regulations.

The second step was to invest the absorbed financial credits in some selected state-owned enterprises and to reconstruct them into joint-ventures with an American or European company. Although ideally Nande should own 51 per cent of each joint venture, Nande only needed a small amount of investment to get the new business registered, because China's Law for Joint Ventures only required 15 per cent of the registered capital to be shown on the owner's account. Suppose the average investment for a joint venture was 100,000 US dollars. Nande did not really need 51,000 dollars in order to control the joint venture. Rather, it only needed 15 per cent of the 51,000 dollars, or 7,650 dollars. Hence the project's name '765'. Mou confidently claimed that under the management of his well-trained managers,[9] the joint ventures would soon make enormous profits and consequently, the state-owned enterprises would be revived.

---

9   On more than one occasion, Mou proclaimed that 'if Harvard Business School produces CEOs, then we at Nande Group produce chairmen of the board of directors'.

Finally, once these enterprises proved successful, they would be ready to sell themselves on the US stock markets. Then they would attract even more investment, which in turn could be used to revitalize more state-owned enterprises in China.

If this plan had worked, it would truly have been 'the biggest business opportunity in human history', as Mou declared. But it must have appeared to be a scary scenario for the Chinese State. If Mou were successful in carrying out his plan, then a large share of China's state economy would have been under his control. The plan was nullified before it even got started. Some serious allegations were made against Mou, accusing him of stealing state property, which we shall see in more detail in the next section. According to Mou himself, he had to abandon the project not because of these accusations but because he had discovered a more efficient way of achieving the original goal, which was to construct the most efficient and the largest financial system in the world. That was the last time, however, that he mentioned the new plan.

Dealing with legitimacy crises

Mou deeply believed that his businesses represented the forefront of China's new economic policies and was absolutely in line with Deng Xiaoping's economic pragmatism. To him, any doubt about the legitimacy of his business arose not because his business strategies were contrary to China's economic institutions but because of the outdated values held by state officials, competitors, and ordinary people. During his entrepreneurial career, Mou experienced some attacks on his strategies and transactions, either in the media or through lawsuits, but every time he believed that not only were these attacks wrong and unfounded but more importantly they were actually attacking state policies and Deng's principles. In this section, I plan to discuss how he attempted to justify and legitimize three important issues in his entrepreneurship: the validity of his firm's ownership, the appropriateness of his cross-trading strategy, and the legitimacy of his use of state assets.

Ownership: private or collective?

After Mou Qizhong successfully accomplished some business deals, local authorities in his hometown started to question the legitimacy of the way he made the profits. What kind of business was he running? Was it politically correct to allow businesses like his to exist? In the end, the authorities concluded that Mou's business was both financially and politically unacceptable. Financially, his profits came from speculation and profiteering. That is, what Mou had done was no more than moving commodities from one place to another so that he could make money from the difference in local prices, which were absolutely not allowed according to the Chinese government's financial regulations at that time. Politically, a deputy Party secretary in charge of legal matters believed that Mou's objective was not merely to make money but to undermine the socialist regime. Therefore, Mou's business was on the capitalist track and should be shutdown immediately. In September 1983, the bank account of Mou's trading firm was frozen, and he was arrested with some other members of the firm.

Living behind the bars for the second time, Mou believed he was wrongly convicted again, just like the first time during the Cultural Revolution. To demonstrate that his business was squarely consistent with the general principles of China's economic reform and to disprove the local leader's narrow-mindedness, he wrote a 17-page application for joining the CCP and two other essays in defence of his political innocence. In one of the essays, he argued that his arrest and the shutdown of his business were a clear example of how the local authorities were holding back the progress of economic reform. The other essay was a grand statement on the mission of China's socialism, quoting extensively from Marx, Engels, Lenin, Mao, Deng, and many others. Although he never made it explicit in the essay, he wanted to demonstrate clearly that, albeit a businessman, he understood the historical significance and fundamental principles of China's economic development; further, he should be seen as a pioneer of the whole mission of economic reforms.

With the help of some sympathetic journalists, his papers seem to have drawn attention from top political leaders. About one and half years later, he was released, cleared of all charges, and allowed to restart his business.

But that does not mean he did not need to defend the legitimacy of his business. He made several attempts of diluting the private ownership of his enterprise. Nevertheless, he could never escape the suspicion that he and his family members were the actual owners of Nande. Till 1995, Mou repeatedly claimed that he opened the first private business in the People's Republic of China and accepted the designation that Nande was a private or civil (*min ban*) company, which is however not confirmed.[10] In January 1995, he created a new term for describing Nande's ownership, 'the cooperated labour system', declaring that 'from now on Nande Economic Group belongs to all staffs and employees'.[11] 'We the Nande Economic Group declare ourselves not a private enterprise', he explained, 'not because we are afraid of any political problems but because private ownership has seriously hindered the development of our company, and because it does not truly represent our company's reality'.[12] But he was vague about just how Nande belonged to the employees in institutional terms. Nande had a Board of Directors, of which Mou was the Chairman, but there was no information about how much each member owned of the company. At one point, he seemed to accept that all assets of Nande belonged to himself. In June 1996, *Forbes* listed Mou Qizhong as one of the wealthiest people in China, with a total *personal* asset of about 0.1 billion US dollars, which was supposed to be the total asset of *the whole company*. Surprisingly, Mou acknowledged that the

---

10 Literally, *min ban* means being established and managed by people themselves, as opposed to those by the government (*guan ban*). More precisely, the category of *min ban* covers four types of non-state economic enterprises in China: private enterprises (including individual household businesses), town-and-village enterprises (TVE), partnership technology enterprises, and enterprises with foreign investments. For example, Mr. Jing Shuping, Chairman of China's National Business Association, adopted such categorization in his speech at a conference of non-state entrepreneurs in September 1994.

11 Mou, *An Optimistic View of China's Economy*, p. 80.

12 Ibid., p. 76.

estimate was approximately correct. It is thus unclear in what sense he saw Nande as an enterprise collectively owned by all employees.

He had to try even harder to justify the nature of his business when proposing to buy out state-owned enterprises and then sell them to American stock markets after some reconstruction work. Unlike people in the West, who usually see the listing of a company's shares on a stock market as a way of 'going public' (the public owns a company by holding its shares), many people in China view shareholding as a form of private ownership because the shares are each individual shareholder's private assets. Therefore, Mou's proposal was perceived to be an attempt of privatizing the state sector. To clear himself, Mou had to repeatedly argue that stockholding was a type of public ownership because nearly all the firms in the West were owned by a large number of people rather than an individual or a family alone. To show that even the great masters of Marxism were on his side, Mou's assistants collected a number of statements from the works of Marx and Engels and printed them in a pamphlet titled 'Stockholding System is Public Ownership'. Obviously, their intention was not to clear up the confusions in understanding an economic jargon but to prove the legitimacy of Mou's overall plan.

Cross-trading: smart deals or illegal transactions?

As said before, Mou believed that Deng Xiaoping's economic policies had offered an extraordinary opportunity for entrepreneurs in China; to make full use of this extraordinary opportunity, one had to adopt extraordinary strategies, especially for a person like him, who had nothing but his own human capital. He explained to a journalist:

> In a market economy it is a universal truth that you have to possess some capital in order to compete with others. For a private enterprise to survive in China, the popular strategy has been to find a 'father' [sponsor] with either money or power. The success of your business thus depends on your father's capital. But I had nothing. How could I compete? ... The only option for overtaking the others was to search for something more effective than money and power.[13]

That 'something' was the strategy of cross-trading with businesses geographically and institutionally unconnected with each other.

There is a risk, however, of making such connections. As each party in the deal has to operate within the designated institutional domain, crossing the domain's boundaries would mean manipulating, if not ostensibly breaking, institutional rules. It is possible that under a particular circumstance the connections could be made without seriously violating a set of rules, but these situations are rare. An exception was the South Korean refrigerators deal. In 1987, there was a great demand for household refrigerators in China. To protect domestic manufacturers of refrigerators, the Chinese government placed strict restrictions and very high tariffs on the importation of refrigerators from abroad. Soon Mou found out that the refrigerators

---

13 Yuan Guanghou, *Mou Qizhong: A Business Giant* (Beijing: Author's Publishing House, 1994), p. 76.

made in South Korea offered good value for money. But to successfully ship the South Korean refrigerators to China, he had to jump two institutional hurdles: one, government restrictions on importation, and two, the fact that at that time South Korea did not have direct trade relations with China. He believed that there must be a grey area in the rules in which he could get around the restrictions, and he did make a discovery in an appendix at the end of an official document: refrigerators of the volume of 360 litres or more were categorized as 'work-related machines', not 'household appliances'. Next, he found a business partner in Hong Kong who could purchase the refrigerators from a South Korean manufacturer and transfer them into Mou's hands.

Even in this auspicious event, the successful completion of cross-trading depends on the legitimacy of each business partner's status and the certainty that they will not withdraw their participation. Mou soon found out that it was very hard to satisfy these conditions. It is particularly difficult when the deal relates to a field under the close scrutiny of state officials. For example, Mou often had to rely on local branches of state banks for access to financial credits. Officials in these banks may take an order from the top more seriously than the contracts that they signed with a company like Nande. We may even say that the banks are part of the State, having the right to change financial policies.

Financial blows struck at least twice in Nande's history. In 1985, just stepping out of prison for the second time, a local branch of the Bank of Agriculture granted Mou a loan of 10 million yuan. Although it was never confirmed, the loan was very likely offered under the instruction of high profile officials as a gesture of support for Mou's liberal economic ideas. From the point of view of the branch, the loan was made to bargain for a higher quota of reserved credits for the next year; that is, the more the branch lent out that year, the more it could ask from the top for the next year. Mou was more than happy, of course, receiving such a large sum of money and soon invested it into many business projects. Several months later, however, the branch asked him to return the money. Nande claimed that this was almost three years earlier than the time dated in a contract between Nande and the branch, all due to the fact that the national government had decided to tighten up financial credits. To avoid inflation, the Bank of China set up a rule that all credits made to non-state enterprises be returned as soon as possible and that no further credits be issued to these enterprises. The rule forced many ongoing projects to abort, and Nande barely survived the crisis. In 1993, Nande found itself in a similarly difficult situation when Mou invested more than a 100 million in a few large projects, most of which, however, had to be abandoned due to the new state policies. Mou sent many complaints in writing to some top leaders of China, but to little avail.

Mou Qizhong: 'The Richest Man' or 'The Biggest Swindler'?

Whilst before it was Mou Qizhong who made use of the media for enhancing his 'invisible assets', since 1996 he found that that was a dangerous strategy after some journalists became suspicious and even belligerent of his business. At the beginning, the journalists with the intention of revealing the true reality of Nande came mostly from news agencies outside of mainland China, such as *Asia Inc., Singtao Daily, The*

Wall Street Journal, Los Angeles Times and *The Guardian.* These reports, published in English and circulated outside the mainland, did not influence Nande's daily business much. Journalists within China were still reluctant to offend this popular star of business.

Serious allegations against Mou and his enterprise were published for the first time in August 1997. A booklet titled *Da Lu Shou Pian Mou Qizhong (Mou Qizhong: The Most Notorious Swindler in Mainland China)* was distributed for sale in a national book fair in the northeast city of Changchun. The author's name was printed as Lu You, obviously a pseudo-name because Lu You was a well-known poet in the South Song Dynasty. The author's true identity was not revealed until 1999, after Mou was arrested for committing some financial frauds.[14] The publisher was *Shi Chang Yu Fa Zhi Dao Bao (Guide to Market and Legal Matters)*, a magazine under the sponsorship of *Fa Zhi Ri Bao (The Legal Daily)*, the official newspaper of the Ministry of Justice. The booklet was published as a supplement rather than a regular issue. Twice, the magazine disclaimed any responsibilities for such an added issue. The first announcement was made on 15 September, claiming that it never published any supplementary issue and thus would not take any responsibility for any consequence. The second was made on 9 October, stating that 'This magazine has not officially published a supplementary issue in any form. Although we applied for publishing a supplementary issue, it was never published because of technical problems'. This means that there was a supplementary issue, although its official publication was aborted. Clearly, there must be someone who knew the inside stories and managed to take the opportunity to make a good sale. As the magazine asserted, some illegal book dealers embezzled the issue, made illegal copies, and finally published it. Since then, nobody has been charged with the embezzlement.

The most important piece of this illegally published booklet was a letter written by five employees of Nande, who also claimed themselves members of the CCP.[15] It listed '13 criminal facts' committed by Mou Qizhong and his closest assistants, including defrauding huge amount of loans from many banks to breaking contracts by investing no money into projects that Mou had promised to support, causing a huge amount of loss of state assets. It also claimed that Mou bribed some government officials and moved a lot of money to the United States.

As the letter was sent out to China's security agencies and the Bank of China about one and a half years before it was circulated among the public, we can see whether the letter indeed drew any serious attention from the state authorities by examining what happened to Nande since April 1996. A journalist did the homework

---

14 It is reported that the author's true name is Wu Ge, but it is not clear whether he was the only author or if there were some others. Wu intended to write the booklet as a serious report, but there has been no explanation of how his report fell into the hands of some underground book dealers, who made a big profit by selling the booklet.

15 There were some confusions with the date on which the letter was written. Most media reports say it was 21 March 1996, but one report disagrees, saying that was the date the letter was sent to the government and it was actually written on 12 May 1995. If the latter was right, then it is not clear why the letter was not sent out during the ten months. Fortunately, this does not seem to be a major issue for understanding the whole incident.

and found that Nande was truly in a very difficult situation in 1996,[16] under close scrutiny of state officials due to its involvement in many legal disputes:

- 31 May, a local court pronounced that Nande pay 4.85 million yuan to a food company in Langfang, a city located in between Beijing and Tianjin;
- 12 June, a local court in Beijing asked Nande to return 4 million yuan to a bank;
- Early July, the Capital Steel Company (*shou gang*) sued Nande for an unpaid loan of 50 million yuan;
- 13 August, China's Trust and Investment Company for Agricultural Development sued Nande for not returning 9 million yuan;
- 28 August, two cars, some office equipment, and other properties were removed and kept under custody under the instruction of a court in Mongolia Autonomous District;
- 26 September, The New Technology Investment Company of China sued several subsidiaries of Nande for a debt of 1.951 million yuan.

These financial troubles were later verified by Mou Qizhong himself, who admitted that there was no salary paid to Nande's employees for several months in 1996 and the first four months in 1997.

What posed a threat to Mou's business was not really the financial disputes themselves. Such disputes were commonly seen in China when the national government's banking polices kept changing. In addition, for the purpose of this study, I do not need to make a judgement on the responsibilities that Mou had to take in each dispute. To me, a more important question is whether Mou and his associates brought themselves into these disputes because they violated legal and moral rules. More specifically, it was vital for Mou to dispute the allegations made in the booklet even though it was published and circulated without going through a legitimate channel. He simply could not ignore the attacks and keep people confused or suspicious of his business.

On 23 September 1997, Mou finally faced the media in a press conference. A theme was designated to the conference: 'The Fifteenth Plenum and The Development of the Nande Economic Group: Mou Qizhong Answers the Press'. It seemed that he did not plan to confront the allegations head-on. Rather, he spent most of the time discussing how the Fifteenth Plenum had offered a perfect opportunity for Nande. The Plenum was held during the week of 12 to 18 September, in which Jiang Zeming, then the General Secretary, denounced the leftist view of China's economic development and asserted that non-state enterprises should be treated as an important component of, rather than merely a supplement to, the national economy. Jiang also claimed that stockholding systems should be adopted as an effective way of reconstructing state-owned enterprises in the next stage of the economic reform. Mou argued that all his strategies and ideas were perfectly consistent with the new policies Jiang had just proposed.

---

16 See the review article by Ren Sen in *Dong Fang Qi Ye Jia* (*Eastern Entrepreneurs*), No. 2, 1998.

In the rest of the press conference, some journalists got the chance to question Nande's financial situation, Mou's business strategies, and his reactions to the allegations made in the booklet. One of the journalists at the press conference, Mr. Fang Jinyu, a reporter with the newspaper *Nan Fang Zhou Mou* (*Southern Weekends*), appeared to be especially sceptical of the legitimacy of Mou's business. After the conference, Fang published a long report '*Shou Fu Hai Shi Shou Pian*' ('The Wealthiest Man or the Most Notorious Swindler?'). Mou and his assistant then fought back with another long article published in their own newsletter *The Land View* on 17 October. Such confrontation lasted till the end of the year. There is no need to present the details of the dispute here.

It is important, however, to understand the issue at the centre of the confrontation – swindling, because it serves as a moral criterion for judging the entrepreneur's legitimacy. In this case, Mou was accused of 'swindling' for three reasons. First of all, Mou's strategy of cross-trading can be seen as a behaviour of swindling because he kept his business partners in the dark. In China, there are two expressions for such behaviour, *mai kong mai kong*, purchasing without money and selling without goods, and *kong shou dao*, making deals without products at hand. For most Chinese people, they are morally wrong and ideologically unacceptable. Business transactions like these were completely banned by the State until the early years of the economic reform. Currently, although no specific legal codes prohibit such behaviours, they are widely perceived as business frauds in the Chinese society.

But Mou disagreed:

> The market economy is essentially a contract economy. As long as both sides [the buyer and the seller] behave according to the contract, their behaviours should always be seen as legitimate, no matter how illegitimate it seems to be from the point of view of a third party and whether it is consistent with his [the third party's] moral values or not. This should be the life of a businessman, and this is the specific meaning of credibility that we are talking about everyday.[17]

In short, as long as Mou's behaviour does not violate the terms of the contract that he signed with A and B, respectively, he should have no obligation whatsoever to tell A what he would do with B or tell B his business with A. He thought that such strategy was morally impeccable and all accusations were ethically outdated.

The second reason that some people thought Mou a swindler was that he repeatedly made unrealistic proposals and then either could not keep his promises or left some projects unfinished. For example, among the most daring proposals were the plan to blow up the Himalayan Mountains in order to produce rains for the eastern provinces of China. The Himalayas form a natural barricade between the Indian Sea and the northwest China, a geographical fence blocking the northwest area from getting sufficient warm airflow and thus rain. On February 16 1996, Mou invited many specialists in meteorology, global physics, and explosion engineering to his headquarters, discussing how to carry out the project. It soon turned out that to make a tunnel for the warm airflow through to the northwest was only a fantasy. Some

---

17 Quoted from an interview conducted by a journalist at Nande's headquarters in Beijing on 17 October 1997, *Dong Fang Qi Ye Jia* (*Eastern Entrepreneurs*), No. 2, 1998, p. 38.

other imaginative ideas were to build the fastest computer processor in the world, to save The Yellow River, and to construct a telecommunication network with 88 satellites. Here are some less dazzling promises Mou made in various occasions:[18]

- In June 1993, after talking to the President of Sichuan University, Mou promised to invest 200 million yuan in a joint-venture with the University for developing a chain of fast food restaurants based on a special local recipe of spicy pot. *Sichuan Daily*, the official newspaper of Sichuan's provincial government, published a special report as a token of appreciation. Then, the University established an institute responsible for academic research. It is not known how much Nande actually invested in the project, but it is clear that it was far less than what was promised. Consequently, the whole project soon disappeared.
- 5 September 1995, Nande American Roosevelt Investment Company signed a contract with Taian Papermaking Company in Liaoning Province to construct the Taian-Roosevelt Paper Company. No results followed.
- 20 September 1995, Nande American Roosevelt Investment Company expressed its intention to establish Zhangjiakou-Roosevelt Citric Acid Company with Wanquan Factory of Citric Acid, located at the City of Zhangjiakou in Hebei Province. No further information is available.
- 7 October 1996, Nande registered a petroleum company in the City of New York. Using a technology innovated by a university professor, Nande would invest in recycling abandoned oil fields. It was claimed that the rate of success could be as high as 90 per cent. Later on 7 November, in a conference for this project, Mou announced that Nande would invest 20 million US dollars in establishing 20 such companies in twenty different countries.
- 11 October 1996, Mou had a conversation with the vice president of the British company Sedgwick Group. The two sides reached an agreement to establish a risk insurance management company, but nothing happened from then on.
- 13 October 1996, Mou met a businessman from Taiwan and the director of China's National TV Station, planning to set up a global Chinese television network. He hoped that it could be done by the end of 1997.
- In an interview in March 1997, Mou said he planned to build highways, railways, and communication systems for each province. When asked where the money came from, he answered, 'from the West, of course'. In his mind was a plan to establish an overseas financial system within three years, including commercial banks, investment banks, securities, insurance, etc.
- 19 May 1997, Nande signed three contracts with the City of Leshan, according to which Nande would invest in the city's tourism, including a hotel, an international conference centre, a skiing resort, a nature protection area, and a highway.
- 20 July 1997, Mou and the President of Beijing Film Company announced that Nande would invest 20 million yuan in movie productions.

---

18 *The Land View*, various issues.

- 1 August 1997, Nande would invest 250 million yuan for developing a deserted area of 20 million Chinese acres in Mongolia Autonomous District.

To Mou Qizhong, it was more important to publicly announce these attractive plans than to actually accomplish them, because the media would help him make those plans widely known, which consequently would become his 'invisible assets'.

If the previous two are controversial issues about business ethics, then the third allegation of his swindling is easier to grasp, which pertains to the legality of Mou's business. It was not the allegations published in the illegal booklet that eventually put Mou in jail, however. Although Mou and Nande were under investigations for several months, there were no formal charges until 7 January 1999, when Mou was arrested for financial frauds. That it took more than two years for the investigators to collect sufficient hard evidence indicates that it was not straightforward to make serious charges against him. On 30 May 2000, a court in the city of Wuhan sentenced Mou to life imprisonment and deprived him of all his political rights. Mou made an appeal to a higher court, but it was rejected on 22 August. The main charge was that Mou instructed some of his employees to swindle the Bank of China's branch in Wuhan of 33 credit certificates with falsified import contracts. The total loss caused to the branch was claimed to be more than 35 million US dollars.[19]

Concluding observations

Among entrepreneurs in China, Mou Qizhong is certainly unique. Other entrepreneurs would not copy his strategy and style of doing business, although they may admire Mou's imagination and agree with some of his ideas. They would not fancy making huge profits simply by following a brilliant idea and making connections with companies isolated from one another. To them, discovering and filling a supply gap in the market would be good enough.

Nevertheless, Mou's story may not sound so surreal if we could ignore the details of his projects, at least temporarily, but focus on the basic logic of his strategy. In fact, what Mou has practised is the market mechanism – a market arises when the exchange between a seller and a buyer becomes possible. Mou was simply quick enough to learn that the seemingly straightforward exchange was in reality very difficult for many enterprises in China due to the nation's socialist planned economy. State policies representing Deng's pragmatism have provided the institutional conditions for earning profits by connecting businesses with supplementary but still segmented resources. Households in Sichuan were allowed to make rattan chairs but wholesales over a long distance were judged as profiteering and illegal. The military factory was ordered to make a living by manufacturing civil appliances,

---

19 Recent reports suggest that there have been some new developments in the lawsuit. For example, see the news summary at http://news.xinhuanet.com/ on 12 April 2004. The sentence has been reduced to 18 years, and it seems that he could have another chance of making an appeal. My presentation stops here, however, as I am not in a position to comment on the legal case and there have been enough materials for illustrating the basic points of this book.

but desk clock manufacturers in Shanghai stopped their production once the state quotas were fulfilled. Goods were overstocked in thousands of enterprises, but there was a rule discouraging these enterprises from selling their products to buyers in other countries. The Sichuan Airline needed new planes to expand; nevertheless, they were ignorant of the manufacturers in Russia who could produce the airplanes that they could afford. Many local authorities would like to air popular television programmes; unfortunately, satellite renting was once reserved only for national stations. There was nothing wild even in his proposal of transforming thousands of state-owned enterprises by making use of western financial capital – China overtook the US in attracting direct foreign investment in 2002.

In fact, many entrepreneurs in China have followed the same line of thinking. That their businesses are less visible than Mou's is largely because they do not cross so many institutional domains. But they do recognize and utilize the opportunities embedded in institutional holes, as we saw in Chapter 4. When they found that it was costly to register a private firm, they claimed that theirs were collective or joint-venture, or they became a part of a state enterprise. When they could not afford an expensive patent, they offered an attractive salary to a technician of a state firm who would provide the know-how. They complained about unreasonable charges and fees imposed by local bureaucrats on the one hand, but they escaped a larger amount of tax on the other hand. In order to obtain a better deal with the government and to show off their financial prowess, they offered the status of nominal trustees to relatives and friends who actually contributed nothing to the business. To shake off administrative constraints on their development, they helped local governments build hospitals, schools, libraries, and other public facilities, and claimed that they did so to return the favour to their fellow residents. Many private enterprises transformed themselves into shareholding companies, but those holding the largest number of shares turned out to be their family members. Crossing the lines of institutional sites is the norm.

There are two main differences between Mou Qizhong and many other private entrepreneurs in China. First, whilst most entrepreneurs cross institutional sites only when there are no other institutionally more legitimate routes to profit-making, Mou thought that making deals across multiple institutional sites was actually the most effective business strategy. He did not pay much attention, however, to the strong conditions under which the strategy would succeed or fail. Suffice it to mention two such conditions. First, it may be usually fine to manipulate the rules or to enter 'a grey area', but some transgressions can induce a price too high to pay. This is especially true when the behaviours of the business partners are beyond control. Mou however seemed to be ignorant of the legal consequences of manipulating state policies and administrative regulations. He deeply believed that as long as he could prove he was standing at the frontier of China's economic reform by writing letters to top leaders, he and his business would be eventually left intact. In addition, very few of his senior assistants had the interest or the competence to offer legal advice to him. In the end, he landed in jail not on political or moral charges but on legal charges.

Another condition for his strategy to operate successfully is that the resources have to be readily available for combination. In other words, for the last one degree of heat to bring the water to the boiling point, the water must have already reached

99°C. After the success of the Russian aircraft deal, only the last degree seemed to be important to him, which explains why he kept throwing out attractive but unrealistic plans, ignorant of the fact that the other 99 degrees were not there yet and it would take a long time, a large amount of resources, and a lot of hard work on his side to make them ready.

The second difference between Mou and other entrepreneurs in China is that the latter do not seriously take the legitimization of their businesses as a part of their job; they only argue and fight for their businesses' legitimacy after the legitimacy is challenged. Initially, Mou was also forced to prove the legitimacy of his business, but later he started to put defending his firm's legitimacy as an important item in his agenda. He seemed to have no interest in the technical aspects of his projects, such as finance and accounting, technological details and employment relations, leaving all these matters to his assistants while spending most of his time writing articles, delivering speeches, meeting journalists, and so on. His hope was that these activities would earn him 'invisible assets', which would constitute his competitive advantage. In fact, he showed little interest in winning the hearts and minds of the journalists, the people on the street, and his own employees. All these people, however, have had their own say on the legitimacy of his business from legal, moral, and cultural perspectives.

For private entrepreneurs in China, to be financially big as well as politically safe is a tricky business. In the next chapter we shall see how the double missions can be accomplished at the same time.

Chapter 8

Entrepreneurial Authority and Institutional Autonomy: Xu Wenrong and the Hengdian Group

The two entrepreneurs studied in the preceeding chapters, Mou Qizhong and Huo Hongmin, both ran into difficult confrontations with state officials soon after an initial success. In this chapter, we turn to an entrepreneur who managed to keep his enterprises clear of governmental interventions – Mr. Xu Wenrong, the founder and leader of the Hengdian Group in the province of Zhejiang. If the puzzle for the previous two cases is how the entrepreneurs exploited institutional holes but were later trapped into disputes with state officials, then the puzzle for Hengdian is its very success: how has it survived waves of institutional changes and sustained its status at the top of non-state enterprises in China?[1]

First of all, it is a success in financial terms. When Xu started his first factory with less than 300,000 yuan in 1975,[2] most residents at Hengdian had no experience of working in a factory at all. Thirty years later in 2005, Hengdian grew into a business giant, with a total asset more than 16.6 billion yuan,[3] ranking one of top three non-state companies in China and one of the top 500 ethnic Chinese businesses in the world. With more than 200 companies under its direct control and many other loosely controlled firms, it contributed more than 1.2 billion to China's national revenue in 2005 alone. Today, Hengdian boasts itself to be the second largest supplier of magnetic materials in the world and is on its way to becoming China's Hollywood, operating a joint-venture with the China Film Group and Warner Brothers.

But the financial success is only a consequence of another success in the institutional arena. And it is these institutional aspects of Xu's entrepreneurship, including his authority, his relations with local officials, his mobilization of resources,

---

1   Xu Wenrong believes that the amazing development of Hengdian is a puzzle that deserves serious attention from some of the best minds in the world. He has invited ten Nobel laureates in economics to Hengdian to find out what has made the achievement possible. According to the company's website (http://www.hengdiangroup.com), so far three Nobel Prize winners have agreed to pay a visit.

2   In his book, *Heng Dian Zhi Lu* (*The Road of Hengdian*, Beijing: People's Press, 1994, p. 1), Xu claimed that he started with only 2,000 yuan. That was the amount of money he borrowed from local residents, not the total start-up capital. In fact, most of the start-up capital (about 240,000 yuan) actually came from bank loans.

3   Xu Yongan's speech at the conference held on 8 February 2006, published on the Hengdian Group's website. Xu Yongan is Xu Wenrong's son, currently the Chairman and Chief Executive of Hengdian Group.

and the transfer of his power to his son, that my study in this chapter will focus on. Many economists in China have visited Hengdian and they have made some valuable contributions to the study of Xu and Hengdian.[4] Most of them, however, seem to be happy with a sketchy account of the institutional conditions for Xu's entrepreneurship. To my knowledge, the number of academic studies published in English remains very small, and they are more interested in business activities themselves than in the institutional environment in which the activities take place.[5] One of the reasons for the lack of attention to Hengdian outside China is perhaps the very successful nature of this enterprise – unless in business-schools, social scientists in the West usually shun the analysis of a single successful case. Perhaps they are concerned with the external validity of a single case and the suspicion of being biased in selecting the case. I think that these concerns are unnecessary. For a case study, the most important thing is what it can, not what it cannot, tell us. If we want to learn more, then we should study another case. Whilst the researcher is obliged to keep the study as analytical as possible and provide the necessary information for others to understand the case, eventually whether the researcher has taken a biased view in selecting and analysing the case is a judgement to be made by the reader.

I choose to study Xu and Hengdian mainly for two reasons. In the first place, the institutional aspects of Hengdian's development are of direct relevance to the theme of this book, i.e., the institutional dynamics of entrepreneurship in China. The fast and nearly uninterrupted growth of this remote and impoverished village can help us to better understand the institutional sources of economic development in rural China. For example, one distinctive feature of Hengdian is its property ownership. Though being honoured as one of the best TVE both provincially and nationally, Hengdian

4   Shen Weiguang and his associates published several books in 1993 and 1994, which provide some basic materials about Xu and Hengdian, including *Hengdian Mou Shi* (*The Hengdian Model*), *Heng Dian She Tuan Jing Ji Mou Shi Yan Ju* (*A Study of Hengdian's Model of Community Economy*), and *Heng Dian De Jing Shen Wen Ming Jian She* (*The Construction of Spiritual Civilization at Hengdian*), all by People's Press. Shen, with He Wei and Wei Jie, also compiled a collection of comments and short essays by some of the most prominent economists in China on Hengdian – *Zhu Ming Zhuan Jia Xue Zhe Lun Heng Dian* (*Observations by Prominent Scholars on Hengdian*, People's Press, 1994). Later, Sun Shiyan, who is now in charge of a research institute at Hengdian, published two books about Hengdian: *Wen Hua Li: Heng Dian De Qi Shi* (*The Power of Culture: Lessons from Hengdian*), Beijing: Zhong Yang Dang Xiao Chu Ban She (School of the Chinese Communist Party Press, 1995) and *Shi Chang Xing Gong You Zhi: Hengdian Chan Quan Zhi Du Xi Tong Kao Cha* (*A Market Type Public Ownership: A Systematic Investigation on the Hengdian Model's Property Ownership Institutions*, Shanghai: San Lian Press, 1998). In 1997, the journal of *Economic Research* (*Jing Ji Yan Jiu*) organized a forum on the case of Hengdian.

5   Jianbao Chen and G.H. Jefferson, 'Development of the Hengdian Township Enterprise Group: A Case Study', pp. 279–287 in Gary H. Jefferson and Inderjit (Hg.) Singh (eds), *Enterprise Reform in China: Ownership, Transition, and Performance* (Oxford University Press, 1999). From a process perspective, David Brown, Hantang Qi, and Yong Zhang compared Hengdian's strategic development with that of Shangfeng, anther enterprise in Zhejiang, 'Insights into strategy development in China's TVEs', pp. 72–86 in David H. Brown and Alasdair I. MacBean (eds), *Challenges for China's Development: An Enterprise Perspective* (Routledge, 2005).

is not a TVE in the sense commonly taken in the current literature. For most TVE, their assets belong to the local community *de jure*, although local officials may act as the chief executives or closely supervise the business's operation. Andrew Walder, Jean Oi and others have contributed this tight coupling between business and local government to the fast development of rural China.[6] As we shall see below, Hengdian does not seem to fit into this model. After several years of initial growth, Xu felt that the connection of his enterprise to the local authority was a pain to be removed rather than an advantage to enjoy. He believes that the severance of its tie to local officials is a major reason for the success of the Hengdian Group. With the administrative affiliation to local governments gone, Xu has declared that the Hengdian Group is owned by all who are working for it, which he dubbed 'community ownership', another important institutional source of business success. In this chapter I shall make a sensible connection between Xu's entrepreneurial authority, Hengdian Group's institutional autonomy, Xu's entrepreneurial strategies of mobilizing resources, and future challenges to the enterprise's institutional structure.

Xu Wenrong's ideas and strategies offer a useful reference in comparison with those of Huo Hongmin and Mou Qizhong, which is the second reason for choosing this case. In addition, it is also interesting and informative to compare Xu with Mr. Yu Zuomin, who has drawn much more attention from academic researchers in the US.[7] Yu was the founder of Dayu Group in the village of Daqiu, located in a suburb of Huo's hometown, the metropolitan city of Tianjin. Both Xu and Yu were born, and grew up, in a poverty-stricken remote village. As young leaders of their villages, they were desperately searching for a way out of poverty. They didn't share Mou's grand ambitions and would not try his tricks of making business connections. Like Huo, they wanted to become rich by selling tangible products. They have proved that an entrepreneur in China does not have to adopt Mou's fanciful strategies in order to achieve an enviable success in market competition. Rather, entrepreneurs in China will become even more successful if they do not make use of institutional holes as Mou did. Xu and Yu have something that Huo and Mou could do nothing but envy: Xu and Yu could mobilize all the resources in their villages and, once they showed their initial success, they could enjoy recognition and support provided willingly by upper-level governments. What distinguishes Xu from Yu is Yu's arrogance toward state agents. As we shall see below, Xu has been much more careful in cultivating collegial relations with upper-level officials, another contributing factor to his success. Of course, these cross-comparisons will not come into a comprehensive analysis of the parameters and corresponding scenarios of entrepreneurship in China, but I believe the comparative study will shed light, in a complementary manner, on

---

6   Walder, 'Local Governments as Industrial Firms: An Organizational Analysis of China's Transitional Economy', *American Journal of Sociology*, 101/2 (1995): 263–301. Oi, *Rural China Takes Off: Institutional Foundations of Economic Reform* (University of California Press, 1999).

7   Bruce Gilley, *Model Rebels: The Rise and Fall of China's Richest Village* (University of California Press, 2001). Nan Lin, 'Local Market Socialism: Local Corporatism in Action in Rural China', *Theory and Society*, 24 (1995): 301–354.

different aspects of entrepreneurship, especially the conditions and growing patterns of entrepreneurship during the initial periods of China's institutional changes.

I shall start with an overview of Xu and Hengdian Group, thereby setting up a backdrop for the following more specific discussions. Then my presentation will focus on three questions, all pertinent to the institutional dimensions of Xu's entrepreneurship. First, how did he establish and maintain his authority as an entrepreneur in an institutionally hostile environment? What is the foundation for his entrepreneurial authority? Second, what is 'communal ownership', which Xu has insisted on but recently struggled to keep under pressures from all sides? Why does it matter to him so much? Third, how have his entrepreneurial authority and communal ownership enabled him to mobilize local resources for bringing Hengdian to a fast track of enormous development? How has he been entrepreneurial in setting up Hengdian Group's internal institutional structure? I shall finish the chapter by summarizing comments on the Hengdian model and pointing out some institutional challenges to Hengdian Group's future development.

An overview

Zhejiang is a coastal province in eastern China, bordering the metropolitan Shanghai to the north. About 70 per cent of its area is covered by mountains and hills; plains at the coastlines, and valleys near the rivers. The town of Hengdian is right in the middle of Zhejiang. As it is surrounded by hills and there is no major river within commutable distance, for decades transportation was a problem. It also has been troubled with a very low rate of arable land *per capita* – in 1992 the total population was approximately 30,000, with each individual having less than half a *mu* (or one-twelfth of an acre). The natural environment was so hostile to agricultural activities that it became clear to local residents that it would be impossible for their material life to improve if they did not do something other than toiling in the field. For hundreds of years Hengdian was well known as a centre for markets and trades, with generations of craftsmen, merchants, and traders. Despite its commercial tradition, this highly populated place suffered from impoverishment since the establishment of the People's Republic in 1949, especially in the 1960s.

One positive thing about the politically and economically devastating conditions is that they supplied a powerful motivating force for Xu Wenrong and other capable young men, who desperately wanted to get out of poverty. With nothing to lose, they embarked on a venture of setting up some factories, such as crop processing, metal appliances, wood carving, and so on, taking economic as well as political risks. Indeed, the venture proved to be a rollercoaster. They started to organize and operate several factories in the early 1960s, when the State issued some liberal economic policies under the leadership of Liu Shaoqi. With the Cultural Revolution spreading out across the whole nation and Liu being arrested and tortured by Red Guards, the factories built by Xu and his associates were labelled as 'capitalist' and consequently shut down. Like other rural areas in China, Hengdian was quickly transformed into a People's Commune, which brought local residents even deeper into poverty. These young men had no other choice but to start again. To avoid political harassment, the factories were established and operated in the name of 'developing the economy of People's Commune'. When the Cultural Revolution came to its end in 1976, these young entrepreneurs had accumulated the experience of operating seven businesses, although not all of them survived.

Xu and his fellow residents believe that Hengdian's industrialization started from the construction of a silk factory in 1975. Similar to the liberalization of state policies on setting up individual businesses (*getihu*) in urban areas, the provincial government of Zhejiang approved Hengdian's application for building a silk factory to solve an urgent and practical problem. The year 1975 saw a big harvest of silkworms, the raw material for silk production. Before, most of the silkworms would be purchased by Zhejiang's Bureau of Light Industries and then distributed to state-owned silk factories. Like many other state enterprises, these silk factories were in a state of stagnation or even on the brink of collapse as a result of ten years' political turmoil. The harvested silkworms seemed to have nowhere to go. Running out of options, the Bureau finally gave the farmers the green light to set up 16 silk factories in Zhejiang. Learning of the new policy from a friend, Xu immediately realized that this was a valuable, and rare, opportunity. After rounds of networking to put the needed 'red stamps' on their application, he eventually obtained a permit from the Bureau.

To Xu Wenrong and other residents at Hengdian, this was a significant event, because it was the first time that they had the authorization from the provincial government for constructing a factory. As the Party Secretary of the village, and the person with perhaps the most experience of business management, the entrusted Xu was put in the leading position of setting up the factory. Everything seemed to be ready for making the new venture into a successful operation: the raw materials were already there, technicians from a state-owned enterprise would come to offer technical help, and the Bureau would purchase the silk as a part of the State's purchasing plan. Therefore, Xu's entrepreneurship was not manifested in recognizing the opportunity. Rather, his entrepreneurship was expressed in mobilizing and organizing the necessary resources in setting up the business on the ground. What he needed most urgently were two things: money for purchasing the machines and workers who could operate them. Training the workers was not a problem; some people were sent out to state enterprises to learn the skills and came back to train others. For the start-up capital, Xu did make a great effort to borrow money from local residents, but he ended up only with 2,000 yuan. It was obvious that they would not have their factory ready without borrowing money from a state bank. In the end, the Bank of Agriculture agreed to grant them a loan but demanded that they show some evidence of repaying capacity. Xu then borrowed another 50,000 yuan from the residents of 39 nearby villages. In the end, he successfully secured a loan of more than 240,000 yuan.[8]

The successful acquisition of bank loans would be impossible if their factory were not registered as a town enterprise, a legitimate component of China's national economy albeit of a lower status at that time. State banks set aside a certain amount of credits for supporting community enterprises in rural areas. Not every village enterprise could eventually obtain such a support, of course, but local leaders like

---

8   Shen et al., *The Hengdian Model*, p. 10.

Xu could *argue* for their entitlement to the support. But in order to obtain permits and supports from the State, this new enterprise had to put on a 'red cap' from the outset. As we shall see later, Xu denounced that the assets of the enterprise belonged to any local government.[9] Note that, although Xu's silk factory and Huo's beverage factory were both wearing a 'red cap', Xu's was much more 'collective' than Huo's. This explains why the town leaders at Dazhong would not support Huo as much as they supported their own businesses, although she registered her company as a TVE in the name of the town. Indeed, as later events show, Xu's dual statuses as an entrepreneur as well as a local leader put him in an advantageous position, particularly for mobilizing local resources and having access to resources controlled by the State.

The silk factory started to operate in February 1976. Within only two years they made a profit of 360,000, more than enough to pay off what was borrowed from the bank and the villagers. Since then the number of factories built and operated at Hengdian has multiplied. Although not all of them have been successful, Hengdian's industrial output has increased at an extraordinarily fast speed (Table 8.1).

Table 8.1 Selected indicators of Hengdian's growth (million yuan), 1983 to 2005

Year	Industrial output	Total sales	Total asset
1983	12.24	–	3.57
1984	19	–	–
1985	38	–	–
1987	110	–	–
1990	180	–	133
1991	305	–	–
1992	600	–	205
1993	1,080	–	–
1994	1,750	–	–
1999	5,400	–	5,580
2002	–	–	7,181
2003	–	12,020	12,990
2004	–	14,225	14,249
2005	–	14,750	16,668

Source: Shen, et al., *Hengdian Mou Shi* (*The Hengdian Model*); Sun, Wen Hua Li (*The Power of Culture*); Hengdian website.

Since then, Hengdian has enhanced its administrative status by absorbing many other less developed surrounding villages. Almost every family has at least one member working at a Hengdian enterprise. With the addition of immigrant workers,

---

9   Xu confessed such experience to Zhu Huoze, see p. 19 in He Wei, Wei Jie, and Shen Weigang (eds), *Zhu Ming Zhuan Jia Xu Zhe Lun Heng Dian*.

the total population of Hengdian in 2005 reached nearly 80,000, more than doubling the figure a dozen years ago.

People at Hengdian see the silk factory as the hen and all other enterprises as the 'hatched chickens'. The metaphor suggests a very high rate of reinvestment, a factor critical to the speedy development of Hengdian and most of other non-state enterprises in China.[10] Another contributing factor at the macro level is the liberalization of state policies right after Hengdian accomplished its initial success. But both factors exist for other non-state enterprises as well, so they do not offer a convincing explanation for Hengdian's extraordinary success. To me, Hengdian can get ahead of others largely because of its institutional autonomy, which in turn depends upon the leading entrepreneur's personal authority. In other words, I see the establishment of Xu Wenrong's entrepreneurial authority as the major source of Hengdian's growth. Without his authority, it would have been impossible for Hengdian to obtain its institutional autonomy at a level rarely seen in other rural areas. The institutional autonomy then provides a platform on which Xu and his associates can mobilize, consolidate, and make full use of all resources available to them.

Entrepreneurial authority

With the success of the first silk plant, Xu proved himself a capable business leader. From then on he reinforced his authority at Hengdian through a series of strategic decisions. Such entrepreneurship-based authority deserves careful discussion because it drives the development of many local enterprises in rural China, with Yu Zuomin at Daqiu and Shi Laihe at Liu Zhuang (Henan Province) being the most well-known examples.

Entrepreneurial authority can be seen as a special type of charismatic authority, although we can not expect an entrepreneur to carry all the characteristics of a charismatic authority defined as an ideal type.[11] An entrepreneur distinguishes himself (or herself) from the followers by some extraordinary qualities, such as the ability to recognize a business opportunity, the capacity to put different resources together in an organized form, etc. Obviously, entrepreneurs do not have supernatural or superhuman qualities that shamans and prophets are usually believed to possess. For entrepreneurial authority, the most two distinctive qualities are recognizing opportunities and transforming available resources into profits. The greater the contrast between an opportunity's uncertainty beforehand and the success later achieved, the more authority the entrepreneur will have. Similarly, the higher the ratio of profits to resources, the more established the authority will be. One feature shared by Hengdian, Daqiu, and Liuzhuang is their disadvantaged natural conditions.

---

10 According to Xu, no dividends were paid within the first three years of operation of the silk factory, suggesting an almost 100 per cent reinvestment rate (p. 7 of Volume 1 and p. 33 of Volume 3 of his *Collected Works*, People's Press, 2005). For the whole TVE or private sector, I am not aware of any specific and reliable measurements of the reinvestment rate.

11 Max Weber, *Economy and Society*, vol. 1, pp. 241–245 (University of California Press, 1978).

This low starting point ironically serves well to sharpen a great contrast with the earnings made, thus enhancing the extraordinary charisma of the entrepreneur. The entrepreneur's exceptionality can also be established and reinforced by contrasting the entrepreneur's personal background with the achievement. Again, the higher the ratio of achievements to background, the more magical the achievement seems to be, and the more undisputable the entrepreneurial authority will be.

Born in 1935, Xu had the misfortune to spend his childhood during the wars (the anti-Japanese war from 1938 to 1945 followed by the civil war till 1949). He became terse when talking about himself:

> I am not a very capable man. I only have primary school education. But I started to learn business management when I was still very young, following my father to do some small businesses. I started to work in commerce at the age of 18 [1953], so I understand cost accounting.[12]

In China, being humble is a great virtue, especially after one has made a name in the public memory. However, Xu would not let his humbleness compromise the evaluation of his capacity. No doubt, he knew he was one of the most capable men in his town, if not the most capable. The trick of balancing humbleness and self-efficacy is to make a distinction between two types of capacities: one measured by formal education and the other represented by first-hand business experience, which he emphasized in the above words. The contrast between his rich experience and his low level of formal education made the experience even more valuable.

In fact, residents of Hengdian have somewhat mythologized Xu Wenrong's extraordinary quality. According to a popular folklore, many and many years ago a golden buffalo turned up at Hengdian. When people were chasing it down, the golden buffalo had nowhere to go but to rush into the Mountain of Eight Facets (*ba mian shan*). Then it told the people that it would not come out until someone could walk around the mountain with 1,000-year old rice straws in hand. Xu has been believed to be the man who can lead the golden buffalo out of the mountain.[13]

The folklore suggests another basis of entrepreneurial authority. As Weber points out, the legitimacy of charismatic authority does not really lie in the genuineness of the charisma but in the 'recognition on the part of those subject to authority'.[14] That is, the circulation of the folklore among the residents of Hengdian *per se* is a proof that they have recognized Xu's entrepreneurial leadership. Furthermore, the legitimacy of charismatic authority is usually based on the subjects' enthusiasm, despair, and hope.[15] Indeed, it was the local residents' desperation in searching for someone who could lead the golden buffalo out, i.e., make them rich, that made Xu's entrepreneurship possible in the first place. Of course, in the meantime, Xu had to show his charisma by producing a 'miracle' – a profit of tens of thousands of yuan was enormous in those years in rural China. It was the combination of despair, desire,

---

12 Shen et al., *The Hengdian Model*, p. 23.

13 Ibid., p. 24.

14 Weber, *Economy and Society*, p. 242.

15 Ibid.

and miraculous business profits that eventually established Xu's entrepreneurial authority.

Xu could not sustain his authority simply with the success of a single silk plant, of course. He had to constantly recharge the legitimacy of his authority with further 'miracles'. One of these sustaining miracles was his strategic decisions on restructuring the enterprises at Hengdian. On 22 November 1984, under Xu's request, the 28 town-enterprises and 481 other smaller enterprises were incorporated into Hengdian Industrial Corporation, laying the foundation for remarkable growth and the establishment of the Hengdian Group. In 1987, Xu came to believe that, with the gradual recovery of state enterprises, the textile market in general and the silk industry in particular would become more and more competitive. Although most of the factories at Hengdian were still making money, he decided to shutdown three large silk factories, sell two not profitable enterprises, and lease out more than ten other businesses. He then reinvested the money in magnetic and pharmaceutical products, which later became Hengdian's two pillar industries. In 2001, while helping a prominent movie director produce a film on the Opium War, he had the idea of turning Hengdian into a centre of movie production and tourism. Now, Hengdian boasts itself to be 'Chinawood', with a movie production area almost as twice the size of Beverly Hills and more than 3 million visitors each year.

What is equally important to his authority, but has not been fully appreciated, is Xu's extraordinary talent for nurturing a collegial social environment at Hengdian. Unlike many successful private entrepreneurs in China, who usually set up their businesses in large urban areas, for the initial years Xu and his enterprises were bound onto the land of his hometown. It meant that he was under constant and close monitoring of his fellow villagers. If he could deliver what was expected from him without putting his own interest before those of his fellow villagers, then the villagers would lend their support wholeheartedly, and the good relationship itself would be a valuable asset. Otherwise, the villagers could turn into a powerful force against him. Later when Hengdian had to invite and employ a growing number of workers, technicians, officials, and specialists from places far away from Hengdian, the job of maintaining friendly social relations became even more critical to success. Among the managers employed were some important officials from the local county Dong Yang and the city of Jin Hua. Many technicians and specialists were from privileged research institutions in China. Like the villagers, they recognize Xu's entrepreneurial authority out of despair and hope. Xu understood perfectly that these people wanted not only a decent material life but also his generosity; he allowed them to try, to fail, and even to become not as outstanding as claimed before. No information is available to tell us the turnover rate, but the growing number of highly skilled employees – from several in the early 1980s to more than 2,000 in 2006 – suggests that his authority has made him very successful in recruiting employees as well.

Institutional autonomy

Hengdian's success would be impossible without its relatively high institutional autonomy, which in turn would be impossible without Xu's entrepreneurial authority. Being asked about the contributing factors to Hengdian's success, Xu firstly said he never carefully thought about this question, but soon it became clear that institutional autonomy was the primary reason, because the separation of enterprise from government was the first explanation that came to his mind. It means that:

> All issues about our enterprise, such as strategic decision making, development, management, personnel, redistribution, and others, are to be decided by Hengdian Group; local governments do not intervene, which we call 'govern with no actions' (*wu wei er zhi*).[16]

Readers familiar with the current literature of China's economic development will find these arguments at odds with some of the institutionalist explanations. For example, according to Andrew Walder and Jean Oi, the key institutional source of rural China's remarkable growth is exactly the coupling of local governments and industrial enterprises – the core of the 'local governments as industrial firms' thesis.[17] They argue that China's fiscal reforms since the early 1980s have hardened the budget constraints on local governments, thus turning them into highly self-reliant cost centres. The motivation for improving the welfare of their own and their local residents, combined with the capacity of directly administering and monitoring industrial enterprises in their jurisdictions, has become a powerful source of energy for engaging in profit-making industrial actions.

As the former Party Secretary of a production brigade (an administrative unit right below the commune or town), Xu was one of the local cadres. But his experience defies the above theory not because he was not motivated by the deal of retaining an attractive portion of the profits made – his enterprises started years before the fiscal reforms – but because he completely rejected the idea of running industrial firms as governmental businesses *even after the fiscal reforms started*. According to him, the involvement of local officials in business activities can only be counterproductive, because it is impossible for a local government to have extra energy to manage businesses properly when its main responsibility is administration. More importantly, it is detrimental to China's socialist market economy to allow local governments to penetrate into business enterprises; if every leader in a town (the Party Secretary, the Governor, the Director of Industries, etc.) manages his (or her) own enterprises, then soon they will end up in 'internal wars', weakening their managerial power.[18] What they care about the most is their records of political performance during their tenure, not the long-term economic performance of the enterprise.[19]

Both points are controversial. Whether local governments have energy or not to manage industrial businesses is a matter of choice. If they can handle other

---

16 Shen et al., *The Hengdian Model*, p. 13.
17 Walder, 1995. Oi, 1999.
18 Shen et al., *The Hengdian Model*, p. 13.
19 Xu, *Collected Works*, volume 3, p. 36.

administrative matters, why can't they handle the task of opening and operating new businesses? Furthermore, it is true that in some rural areas different local leaders are in charge of different enterprises, but that does not necessarily lead to irreconcilable conflicts or 'internal wars'. Again, if Xu can manage all the enterprises at Hengdian, why can't another local Part Secretary provide effective leadership? If he can delegate some of his responsibilities to his deputies, why does division of labour among local leaders of other areas have to end up in chaotic confrontations?

In my view, the very reason that Xu does not want to follow the 'government as business' model is to secure the institutional autonomy of his business empire. An assumption of this model is that local government officials care about their political careers. In other words, while promoting local enterprises, they still want to keep their political positions; the increased financial incentives are a wonderful bonus, but they are bonus only, not attractive enough to make them give up the political power in their hands. There are some local officials who eventually 'step into the sea' (take a career in business), but there is no evidence that the majority of local officials have abandoned their political statuses; most of them have managed to straddle two domains. For them, the ideal is to let their political power and financial gain strengthen each other. What distinguishes Xu from most other local leaders is that he values his business more than his political career. And he realized that in China's institutional environment it is much easier to exercise control over one's commercial business than over the political system. Therefore, for the business to enjoy sustainable growth, it is better to take it out of the political system than to keep it inside.

During the initial years of managing the factories, Xu did not receive much incentive from upper-level governments. On the contrary, what he received was distrust, envy, administrative hassles, and even harassment. For several years after he started the silk factory he was not designated the factory's Party Secretary. In the early 1980s, based on some unfounded allegations, a group of officials spent several months investigating his misconducts.[20] What Xu felt the most unacceptable was the fact that his hands were tied up although he was the one who actually managed the factories and made them profitable. It was the Party Secretary of Hengdian Commune, not him as the factory manager, who had the final say on recruitment of employees. In addition, although employees worked in the factory, it was the village leader who decided how much each employee should get paid, because the factory was under the administration of village. Any proposal for expansions or new projects would have to be approved by the Commune leaders, who nevertheless did not take any supporting responsibilities. All middle and upper level managers at the factory were appointed by the Commune. For a long time, it was an accountant directly responsible to the Commune who took charge of the factory's finance. The Commune and the County could intervene at any time they wanted. Finally, despite the factory's financial situation, a predetermined proportion of profits and fees had to be submitted to upper-level governments.

To break free of these administrative constraints, Xu and his fellow residents 'drove away' five local officials in charge of the town's industries. He also made

---

20 Ibid., p. 25.

many visits to county leaders, asking for a more 'hands-off' Party Secretary. However, such manoeuvring did not help very much because it was not about any particular individual above Xu; whoever it was in the position, as part of his duties, the local leader was supposed to do something about Xu's enterprises. Therefore, something dramatic had to be done.

The year of 1984 was a turning point for Hengdian. The Central Committee of CCP and the State Council issued a document calling for an accelerated development of industrial enterprises in rural China. Backed by the support of state policies and armed with an impressive record of industrial performance – millions of profits, 28 core enterprises plus hundreds of smaller businesses, Xu Wenrong believed that it was time to completely sever the administrative tie with local government. Under his request, Hengdian Industrial Corporation was established as an economic organization independent of government administrations. In the meantime, Hengdian Town's Office of Industries, once the government agent directly on top of Xu's enterprises, was abolished. The following points would define the new relationship between the town government and the enterprise:

1. The government shall no longer intervene into the Corporation's managerial activities, including employment, expansion, distribution, investment, etc.;
2. The local government shall no longer take profits made by the Corporation, as the Corporation shall be financially independent and responsible for its own performance;
3. Responsibilities of the former Office of Industries will be taken over by the Corporation, including helping village and household enterprises;
4. Depending on its capacity, the Corporation will voluntarily provide financial support to the construction of local public infrastructures, while at the same time, the town government shall not impose any unreasonable fees and charges in the name of constructing public projects;
5. The Corporation will fulfil all other political or social responsibilities, including environment, hygiene, birth control, public security, etc., but how these are to be done is a matter to be dealt with by the Corporation.

All these points were approved by upper-level governments. How the town leaders reacted to such an arrangement is unclear, but it is clear that the resistance, if any, was not strong enough to reverse Xu's proposal. One possible explanation for the smooth transition would be the exchange of financial contributions for administrative independence, perhaps another example of symbiotic relationship between a non-state enterprise and local government.[21] For local officials, to reject Xu's request would be economically disastrous and politically suicidal; a smart move

---

21 Xu once summarized such relationship as the following: 'Our enterprise is grateful for the government's guidance and service, and the government praises the enterprise's cooperation and support' (*Collected Works*, volume 1, p. 287). More generally, David Wank has focused his analysis on the symbiotic relationship between private businesses and local governments in his book *Commodifying Communism: Business, Trust, and Politics in a Chinese City* (Cambridge University Press, 1999).

was to reap the economic contributions by the enterprise and keep it as a feather on their cap. In return, Xu needed to demonstrate how his model of 'industrial firms as local governments' would be a good deal for local officials. Xu claimed that his enterprises had invested more than 1 billion yuan in public projects at Hengdian in 20 years, between 1975 to 1995, including the town government building, police stations, nurseries, schools, hospitals, libraries, theatres, museums, parks, etc.[22]

Such a symbiotic relationship would not be sustainable if it were not set in the context of liberal state policies and Xu's entrepreneurial authority. Recall that 1984 witnessed one of the most liberal periods in the history of China's economic reforms, and it was in that year that Xu's business showed the potential of becoming a business giant. Xu is clearly aware that his business cannot operate completely outside of China's political system. After all, he is still a member of the CCP and there has to be a Party Committee *within* his business. Although interventions from local governments have been kept at bay, further denunciation of the relationship with the dominant ruling party will mean the end of his business. The question is how to keep a working relationship with the Party while minimizing the hassles that the relationship would potentially entail. Obviously, just as he would not accept someone at the local government telling him what he has to do, nor would he work with a Party Secretary in his corporation who may disagree with him or ask him to act against his will. The easiest solution was to make the conflict impossible by setting up the necessary institutional arrangement. Before retreating to the backstage in 2001, Xu was both the chief executive as well as the Party Secretary of Hengdian Group, and he justifies that the concentration of power will be in the best interests of the enterprise by ruling out the possibility of 'internal wars', although he never specifies the foundation of his consolidated power and never discusses whether his power should be checked or monitored.[23] The enterprise's link to the Party is via one of his deputies. That is, daily businesses of the Party Committee, such as sitting in meetings, report-writing, handling problematic cases, etc., were all handled by a professional bureaucrat as Hengdian Group's Deputy Party Secretary. The essential function of this deputy, however, is to shield Xu from wasting his time on matters not related to profit-making activities without giving the deputy any institutional basis for challenging Xu's authority.

What we should discuss next is the effect of Xu's institutional autonomy on his business strategies and practices. But before doing that we need to learn about the ownership of Hengdian's enterprises, as the ownership determines where the strategies come from and where they are to be implemented.

Communal ownership

At the time of writing (April 2006), the ownership of Hengdian Group's assets and its transformation are still under consideration and discussion. As we have seen in

---

22 Xu, *Collected Works*, volume 1, p. 270 and volume 2, p. 158.
23 Ibid., p. 15.

previous chapters, ownership has been a sensitive issue for both politicians and entrepreneurs in China. It is perhaps even more so at Hengdian after Xu declared that the assets of Hengdian Group were neither state-owned, nor town- or village-owned, nor privately owned, but were communally owned. Economists in China disagree over whether Hengdian's ownership structure is clear, whilst those in the West hold different points of view as to whether clear ownership is a precondition for better economic performance. To those involved in Hengdian's businesses, this is more than a theoretical issue – clarification of ownership means who deserves how big a piece of Hengdian's total assets. To me, Xu's effort of arguing for communal ownership represents his entrepreneurial strategy of acquiring and maintaining institutional autonomy.

The issue of ownership started to draw serious attention from Hengdian and Xu Wenrong in 1993, the year in which the enterprises at Hengdian became united as the first TVE Group approved by the Office of Economy and Trade, an agent of the State Council. The approval not only represented the national government's recognition of Hengdian Group's economic achievements but more importantly it granted Hengdian an economic status at the national level with privileges that most other TVE were envious of, such as access to technology, financial credits, imports and exports, etc.

In the same year, the call for transforming nearly all types of domestic enterprises into share-holding companies gained enormous momentum. The neo-classical institutional theory found its biggest audience in the world. It was widely believed that the share-holding system represented an advanced economic structure because property rights were clear, which would in turn generate strong incentives for economic actors. Successful enterprises were expected to take the lead in a movement like this, and Hengdian was no exception. Leaders of Zhejiang Province and other government agents came to Hengdian in an attempt to convince Xu to join the crowd. It was estimated that Xu could be granted more than 10 per cent of Hengdian Group's total assets; that is, he could become a multi-millionaire overnight.

But Xu had his own ideas. He had declared that he is against the idea of quantifying Hengdian's assets into shares and distributing them to individuals because privatization would weaken rather than strengthen Hengdian's overall economic development.[24] First and foremost, he argued that it is almost impossible to identify the 'true owners' of collective assets, and the cost of arbitrarily assigning ownership to particular individuals is likely to be unbearably high. In theory, every individual who has contributed to the development of Hengdian, regardless of the way in which the contribution was made, deserves a certain number of shares. In practice, however, it is not so straightforward. It might be easy to identify the contributions made by key employees, but how about other stakeholders who once provided a variety of support to the Group, especially during the initial years. For example, officials at local governments offered some administrative support to the enterprise, and some residents introduced their highly skilled relatives or friends to Hengdian. It is not at all clear how to determine a 'fair' number of shares. In

---

24 Xu, *Collected Works*, volume 1, p. 311.

addition, Xu has been concerned about the return of 'internal wars'. That is, once the share-holding system is established, conflicts are hardly avoidable between 'the three old committees' – party committee, labour union, and employee representative committee – and 'the three new committees' – the shareholder committee, the board of directors, and the monitoring committee. Xu has worried that the cost of solving these problems is so high that the business empire built with his whole heart and life will have already collapsed before the new system shows its claimed advantages.

These concerns may be valid, but the fact is that the number of TVE and private enterprises that have transformed themselves into share-holding companies is increasing, and there is no evidence to show that they have performed significantly worse than they did before the transformation. Therefore, Xu needs stronger arguments than simply expressing his worries about the potential risks of introducing the share-holding system.

His direct answer to the question of ownership is that the assets of Hengdian Group belong to the members of the community. His logic runs as follows. The first factories were built up with the funds collected from local residents, other villages and state banks. After the money borrowed was paid off with part of the profits made, the newly built enterprise had no economic relations with the residents, the villages, and Bank of Agriculture anymore. In addition, the enterprise also paid the local government for using the land.[25] Therefore, it is obvious that:

> the Group's asset does not belong to the State, nor to the town, let alone to some individual persons; it can only belong to the Group. But our Group is unlike any ordinary business, because it is composed of enterprises at different levels. From a social perspective, it is a community, so we call our Group communal ownership.[26]

But the problem is not solved: if a certain amount of asset belongs to a community, why cannot it be quantified and distributed to each member of the community? The answer is the lack of a widely acceptable logic for determining each individual member's weight, i.e., how many shares of the collective asset a member deserves. In principle, this is doable, particularly when all members agree on the distribution of shares *before* the asset is used or invested. To me, this is an important practical reason why it has been so difficult for Hengdian Group's asset to be quantified and individualized – no agreement was made among the entrepreneur, the villagers, the town government, and the bank about how many shares each of them possessed out of the total so that each party could claim a corresponding number of dividends after the business started to make profits. In other words, it is simply too late to determine the relative contribution of each party involved in the very first enterprise.

If his above logic makes sense, then Xu becomes ambivalent of the following questions: Who is the Group? How do they own the Group's assets? Xu asserts that (1) all working for the Group are the Group's members, (2) no member owns the

---

25 The responsibility of paying off land rentals has been reportedly centralized at Hengdian Group, with a foundation collecting charges from member enterprises and paying villages for using their land. See p. 22 in Shen et al., *A Study of Hengdian Communal Economic Model*.

26 Xu, *The Road of Hengdian*, p. 72; *Collected Works*, volume 1, pp. 302–303.

Group's assets in the sense of taking dividends or interests, (3) membership of the Group is neither transferable or inheritable, and (4) one is not allowed to take away any piece of the Group's assets upon leaving the Group.[27] These points amount to turning the Group's ownership into an abstraction, because in no way can ownership have a concrete meaning here. Common rights of owning a particular property, such as using, moving, transferring, benefit claiming, inheriting, etc., are all prohibited. What the employees have are only the right to work and the right to be treated fairly according to the rules set up by the Group, but these rights are not unique to employees of Hengdian Group and therefore cannot be used to distinguish its communal ownership from other types of ownership.

Clearly, this unusual ownership demands some justifications. Like Mou and many other entrepreneurs in China, Xu has searched for and found some supporting words from Karl Marx. He argued that communal ownership was consistent with or even represented a preliminary form of the economic relations in the Communist society. For example, as Marx points out, in a Communist or co-operative system, 'no one can give anything except his labour' and 'nothing can pass to the ownership of individuals except individual means of consumption'.[28] Communal ownership thus represents an advanced form of social ownership, which does not involve individualized ownership of properties or means of productions. Although communal ownership is not divided into individual pieces, its organizational or communal boundaries make it clearer than ownership structures in most enterprises nominally owned by town and villages. Finally and perhaps most importantly to Xu, communal ownership grants an independent status to the enterprise and thereby allows self-reliant and self-responsible actions, which is a key condition for a market economy to function effectively.[29]

Ownership does not matter very much if it does not show its effect on economic performance. At the core of the debate over ownership is the question of which type of ownership is more likely to provide a reliable and durable basis for better economic performance. It is thus more fundamental to study the effect of communal ownership on managerial and entrepreneurial behaviours than to argue about the exact nature of ownership at Hengdian;[30] otherwise, the concept of communal ownership tends to isolate ownership from management.

---

27 Ibid., p. 74.

28 Marx, 'Critique of the Gotha Program', in Robert C. Tucker (ed.), *The Marx-Engels Reader*, 2nd edition (W.W. Norton and Company, 1978), p. 530.

29 Xu, *The Road of Hengdian*, pp. 81–84.

30 However, one point should be briefly mentioned here, as it has drawn little attention. In an extreme situation that all employees denounce their Group membership or pass away at about the same time, there would be a huge amount of assets to which no one would be eligible to claim as an owner. These situations are imaginary, of course. The point is that the ownership of certain properties is hardly tenable without allowing individual members to do something about the properties. A less dramatic situation would be that Hengdian Group relocates to another place while most local residents, most of which are employees of Hengdian Group as well, would prefer to stay at Hengdian. It would be hard to imagine that these residents would voluntarily give up their membership.

Rarely has Xu made an explicit connection between communal ownership and his entrepreneurial behaviours, but a careful reading of his published words indicates that, just as he endeavoured to keep his business free from governmental influences, his insistence on Hengdian Group's communal ownership is part of his overall strategy of enhancing the Group's, and thus his, institutional autonomy. He made the point most clearly in April 1994, when he was interviewed by two news reporters from School of the Chinese Communist Party. Being asked what he thought the ultimate goal of ownership reforms should be, he said it was for enterprises 'to obtain an independent, comprehensive, and legally protected status in the market'.[31]

Indeed, after severing the Group's administrative connection to local governments, the call for transformation into a share-holding company is perhaps the last threat to its institutional autonomy, and communal ownership, as is specified by Xu, is by far the most reliable institutional structure that can protect his control over the Group. Although there is a Board of Directors within Hengdian Group, it has not functioned in the way expected from similar organizations in a developed economy. In addition, Xu Wenrong was the Chairman of the Board until his semi-retirement (now his son Xu Yongan is in the position). And Xu has not been shy in telling others about this, because the concentration of power in his and his son's hands means efficiency.[32] Any serious introduction and establishment of a share-holding system will mean the end of such a concentration of power, and he could always defend himself with the argument of maintaining managerial efficiency. A key precept of a share-holding system is the separation of management from ownership, an institutional basis for corporate governance. If that is adopted at Hengdian, Xu may hold the largest number of shares as a reward to his contributions, but the institutional foundation of his autonomy will be seriously weakened.

Thus, Hengdian Group's communal ownership represents an irony. On the one hand, all employees are claimed to be equal as Group members because without individual ownership, it is impossible to tell who owns more than others. Xu proclaims that the goal and canon of communal ownership is to work, own, prosper, and enjoy together.[33] On the other hand, the employees do not manage together in a democratic manner; all important decisions including investment in new projects, personnel, distribution of profits, etc., have been finally made by Xu Wenrong, although consultation is usually provided by a group of senior managers. The discrepancy between communal ownership and Xu's personal control cannot be sharper.

Again, the question is: how could the concentration of power in Xu be possible? The answer is: he has established his authority among the employees, which is why

---

31 Quoted in Sun Shiyan, *Wen Hua Li*, p. 84. Later he made a very similar point in his *Collected Works*: 'The transformation of ownership structure is only a tool, so the autonomy and independence of enterprises should not be sacrificed as a result' (volume 1, p. 256).

32 In an interview, Xu was proud of telling some researchers that his enterprise was run like a military army. See Shen, et al., *The Model of Hengdian*, pp. 13–14.

33 Xu, *Collected Works*, volume 1, p. 304.

I discussed his entrepreneurial authority before analyzing Hengdian's institutional autonomy and communal ownership.[34]

Mobilization and deployment of resources

The establishment of Xu's entrepreneurial authority and communal ownership constitutes the institutional foundation for the following full play of Xu's entrepreneurship. With his entrepreneurship now highly institutionalized, Xu enjoys the autonomy of effectively mobilizing and deploying local resources for achieving the common goal shared by all residents of the community. In this sense, Hengdian is not an exceptional case; we can recognize the same path of growth in other cases, such as Daqiu and Liu Zhuang, now popularly known in China. One thing that clearly distinguishes these industrial enterprises in rural areas from other types of enterprises in China is a local identity, which is recognized, shared, and maintained firstly because the geographical area is small enough for the residents to develop a strong sense of common identity during years of intense interactions. The shared identity is further sharpened in later successes that confirm the benefits of working as a united force. Finally, the leading entrepreneur's ambition of building up a business empire requires that all members of the community participate in the mission under an established leadership.

According to Xu, the unified as well as centralized mobilization of resources is what defines 'The Hengdian Model':

> Hengdian Group has united all the town enterprises (*zhen ban*), village enterprises (*cun ban*), joint enterprises (*lian ban*), and household enterprises (*hu ban*) in the town of Hengdian ... This is called 'four wheel drive'. The town enterprises have played a major role. They are the most closely connected to the Group, and as the Group's backbones and pillar enterprises they drive the development of the whole Group. We believe we have walked out a path of economic development in rural areas, and I think it is appropriate to call it the Hengdian model.[35]

The first round of unification was accomplished in 1984 with the establishment of Hengdian Industrial Corporation, which consisted of 28 town enterprises and 481 other businesses. Each enterprise was still responsible for its own management, but the Corporation became the centre of strategic decision making, especially on investments. Now there were no institutional barriers that would prevent Xu from being able to decide on which new products were to be introduced and which factories must be closed down.

---

34 Zhou Qiren expressed a similar idea from an economic point of view. His aim was to explain the incentives to Xu's entrepreneurship given the fact that Xu was rewarded only a small part of the total earned profits (about 1.2 per cent). Zhou concluded that the right of control was a compensation for the low financial reward that Xu received. Clearly, the compensation is made under the condition that Xu keeps a good record of performance. My argument differs from Zhou's in that I see Xu's control as a natural outcome of his established authority, not really an intentional arrangement based on financial considerations.

35 Shen et al., *The Hengdian Model*, p. 12.

Centralized mobilization showed its advantage especially in difficult times. In 1985, many TVE suffered from a short supply of financial credits. Originally, Hengdian planned to invest 19 million in 13 projects, but it turned out that they could only collect 8 million. A provincial bank promised to offer a loan of 2.37 million yuan before, but in the end 70,000 was all that the bank could offer. Under Xu's mobilization, people at Hengdian put down 1.5 million and other loosely connected enterprises lent them more than 3 million.[36] In the end, the Hengdian Corporation increased its previous year's profits by 58 per cent. By 1987, Hengdian's industrial output exceeded 110 million, making it the first '100 million town' (*yi yuan zhen*) in Jinhua City.

The newly gained autonomy and unification showed their advantages further in the difficult years from 1988 to 1990, when the nation's economy and politics seemed to be out of control. Non-state sectors suffered from a tightened supply of financial credits, more difficult access to raw materials, shrinking market demands and a hostile political environment. Thanks to his authority and the Group's independence, Xu was able to make prompt decisions to shut down and sell off some unprofitable factories, change the main products of others and invest in some more profitable projects with the money returned. He would not have been able to do so, at least not in such a prompt manner, if he had to report his plans to a number of government agencies and beg for their permission. These wise but risky decisions generated enviable results, which helped establish Hengdian as the first TVE group in Zhejiang on 11 November 1990, with 35 directly controlled enterprises covering seven industries including textile, printing and dyeing, magnetic appliances, organic chemicals, pharmaceuticals, electronic machineries, and trading. Further, in the following three years, Hengdian developed into a national business group of 90 enterprises under direct control, with the sanction by the Office of Economics and Trade of the State Council.

My purpose here, however, is not to conduct a comprehensive study of Hengdian in the light of the current literature about business groups.[37] Rather, I see the construction of Hengdian Group as an entrepreneurial strategy of mobilizing local resources. Members of Hengdian Group were not in a situation where they were isolated from each other and only came together to form a strategic alliance after each of them had grown into an established entity. Like most of the Korean business groups developed in the 1960s and 1970s,[38] Hengdian Group came into existence from some closely connected enterprises under a single entrepreneur's charismatic leadership.

---

36 Xu, *Collected Works*, pp. 31–32.

37 See the reviews by Mark Granovetter in Neil Smelser and Richard Swedberg (eds.), *The Handbook of Economic Sociology*, 1st and 2nd editions (Princeton University Press, 1994 and 2005).

38 Nicole Woolsey Biggart, 'Institutionalized Patrimonialism in Korean Business', pp. 113–33 in Craig Calhoun (ed.), *Business Institutions*, vol. 12 of *Comparative Social Research* (JAI Press, 1991). Sea-Jin Chang, *The Rise and Fall of Chaebols: Financial Crisis and Transformation of Korean Business Groups* (Cambridge University Press, 2003).

After the initial success in silk and textile industries, however, industrial diversifications across companies within the Group were almost exclusively determined by anecdotal recognitions of opportunities in the market. The production of magnetic appliances started simply because Xu came to know that a magnetic technician, whose wife had family relations at Hengdian, visited the area regularly. The idea of developing Hengdian into a base for film production came to Xu's mind when he was trying to help a prominent movie director build up a filming site. Although film production and the related tourism have been very successful, the whole project is not actually in line with a principle that Xu has adhered to for many years – no investment shall be made in products of low technological component.

This style of investing, highly contingent on market situations and personal interactions, usually finds its peak under the leadership of a single iron hand. Besides preventing the CCP Committee from intervening into the business's daily operations, Xu has further institutionalized the subordination of member enterprises to his control. According to the Group's *Constitution*, company chief executives and factory directors are the legal representatives of the enterprises under their management and can make decisions on matters including personnel, organization of production, management, employment, rewards, punishments, etc.[39] From the outset, however, Xu made it clear that it was the Group that had the right to determine on the most important issues, such as investment and finance, appointment of top managers, price control, introduction of technology and technicians, and public relations. Almost all important decisions are to be discussed in a committee composed of top managers, and it is Xu who makes the final decision. Xu has argued that such a structure ensures efficiency, avoids internal competitions, and promotes a unified image to the outside world.[40] It is even unclear how much power a chief executive of a particular member enterprise has over the matters listed above. For example, Xu once pointed out that an advantage of operating as a business group was to deploy technicians to a needed member company.[41] Also, as the rules regarding salary, bonus and other rewards have already been set up by the Group, it is therefore very likely that a member enterprise is only allowed to deal with minor issues. In the end, member enterprises have become production units of the whole business machine.

The sharp contrast between the Group's autonomy as a whole and each member's dependence is perhaps most clearly manifested in their financial relations. Starting as early as 1979, Xu proposed that employment not be permanent but contractual, and every employee be responsible for a pre-determined production value and a rate of profits. Correspondingly, their salary has two components: a basic salary, based on qualifications and experience, and a profit-related salary. It was estimated that on average, the latter constituted about 40 per cent of an employee's total salary. Company executives, factory directors, and other senior managers are not appointed

---

39 Hengdian Group keeps a set of principles, known as the *Constitution* (*zong gang*), for regulating internal economic relations, which are reviewed and, if necessary, revised almost every year. There is also a *Handbook of Management* that specifies managers' rights and responsibilities.

40 Xu, *Collected Works*, volume 1, pp. 267, 273–275.

41 Ibid., volume 2, pp. 131–137.

by local government, as they were before. All have to submit a loss-compensation fee. This is especially designed for managers and contractors who rent an enterprise of the Group. The collateral is worth either 10 times the sum of the contractor's annual salary or 10 per cent of the total asset of the rented enterprise. They will be rewarded with 10 per cent of the extra profits made, but if the business is in the red, they will have to pay 10 per cent of the loss.[42] Xu and his senior managers believe that this institutional structure has maximized employees' motivations.

This seemingly precise system, however, is not without ambiguities and controversies. For example, it is not clear what should be done if 10 per cent of the loss exceeds 10 per cent of the total asset under the control of a manager or contractor, which is very likely. It is also unclear where the 10 per cent comes from in the first place. Two further questions arise in putting the rules in practice: How can each employee's contribution be accurately assessed, which will determine the flexible part of salary? Who takes up the responsibility of quantifying each component of an employee's salary?[43]

Again, this internal problem is handled in a highly centralized way rather than in a democratic manner by all members of the community. This is not only because salary determination is an extremely important and sensitive issue but also because the total amount of salary depends on the Group's total profit. That is, a particular employee's salary can only be approximately determined *after* the proportion of the total amount of salary out of the total profit is determined; thus, it cannot be calculated exclusively based on an employee's performance. As a general rule, 65–70 per cent of the after-tax profit will be retained by the Group and the other 30–35 per cent will be distributed as rewards to the employees and managers who have performed well.[44] It is hard to imagine that the total amount of salary determined exclusively based on each employee's performance will necessarily fall into the range of 30–35 per cent of the Group's total profit earned. Clearly, it is the Group, or managers at the very top, who determine employee salaries, although in practice they will try to link salary to performance as closely as possible. Salary determination is a part of the resource mobilization.

Concluding observations

It is perhaps ironic that a precondition for the remarkable growth of industrial enterprises in rural China is their low starting point. This is not to say that the low starting point makes later development more impressive in relative terms. It means that, to rural residents, poverty has not only inflicted discomfort in their material life but also generated a powerful force for getting involved in industrial productions. Most rural areas at the end of the Cultural Revolution (mid 1970s) were in absolute poverty. The desire to get out of poverty has driven them to break through institutional barriers and to lend whatever support they could afford to entrepreneurs. Xu Wenrong

---

42 Shen et al., *The Hengdian Model*, p. 21.
43 Zhou Qiren has paid attention to these questions in his paper.
44 Shen Weiguang, et al., *Hengdian She Tuan Jing Ji Mou Shi Yan Jiu*, p. 37.

acknowledged that such desire was at the root of Hengdian's development.[45] Consequently, 'venturing on an industrial enterprise in rural China is a fight to win or lose, that is, our only choice is to move on with all our might'.[46] Combined with a strong sense of communal identity and an entrepreneurial leadership, the desire has produced an enormous amount of energy in industrial productions.

Though initially confined in certain industries designated by the State – TVE were only allowed to operate in industries that would directly serve agricultural production – industrial enterprises in rural China have enjoyed a much friendlier institutional environment than their private cousins. They could readily carry the name of collective interest, which could be hardly made illegitimate by local officials, and play with the ambiguities of defining what industries were related to agriculture. But even for them, entrepreneurship remains a mission of dual tasks, especially in their early years. In the case of Hengdian, Xu had to fight on two fronts, i.e., managing the factories and fighting for the right to open new businesses that had nothing to do with agriculture. Even after the achievements were made and the status of Hengdian Group was granted by the State, he had to work very hard to explain why the Group should choose communal ownership instead of a share holding system and why he and his son should have so much control over the business. Like Mou and many other entrepreneurs in China, once the business became highly visible in the public arena, Xu had to spend much of his time labouring in the theoretical domain in order to justify the worth of the business.

We have also seen actions exemplifying the strategy of playing with institutional holes throughout Hengdian's development: putting on 'the red cap' of TVE while repeatedly arguing for the advantages of communal ownership, employing different principles and logics for acquiring and enhancing institutional autonomy and concentration of power, taking advantage of the overlaps of business networks and personal networks in obtaining financial credits, technologies, personnel, and so on. Xu believes that an entrepreneur in China must learn how to exploit the loopholes in state policies; otherwise, the entrepreneur would not achieve anything if always docilely following the rules.[47] Like Mou, Xu also believes that many entrepreneurial opportunities are embedded in the constraining and unsatisfactory institutional structures. He differs from Mou in that he would not build his enterprise entirely through making use of the institutional structures or playing as a half-visible intermediaries between multiple business partners. Rather, he suggests that the constraining rules should all be eradicated once and for all:

> Now there are still some officials whose minds are not liberal enough and who would not let us go. Therefore, if TVEs want to grow, then we have no other choice but to break through the Palace of Hell ... The first Palace of Hell is the incorrect understandings of market economy in some people's mind, and another is the set of rules, regulations,

45 See the interview with Xu by Chen Jiali, published in *Nan Fang Du Shi Bao* (*Southern Metropolitan Daily*), 1 December 2003.

46 Xu, *Collected Works*, volume 1, p. 57.

47 Ibid., p. 24. His original words were '*xue hui zuan kong zi*', or 'learn how to make use of loopholes', which were later reworded by officials and journalists into a politically more acceptable expression 'to maximize the full potential of state policies'.

etc., outside our enterprise. It is of course necessary for our nation to have plans of development, but those plans must be made for controlling the overall balance, not for regulating specific productions.[48]

Like Huo, he would directly confront state bureaucrats in fighting for his institutional innocence if he had to.

As this chapter shows, the reason that Xu would, and could afford to, adopt the above strategies is because he established his entrepreneurial authority in his community, something that Mou and Huo did not have. Supported by a strong sense of shared identity among local residents, the authority allows him to mobilize resources, such as household savings, loans from state banks, land, employees, market information, technologies, etc., in a larger scale and on a more legitimate basis. These resources have found their best use in Xu's hands. Different from many other entrepreneurs in China who are happy with making money by producing low-cost but low technology profile products, such as toys, clothes, foods, and household appliances, Xu proclaimed as early as in 1990 that Hengdian would not invest in any products of low technological profile. High technology generates a high rate of returns, which in turn strengthens his authority, thus forming a benign loop of business development.

So far this model has worked wonders at Hengdian. However, the model's two key elements – a highly centralized but efficient management system under a charismatic entrepreneurial leadership and an institutional autonomy supported by a strong sense of local identity – have come under some challenges. As the leading entrepreneur approaching the end of his natural life, the issue of succession necessarily comes to the top of agenda. In 2001, it was Xu Wenrong's son, Xu Yongan, not one of his senior managers, who took over as the Chairman and Chief Executive.[49] Of course, Xu Yongan does not have to copy his father's style of entrepreneurship and leadership; actually, he may perform far better by following his own ways of running the business. Nevertheless, he cannot afford a less effective leadership. It still remains unclear whether and how the junior entrepreneur will survive the transfer of authority or even outrun the senior. On 9 March 2003, a journalist asked Xu Yongan, 'Your father has greatly relied on his personal authority in managing and controlling the business. What will you be able to fall back on?' His answer was, 'I've never thought about this question'.[50] It is hard to believe that he meant to say that how he would maintain his authority at Hengdian Group was not an important issue in his mind. But it would be equally hard to understand his words as implying that he did not worry about his authority. As a matter of fact, it was himself who acknowledged the challenges to his authority. About five years after taking over, in his speech at the Group's annual conference held on 8 February 2006, he pointed out the existence of serious ignorance, disobedience, and even violations of company rules among

---

48 Ibid., p. 24.

49 It is very difficult to find out and thus explain how this sensitive transfer of power took place at Hengdian. Following the explanation proposed by Professor Zhou Qiren, this could be seen as another form of compensation to his claim of only a small proportion of the Group's profits.

50 *21 Shi Ji Jing Ji Bao Dao* (*21ˢᵗ Century Economic Report*), 9 March 2003.

managers of member enterprises or businesses located outside Hengdian,[51] a problem his father never talked about before.

In the meantime, less power has been put into the hands of the junior entrepreneur. It is Xu Wenrong's brother, Xu Wencai, who took over as the Party Secretary of Hengdian Group. Although the uncle is expected to support his nephew without any reservations, such an arrangement is at odds with the arrangement of designating one person as the chief executive as well as the Party Secretary, a practice that Xu Wenrong had advocated and propagated in his tenure. It is not clear why the split of power was made and whether it has been practiced in each member enterprise. We still need to wait and see what this transfer implies for the Group's future development. More generally, how second-generation entrepreneurs establish their authority in the business created by their parents (mostly fathers), particularly how they create new institutional rules and make use of institutional environments, will be a question of great importance for the development of China's non-state enterprises.

Also challenged are Hengdian Group's shared local identity, institutional autonomy, and communal ownership. First of all, Hengdian's demographic profile has greatly changed with its industrial growth. There are no exact statistics to show how many of Hengdian's current 80,000 population are not long-term residents, but we do know that hundreds of highly skilled persons and thousands of workers have moved to Hengdian. In addition, the Hengdian Group has set up businesses, offices, or branches in many places outside of Hengdian, both inside and outside the mainland, including Hong Kong and the US. The originally strong sense of local identity will be further challenged with the town being opened up as a centre of film production and tourism. It remains unclear whether a shared identify is still necessary for the Group's development in the twenty-first century, and if the answer is yes, what comes as the basis of a shared identity to these people of diverse backgrounds?

Second, it seems that the pressure of changing the Hengdian Group's institutional nature has been growing. It was indeed an entrepreneurial act in institutional terms for Xu Wenrong to keep government interferences out of the business. Nevertheless, it is perhaps impossible to have an economic organization immune from governmental influence in China's current political system. We can have a glimpse of such influences from the many seemingly occasional visits made by many state officials. Anyone who has ever read Hengdian Group's internal newspaper or the list of events posted on its website will be struck by the large number of groups of officials coming to visit. Not all of them have the power of shaping Hengdian's fate, of course, and many go to Hengdian simply to look for business opportunities. But among them are some officials who do have direct influence, either potentially or currently, such as the provincial governors and party secretaries, and officials in charge of TVE, state banks and high technologies. After learning Huo Hongmin's story, we know that executives at Hengdian cannot afford to give a cold-shoulder to bureaucrats for technology inspections, safety, environment, and other agents. Given their tightly booked schedules, it must be a very delicate matter for the top managers to decide who should see whom.

---

51 Hengdian's Group's website.

The influence from the government has grown so strong that Xu Wenrong is no longer able to hold onto communal ownership, which he holds as 'the sun in the heart of the Hengdian people'. On 17 November 2004, in a meeting with the attendance of the Party Secretary and the Governor of Hengdian Town, he announced that 'upon the request by upper level governments', the third stage of institutional reforms at the Hengdian Group will be the quantification of its assets,[52] a step that he has resisted for many years. As pointed out before, the key function of communal ownership is to allow Xu to mobilize all local resources whenever he deems necessary. Clearly, quantification or individualization of the Group's assets poses a serious threat to this mechanism. He expressed his reluctance of following the order from the above by insisting that 'the flag of communal ownership' should not be toppled. It seems that a compromising policy has been made; that is, only the newly added assets will be quantified. Xu emphasizes that this new policy should not jeopardize communal ownership, but it will be difficult to keep communal ownership once the newly added assets exceed the communal assets. Xu also worries about the deterioration of local identity due to the quantification of Hengdian Group's assets by pointing out that, for many local residents, the Group is their backup and home.[53]

It is clear that the most demanding job for the junior entrepreneur is more about institutional transitions than about managerial strategies.

---

52 Hengdian Group's website.
53 Xu, *Collected Works*, volume 2, p. 48.

Chapter 9

Double Gambles

I have focused my attention on entrepreneurship because it serves well as a working mechanism connecting institutional change and economic development in China. Since Joseph Schumpeter published *The Theory of Economic Development* 80 years ago, that entrepreneurship is an engine, if not *the* engine, of economic development has become common sense in both developed and developing economies. Academics and policy researchers have also tried to engineer the science of entrepreneurship by discovering and nurturing the conditions with the highest likelihood of nurturing entrepreneurship, although answers to these practical questions have been less firmly established. As the title suggests, this book is about a special case of entrepreneurship, that is, the entrepreneurship in the People's Republic of China since the end of the 1970s, or China after the economic reforms started.

Entrepreneurship in China is a relatively special case in both aforementioned connections. For the connection between entrepreneurship and economic development, entrepreneurship was not recognized as a legitimate element, let alone a driving engine, of the nation's economic development until only two decades ago. The fierce debate among economists and policy makers in the 1980s over the extent to which China should go in the direction of a market economy is a good illustration of the precarious status of entrepreneurship, because it is only sensible to talk about entrepreneurship in an economy that operates fundamentally by market mechanisms. The indispensable role of entrepreneurship was only formally recognized in the early 1990s after the national economy became more and more dependent on the economic contributions by the enterprises in non-state sectors. In China, the legitimacy of entrepreneurship is hard earned.

More particular to entrepreneurship in China is the link between entrepreneurship and its institutional environment. Here we have a whole array of institutional conditions, from the most encouraging to the bluntly suppressing, with the following in the middle: the cautiously supporting, the strategically allying, the passively cooperating, and the cunningly exploiting. How each of these institutional settings connects to entrepreneurship has challenged our imagination. We may be able to say that the overall institutional environment has become friendlier to entrepreneurs, especially when we measure entrepreneurship by the number of newly established firms. But we will not be so sure about how institutions work when we observe entrepreneurship in establishing the legitimacy of a new type of business, jumping over or steering clear of institutional hurdles, obtaining untitled resources, and entering industries without the privilege needed. To obtain a better understanding of entrepreneurship in China, we need to learn as much as we can about institutional rules while keeping in mind that entrepreneurs can do something about them.

In other words, changing institutional rules are at the root of the chain of connections that we hope to understand. In understanding China's economic development in general and entrepreneurship in particular, we must realize that these changing rules are full of uncertainties, inconsistencies, ambiguities, delays, and unexpected repercussions, because they have been created without a blueprint or a widely accepted logic. Consequently, entrepreneurs in China have to live with, and learn how to deal with, uncertainties in the market as well as in the institutional domain. Hence the concept 'double entrepreneurship', which I defined in Chapter 3 and illustrated in the following case studies.

To survive and thrive, entrepreneurs in China, especially the most ambitious ones, have to play double gambles interactively. They usually start with an initial success to show the worth of their business or at least obtain a basis on which they can establish the business's legitimacy. Then a significant amount of their time, effort, and resources will have to be invested in enhancing their legitimate status, and they do this in the hope of shielding their business from institutional uncertainty or even expanding their business based on its newly gained legitimacy. They have to apply extreme caution in betting on both sides especially when the business becomes visible to the government and the public. The irony is that, although such gambling on two fronts will drain away a substantial amount of resources, most entrepreneurs simply cannot help following the risky route because this is a shortcut for them to grow bigger and faster, and they are strongly motivated to grow bigger and faster.

In the meantime, we should also keep in mind that the Chinese State and its officials are also playing double gambles. How to strike a balance between economic development and political reform has been one of the most demanding jobs for those at the very top of the Chinese State, who have been gingerly forging a mutually reinforcing relationship between the two processes. In doing so, the only recipe they can follow is to try in practice to monitor the consequences of their policies carefully, make the necessary adjustments and avoid irreversible calamities. To the leaders of China, the growth of the economy and the increase in people's quality of life will surely boost their political credentials, so it is in their interests to liberalize the economic environment for entrepreneurship. On the other hand, however, they want to keep the economy under control; that is, by allowing many people to become economically powerful, they have not unwittingly nurtured a new political opponent. They have been trying to maximize the positive effects of their political dominance on the nation's economic development, such as safeguarding a society in which people can be busy making money and improving their material life. This is a tricky business because they have to constantly watch the economic development to ensure that the nation will not slip into a situation in which it is impossible for the economy to move further without significantly reducing the political power of the Chinese Communist Party. Similarly, officials at localities have been thinking very hard about how their political careers can help improve their personal financial situations, and *vice versa*. Too often caught in the middle of institutional change, they need to carefully detect the direction of policy winds, assess the implications for their personal wellbeing, and then decide how far they want to keep the distance between them and the nascent entrepreneurs.

The cross-interactions of these double gambles generate multiple scenarios, which, I hope, can serve as an analytical map for us to navigate the perplexing world of entrepreneurship in China and perhaps entrepreneurship in general. In the rest of this chapter, I shall highlight the key findings at some points in my navigation. There is no point, however, in repeating the details previously presented in cases and statistics. Rather, I shall be talking about types, scenarios, and expected consequences.

The context

It is now a widely accepted insight that entrepreneurship is embedded in a historically specific context. As Arthur Stinchcombe forcefully argued four decades ago, new organizations, consciously or unwittingly, mimic the social structure from which they emerge as they struggle to survive by gaining access to available resources and earning credits of legitimacy. I presented some details of the historical context for the emergence of entrepreneurship in China in previous chapters. Here I offer a concise account of such context.

At its initial establishment, the People's Republic of China was indeed a polity that represented different groups of the people – about half of the members of the new State's governing committee were from political parties other than the Chinese Communist Party (CCP) and half of Ministers of the State Council were non-Communists, many representing the interests of capitalists, merchants, and other businessmen. During the early years of the Republic, leaders of the CCP repeatedly made it clear that, as long as owners of domestic private businesses cooperated with the new government, they would enjoy 'the New Society' in the same way as the working class (workers and farmers), whose interests were represented by the CCP. But it proved impossible to make the antagonism between 'the exploited' and 'the exploitive' history. The capitalists soon learnt that the CCP's collegial attitudes towards 'the exploitive class' were only a temporary tactic of earning time for consolidating the Party's political power. In mobilizing all the nation's resources necessary for building up a superpower, the new State quickly found it frustrating and constraining to rely on an ideologically alien class. The State wanted to become *the* entrepreneur, who would enjoy the freedom of mobilizing all available resources in an authoritative manner. Note that, during the first years of the new regime, to most people in China, this authoritative entrepreneurship was highly acceptable (similarly, Xu Wenrong asserted that, once an organization obtained its autonomy, it would be to the interest of the organization to adopt an authoritarian structure internally for the sake of efficiency).

If entrepreneurship is measured by the number of new organizations created by combining available resources, then the entrepreneurship of the Chinese State was admirably successful, at least in the 1950s and the first half of the 1960s. Even with the costs of the Korean War and some natural disasters, the new State was able to put up an industrial system with hundreds of thousands of factories and enterprises, particularly in the heavy industries. This was achieved, however, by paying two dear prices: one, the farmers were exploited so heavily in supporting the construction of the industrial system that most of them were living in absolute poverty; two, the spirit of entrepreneurship among the people was nearly suffocated. The Great Cultural Revolution of the Proletariat added further detrimental effects to these problems and prolonged their rectifications.

China at the end of the 1970s was the immediate historical context in which entrepreneurship started to grow. Frustrations, confusions, and the desire to improve the quality of life were the dominating sentiments among the people. Their material life was highly impoverished. Even in big cities, everything necessary to a normal life was rationed, including clothes, meat, eggs, vegetables, milk, etc. Families with growing boys had to find other means of feeding their children as the designated amount of food was usually not sufficient. Vegetables were preserved with plenty of salt for future use, and meat was consumed only on holidays. Among the siblings, clothes were passed on from the elder to the younger.

Although most people were employed, work was hard and boring. A considerable amount of time was devoted to prolonged meetings, document readings, and unproductive discussions. Another big chunk of time was spent on playing politics and fighting for limited resources, including housing, promotion, easy jobs, welfare, and so on. In rural areas, the fights were normally about designations of pieces of land, domestic fowls, and basic materials of life. Most people did not work hard because others did not. Workers as well as farmers became good at minimizing their efforts at work. Whenever they could, people working in an office took a long lunch, had a nap, or ran errands during work hours to take care of household matters. Many thought hard about how they could exchange the power or privilege in their hands for valuable resources. On the one hand, everything was under the control of the State, so one had to go through some bureaucratic procedures in dealing with virtually every important matter in life. On the other hand, all these procedures were negotiable if you knew, or made yourself known to, the right person in charge. Valuable goods were bought not for personal use, but for giving away as gifts, and the recipient would store them away for giving to others in the future.

One thing was well preserved in these difficult times: the desire to enrich the material life. I believe that, of all ethnic groups in the world, the Chinese are one of the few who have the strongest desire for living a materially rich life. And this is more so in relative terms than in absolute terms. That is, they would strive and make every effort to ensure that their material life is no worse, if they truly cannot make it better, than that of others. The search for relative privilege on the one hand and the phobia of relative deprivation on the other constitutes the motivation behind the hard work of the Chinese. The longing for a better life was later fuelled when China gradually opened its door to the West, thus opening the eyes of the mainland Chinese to the enviable material life in Hong Kong, Japan, America, and Europe. When the desire could not be satisfied in the official, planned economy, energies were then channelled into underground activities, informal transactions, and the exchange of power and valuable goods. It was from this unofficial world of economic activities that the first generation of entrepreneurs emerged in China.

Given the shortage economy and the popular craving for a better life, there is not much impressively entrepreneurial about most entrepreneurs of the first generation. For the vast majority of new businesses created in the late 1970s and early 1980s, what it took to open a new business was only some simple tools and the courage to let others watch you. The market was close to blank; you could sell everything that people needed in their daily life. Breakfast shops, restaurants, barbers and hair salons, tailors, cleaning shops, street corner groceries, home appliance repairing shops, food processing shops, bike repairing sites on the street, milk deliveries, and many more similar businesses mushroomed during those years. Not everybody could do it, but many could. If entrepreneurship is measured by the number of new businesses, then millions in China could have enjoyed the title of 'entrepreneur'. I am not sure how many people in China would call owners of those businesses 'entrepreneurs'.

What truly made someone deserve the title 'entrepreneur' in China was the institutional, not the managerial, aspect of the business. During the early years of economic reforms, town-and-village enterprises (TVE), individual household businesses (*getihu*), and privately owned businesses were new in China's economic landscape not merely in the sense that they did not exist before in the market but in the more important sense that they were *new institutional entities*. When they started to appear, there were only two legitimate types of business organizations in China's economic system – the state-owned enterprises (SOE) and collective enterprises, all being under the certain control of a particular agency of the Chinese State. One reason for the speedy development of TVE in the 1980s is their institutional affinity to collective enterprises; many of them were indeed commune or brigade enterprises during the Cultural Revolution. Foreign firms and joint-ventures with businesses from Hong Kong or Taiwan, although not directly controlled by the State, enjoyed unquestionable legitimacy as the State had a clear policy of attracting foreign investments and technologies. Nor did individual household businesses encounter much trouble of legitimacy because the Chinese State had no other choice but to let them grow in order to solve the urgent unemployment problem. In the end, being institutionally the newest, privately owned enterprises suffered from the lowest level of legitimacy. This is why I think that entrepreneurship has most strongly expressed itself in the private sector in China and that it is critical to understanding the institutional life of entrepreneurship alongside its life in the market.

To become legitimate is to be accepted according to a certain set of values. It is therefore impossible to ascertain the meaning of legitimacy without firstly specifying the values under concern. Cognitive legitimacy is of low importance for private entrepreneurs in China, because nearly everything is political. In the context of China's economic transition, three sets of values have been very important to entrepreneurship: ideological, regulatory, and moral. Firstly, entrepreneurship, understood as opening commercial business in order to earn or increase personal financial interests, has to be accepted by the ideology upheld by the ruling political party, the CCP. This has proved to be a task much more demanding for the Party itself than for the private entrepreneurs. Some of the most thorny issues are: Should there be any economic components not under the control of the socialist State? Should the exploitation of employees by the employers be allowed? How far should inequality among the people go? One of the significant contributions by Deng Xiaoping is his pragmatism; he made all these issues inferior to the hard work of promoting economic growth. Without his political entrepreneurship, there would be no business entrepreneurship in China.

The second source of legitimacy of entrepreneurship comes from regulatory policies by the Chinese State that determine the acceptance of a particular private business from a variety of perspectives. Compared to ideological values, the policies have been politically less fundamental and controversial, but they are less transparent, coherent, and consistent as well. Different local conditions, different understandings of the underlying ideas, different ways of implementation, and different motivations all contribute to the contingent status of a private business.

Finally, the acceptance of entrepreneurship in China has been examined against a set of moral values. Whilst the act of opening a new business has been widely accepted as beneficial to the nation's economic conditions, how a business has been operated and how the earned profits have been used remain hot topics in the public arena. For a long time, making profits by taking advantage of price gaps in different geographical areas was seen as an immoral behaviour. Many times the line between making use of one's personal connections and bribing government officials is a fine one. Ill treatment of employees, unsafe working conditions, and irresponsible behaviours such as manufacturing fake products, violating copy-rights, and damaging the natural environment, plus corrupted personal life-styles have been the headlines for many years.

These three groups of values are the key components of the institutional context for entrepreneurship in China. Changeability is their commonality; to a large extent, entrepreneurship in China is about navigating the bewildering world of institutional rules.

The first generation

The first generation of entrepreneurs in China – those who started their own businesses right after or even before the launch of economic reforms – have all gone through the turbulent years of the Cultural Revolution. Those in rural areas were already used to harsh conditions of life, of course. Most of those in the cities, however, lived a long period of hard life as well, especially those 'Red Guards' who went to the villages and then returned to their urban homes. No matter where they were, they were politically wounded and tired of politics. In addition, this was not a well-educated generation not simply because they spent much of their youth on political activities and battles during the Cultural Revolution, but also because higher education was still something reserved for a tiny proportion of the population. With enthusiasm for political ideologies painfully faded away, no hope of pursuing an intellectual life, and economic conditions deteriorating, the only thing worth of doing was to make money.

Much of their knowledge came from self-learning, knowledgeable relatives and friends, or working experience. By showing their skills and intelligence in some technical tasks, such as repairing household appliances, constructing a house or building, operating a machine, organizing a public project, or selling a particular product, they earned the reputation of 'capable man' or 'strong lady'. This explains why most entrepreneurs had backgrounds of working as a salesman, a technician, a mid level manager, or a local official with some experience in business. Through their work experiences, they also became versed in the market, the production process, and the management of a business. It was exactly because of their capacities that they often found China's economic system in general, and their work unit in particular, constraining or even suppressing. Motivated to live a better material life and armed with practical skills, they were ready to start a new business.

Rather than waiting for the overall institutional environment to accept their businesses, most of them would deal with the issue of legitimacy only when they had to, after the business was already opened. They would not try to completely sever their connections with their original work unit – in China, to keep as much social capital as possible is a common wisdom of social intelligence. Private entrepreneurs thus took away many valuable resources from the legitimate enterprises: technology, knowledge, customers, personnel, and even hardware. I shall say more about the entrepreneurial process in the next section.

Most nascent entrepreneurs in China took a dominant role in the new business, usually supported by family members and a few very close but capable relatives and friends. Kinships, friendships, and other social ties were all sources of help and support, but private entrepreneurs had to be very vigilant in selecting their aides and managers as they could not afford to pay someone simply because of *guanxi* (personal connections) rather than competence. In other words, social relations supplied a pool of trusted personnel from which the entrepreneur selected the capable partners and assistants. If we would like to call them an entrepreneurial team simply because they work together to achieve a common objective, then it was a team with a hierarchical rather than a horizontal structure. Teams composed of members who have different valuable skills, enjoy equal status and have no strong ties are still rare among entrepreneurial enterprises in China. The lack of trust of those outside the family or a close circle is obviously a reason, but note that the concern is not just with having access to various properties of the business; more sensitive than finance, personnel and other matters are some strategies and behaviours that the entrepreneur would want to share with as few people as possible. If there is an entrepreneurial team, then that team is most likely to be composed of family members. The heavy representation of family relations in private enterprises in China has not only saved much in cost of internal transactions but also shielded these enterprises from examinations of their legitimacy.

Furthermore, the entrepreneurs trust more in people than in institutional rules. To them, people's behaviours are much more predictable once we know what they want and what they can do. In contrast, rules are elusive because they do not have stable properties and predictable behaviours. Worse, many people can do very different things to them, and it is very hard to foresee what a certain kind of person will do to a particular set of rules. Obviously, the two kinds of trust are interlinked to each other – the distrust of rules comes from the distrust of the people who create, use, or manipulate them. At the ideological level, the Maoist model proved to be a disaster for China, both politically and economically. At the end of the 1970s and during the 1980s, China was haunted by a strong sense of frustration, confusion, suspicion toward Mao Zedong Thought, Communism, and the CCP's handling of internal affairs. Although sometimes the overall circumstance became quite liberal, entrepreneurs and others soon learnt the lesson that it was wiser to make use of the institutions set up by the CCP rather than to challenge the Party's legitimacy. Political apathy, followed by a cult of money and luxury life, came to dominate the public mind. Such lassitude and distrust of ideologies and political power then reinforced an opportunistic attitude towards institutional rules at the regulatory level. Once previously held ideological principles were not perceived to be binding anymore and the majority of state officials were seen as rent-seekers, entrepreneurs lost much of their respect for rules, regulations, principles, and even laws. It would be too costly to break the rules or laws, so a more realistic strategy was to twist the rules to serve one's own interest. Many entrepreneurs were much more aggressive in dealing with these types of rules than with the ideological ones. The level of risk was lower, the room for manipulation was more spacious, and it was more acceptable by the State because even the State itself admitted the deficiencies of many institutional rules. Some private entrepreneurs were strongly driven to change the regulatory rules, and the influence made in turn enhanced their chance of growing on the business front, forming a dynamics of growth. Finally, entrepreneurs in China have found moral rules the least worrying. At least in the early years of economic reforms, the State did not seem worried very much about moral values; sometimes, it even encouraged people to adopt values claimed to be consistent with a market economy. Busy making money, the public seemed to have become oblivious of any moral principles, and every individual feels so powerless in waves of commercial transitions that it was better to become ignorant of than to swim against the tide. In sum, to most entrepreneurs in China, rules are created for them to use whenever possible, to twist, manipulate, or even violate if they have to, and to follow only when they find them useful.

The process

The above discussions of the attributes, motivations, and contexts of entrepreneurship will not automatically lead to a definite set of scenarios of the entrepreneurial process. This does not mean, however, that we should withdraw from depicting a big picture of the entrepreneurial process in China. Drawing on the previous empirical studies and keeping some of the important theoretical issues in mind, here I offer an ideal-typical summary.

A process is a sequence of events. A normal or standard entrepreneurial process starts with an initiation – thinking seriously about setting up a new business, discussing the plan with trusted others, and trying to find out what it takes to achieve the plan. A crucial part of passing this stage is the evaluation of potential opportunities and risks. If the idea is found feasible and there are no serious obstacles and oppositions, then the process moves on to legal establishment – filing applications for license and making the business known to a wider circle, including the customers, clients, the industry, etc. After the business is formally established, two resource mobilizations come to the fore. The first is logistical, involving the setup of facilities, equipments, materials and financial accounts so that the business can function smoothly. The second mobilization is organizational, including the establishment of social roles, organizational structures, internal rules and procedures. The successful delivery of the first round of products or services is usually believed to indicate the end of the entrepreneurial process; the business then moves into a phase of routine operations.

In China's early years of reform, a large number of people were forced or pushed into the business world. They became nascent entrepreneurs because opening a business seemed to be the only alternative. Among them were those unemployed, those made redundant, and those virtually made redundant (farmers in poverty or workers whose work units were in poor financial conditions). The force of pushing was much stronger than that of pulling in these years because of several reasons: the State did not wholeheartedly and publicly support private businesses yet, there were many discriminatory regulations against the private sector, few private businesses provided successful examples, and the risk of investing seemed to be quite high. However, year by year the situation was becoming more and more positive: State policies were becoming more liberal, some discriminatory rules were under fire and entrepreneurs learnt some ways of eschewing them, some individual household businesses had successfully transformed into large enterprises and their visibility in the media showed a promising and lucrative future for those still waiting and watching. These encouraging signals pulled a group of 'capable people' into private business: salesmen, technicians or people with special skills, lower level managers, and members of government staff. Whenever they could, they would keep one of their legs in the more stable although less attractive state economy and the other into the water of the risky but alluring world of the market.

Those pushed into the entrepreneurial venture were more likely to follow the steps of the standard process specified above because they needed to get the business up and running as soon as possible, thus it was less affordable for them to aim high. With no jobs to fall back on, they would do whatever they *could* do, not what they *would like* to do. This type of entrepreneur would prefer the whole entrepreneurial process to be as short and quick as possible. Some would even jump over a step or two, such as obtaining a license, in order to see the quick returns. Consequently, the level of technology was very low and organizational structure very simple.

The picture for those pulled to entrepreneurship is much more complex. Most of them were employed in a decent position before they were drawn to start a business of their own, and many times the previous sequence of entrepreneurship did not apply. The idea of starting a new business might come after they found a good opportunity in their employed work. Further, they could afford a certain period of time for mobilizing resources before formally registering the business. Some even accomplished a few transactions, as part of their previous employment before their business came to exist. A minority of entrepreneurs in China could even start a series of businesses, each following a different sequence of development or employing different strategies of mobilizing resources, making it difficult to ascertain the order of events. Obviously, the distinction between 'the pushed entrepreneurs' and 'the pulled entrepreneurs' is somehow arbitrary; there must be some 'cases in between', and a pushed entrepreneur may well become a pulled entrepreneur after a period of growth.

Entrepreneurs in China also differentiate among themselves in terms of their approaches to recognizing opportunities and to developing an overall strategy. It is at this step that entrepreneurship has found its most crude expressions in China. In most cases, opportunities have been often understood as a chance to make a profit by filling a gap in demand. As pointed out before, China's shortage economy and the limited amount of resources needed for starting a small business have created hundreds of thousands of new business organizations. To recognize an opportunity is to know what can be sold quickly. It does not demand much entrepreneurship to know what people would like to buy in a shortage economy: food and catering, clothes and shoes, household appliances, bikes, office supplies, construction of houses and buildings, etc. Small private enterprises in China constantly change their industries and main products, and some are even proud of such a 'market-oriented' approach, not worrying about the costs of entering a new market and the loss of accumulated experience. It is no surprise that the majority of entrepreneurs in China are reproducers, not innovators, generalists, not specialists. Few have the ambition of dominating a particular niche of an industry and would like to invest heavily in technological and organizational efficiency. This kind of entrepreneurship is vibrant, but it is nearsighted as well.

Accompanied with the desire for making quick money is the worry of changing state policies. For many years entrepreneurs were worried that private businesses might become illegitimate again and a new, harsher regulation was on its way out. Opportunities are precious because they will disappear more quickly in an unstable institutional environment, rendering it less preferable to develop a long-term strategy. Many successful enterprises entered unrelated industries without a coherent vision of development; diversification was made simply because of accidental access to a group of customers, a particular technology, or an amount of bank loan. Only a limited number of brave and wise souls had the courage and the resources to drive the market rather than to be driven by the market. An even smaller number of entrepreneurs would surf the waves of institutional changes and make profits out of them. Overall, entrepreneurs in China have been very opportunistic in recognizing and using opportunities.

The lack of strategists among Chinese entrepreneurs is not all their fault, of course. For a long time, most industries were still dominated by state enterprises, making it very hard for non-state firms to enter, let alone to gain a decent status. Moreover, to develop a senior and influential position demands stable supply of resources, including raw materials, financial credits, technology, and qualified employees, which are under the control of state agencies or enterprises. Changing state policies and their interactions with market mechanisms have put the entrepreneurial process in a flux and the development of business visions very difficult. Attracted by so many market *lacunae* on the one hand and put off by such unstable environmental conditions, many successful non-state enterprises can grow big, not because they have accumulated admirable experiences, technologies, and business know-how, but because they have a business portfolio that allows them to survive the vicissitudes of the market and policies.

To establish the legal status of entrepreneurial ventures in China is much less institutionalized than in mature market economies. The market mechanisms were new to the State, and by the end of the 1970s the Party had lost many of its economic and financial professionals. To avoid irreversible and disastrous consequences, it was preferable to follow an incremental approach. In addition, within the Party there were always voices calling for pulling back from liberal economic policies. All created many confusions and inconsistent practices in the administration of private enterprises. For example, it was unclear how a private enterprise should be defined and then registered. Whilst there was a threshold of employing eight or more employees, many private entrepreneurs refused to be labelled as such, claiming that people were working cooperatively and there was no distinction between the employer and the employees. Others resorted to their connection with a state or collective enterprise as a way of establishing a more legitimate and profitable legal status. As long as the State treated different types of enterprises differently, there would always be corresponding strategies for taking the incentives while avoiding the penalties.

Obviously, following these strategies incurred costs that would not normally be taken into account by entrepreneurs in western market economies. Entrepreneurs in China, especially those with an extraordinary desire to get ahead of others, invested in a large amount of time mulling over Party resolutions, newspaper editorials, speeches made by influential leaders, to search for clues of the next big move of new policies. They also spent no less time learning about administrative policies and procedures that had a direct impact on their business, thinking over which particular rule might be used to serve their interests, where was covered by no rules, and which rules appeared to be conflicting with each other so that an argument could be made. Many entrepreneurs have become experts of state policies. A small number of them have actually invented their own ideas, arguments and theories. Whilst it is common for successful business leaders in western societies, mostly retired, to note down their personal views of business strategies, principles, and tricks, some entrepreneurs in China are unique by publicly discussing their ideas and theories as part of their business career. What they have touched is not confined to their own business or relevant industry; more broadly, they have voiced their views on the status of private enterprises, industrial structures, future directions of China's overall economic reform, power, money, and moral values. Making these ideas known to the public is expected to serve two functions: to help legitimize non-state businesses in general and their own business in particular and to enhance their business reputation that in turn is expected to increase the business's profitability. As we learnt from previous chapters, to increase media coverage is, however, a tricky business.

Besides, entrepreneurs in China differ from one another in their preparation for dealing with administrative officials. Some are good at arguing for their legitimacy, armed by their knowledge of Party policies, some are backed by financial strength, others can resort to powerful connections, and still others are able to employ more than one type of resource. Correspondingly, the officials adopt different attitudes and strategies in dealing with different kinds of entrepreneurs, depending on their position, knowledge, calculation of their interests, and available social capital. The enormous number of combinations of characteristics on both sides would constitute a basis sufficient for a large number of novels, television programmes and movies. Students of entrepreneurship and business studies, however, have had a difficult time pinning down any reliable patterns except for gaining a general idea that the successful establishment of an entrepreneurial business in China is highly contingent on the complex relations between the entrepreneurs and the officials.

Perhaps one thing that we are confident in saying about the entrepreneurship process in China is that entrepreneurs have relied much more on resources outside the direct control of the State, because nearly every step of the entrepreneurship process is tightly controlled by state policies and regulations. They learn information about a particular opportunity through friends, relatives, or anybody else they happened to know. They come to know the tricks of the trade by having a banquet with someone with ample experience or an official in charge of such matters. They collect the start-up capital from members of their extended families, neighbours, local communities, etc. They look for competent technicians by snowballing their existing personal connections. To a large extent, and for many years, the private sector in China has remained an informal economy. But sooner or later they have to face the formal procedures: registering the business and obtaining a license, applying for bank loans if they want to grow, purchasing materials and equipment controlled by state agencies, setting up internal organizations such as labour unions and a Party branch, and dealing with rounds of inspections by the police, tax collectors, public hygiene officers, and other state agents. These two parallel processes (formal and informal) are the institutional sources of double gambles by the entrepreneurs – once they find out that their survival and success will be impossible without either informal or formal resources, the conflicting nature of the two suggests to them that developing a mutual reinforcing process is the best strategy.

The need to keep a balance between the informal and the formal is also reflected in the step of setting up the new business's organizational structure. All important positions will be taken up by family members, trusted relatives or friends, and perhaps other key partners. When the scope of control is still manageable, many employees also join the new firm through personal connections. However, in two interrelated aspects the business is crudely organized. First, for the workers in the frontline, responsibilities and rights for secretarial and managerial positions are not clearly specified, and people in these positions usually accomplish a variety of tasks without a clear logic of priority. Which one to do pretty much depends on the task's urgency rather than its importance. The other aspect is the relationship between the entrepreneur, now the employer, and the employees. Whilst relationships between family members or close circles can sort things out amongst themselves informally, those between the employer and the employees are supposed to be formally spelled out. But most entrepreneurs do not have much interest in formalizing their organizational structures because they do not want to be bound by formal contracts and procedures, which naturally increase transaction costs and threaten their authority. Most first generation entrepreneurs are still used to the authoritarian style of running a business. Many decisions are made on the spot by the founding entrepreneur, without even consulting the senior managers, and the complaint most often made by managers and secretaries is that their boss constantly changes their mind or gives very short notice of changes. The founding entrepreneur enjoys a powerful status, which they could easily justify: quick decision is a sign of management efficiency and determination, something the state enterprises can only envy and learn from.

On many issues in life, most people do what they can, not what they should. Entrepreneurs in China do not sign up formal contracts with employees and specify their duties because they do not have to. There is a large supply of cheap labour, much of which is well educated. In addition, even for now, there are very few state regulations on how employees in private enterprises should be properly treated, and if not, what consequences the employer has to face. Thus, there is a large incentive but a tiny penalty for not treating employees in a formal and responsible manner. Private entrepreneurs have little motivation to copy the organizational structures and procedures adopted in state enterprises. In their minds, their newness and liability are only in ideological and regulatory terms, not in managerial terms. They have many reasons for not setting up a labour union in their business, not providing pensions and other welfares, and not letting employees influence their decisions. The institutional environment has made an imprint on newly founded private enterprises, but many times in the opposite direction.

The attainment of a business license, the establishment of the organization, and the delivery of goods and services may indicate the end of the starting period of the business, but by no means do they signal the end of the entrepreneurial process. Defining entrepreneurship as the founding of new organizations clearly assumes that the rest will be nothing but routine. How far this entrepreneurship *vs.* management divide can go has worried many researchers. This book has shown that it certainly does not work very well in the case of China. It is entrepreneurial to set up a new business, especially a private business, in China, but one has to be even more entrepreneurial *after* the business is founded and put into operation. It is certainly not a one-off event. Those who aim to thrive rather than simply survive have become an entrepreneur several times during the life course of their businesses. When new opportunities are arising, they enter into new industries and found new firms. They also show their entrepreneurship in closing down non-performing firms – terminating a business is no less entrepreneurial than establishing one. In either case, entrepreneurial strategies must be developed with regard to the firm's identity, image to the public, relations with competitors, clients, customers and government agents. In accomplishing these tasks, it is truly hard to follow any routine or managerial principles, because the new signals keep coming from the institutional environment.

The effects

The founding of hundreds of thousands of new firms outside the planned economy is the most tangible result of entrepreneurship in China. Many of these new firms have not survived due to newness, illegitimacy, technological incompetence, weak leadership, unwise use of resources, or simply bad luck. There has been, however, an enormous net growth of firms, and the growth means more products and services. The ration system quickly became something of the past, and customers soon started to enjoy a buyer's market. The quality of their material life still remains much lower than that in America, Japan, and Europe, but the speed of improvement is astonishing. There is no need to say more about this.

There is a more fundamental effect. Recall the initial motivation of the Chinese state's permission to allow individual and household businesses to grow – a highly pragmatic tactic to solve the urgent problem of unemployment and extreme poverty. To a very large extent, these targets have been achieved. China has been one of the most successful countries in reducing poverty in the world; it is now among the top three food exporters in the world. The new businesses offer employment opportunities not only to their owners but also to their employees. Further to the satisfaction of the State, non-state enterprises have become the major receivers of those employees made redundant from state enterprises, a step that the state must take in order to rejuvenate the state sector. It is true that non-state enterprises have taken over from the state-owned ones in many industries and markets, such as construction, retailing, light industries, etc., thus forcing many state enterprises into bankruptcy. But institutionally speaking, this is exactly what the reform of the state sector is all about: pushing the state firms into market competition and learning how to survive by themselves. In the end, the non-state sectors have offered much more than what the state asked for. It is obviously wiser to offer these types of enterprises a larger space to grow than to hold on to outdated ideological principles, although the whole process needs close monitoring.

If what entrepreneurs have done to China's economy has been mostly welcomed, things are not so certain with regard to what they have done to the social and political parts of contemporary Chinese society. Here I briefly address three aspects: (1) social stratification, mobility, inequality, and justice; (2) power, political participation, and democracy; (3) belief, moral values, and ideology. Clearly, sometimes we cannot talk about one of them without talking about the other two.

Whether economic development would necessarily increase the divide between the rich and the poor, and to what extent that should be accepted, have been contentious issues in the short history of China's economic reforms, not only among political leaders but among academics and ordinary peoples as well. There is no need to go into the details here; suffice it to say that eventually Deng's liberal policy gained an upper hand, and his key point was popularly summarized as 'Let some people get rich first'.

His original ideas were actually more sophisticated. First of all, he emphasized that this was only a strategy for making the nation's economic development take off. In other words, he would not like to see the increasing gap between the rich and poor, but it is more preferable to let some people get rich first than to keep all people poor. Next, he also emphasized that the rich should then help the poor, because the common goal is to get rich together rather than to keep the gap forever. Third, how to get rich is of great importance. Deng said many times that people should get rich only through working hard, following the rules, and obeying the law.

Obviously, these are complicated issues. The first point, that economic development is more desirable than social equality, holds only under strong conditions. That is, social inequality has to be kept at a tolerable level while the economy is growing. How that can be done in practice is a difficult question. The second point sounds farfetched: there is little ground for believing that the rich and the poor will share the common goal of getting rich together and that the rich would like to help the poor get rich. It is more realistic to assume that the rich would not voluntarily help the poor, so the question is how to encourage them to, or even make them, offer help, such as by granting honours and taxing heavily. But how to do that is a political problem, whose resolution will not simply depend on ideological or moral principles. To Deng's last point, I believe that people in China have paid the least amount of attention. Although they would not dispute the value of hard work in getting rich, it would be naïve to believe that the rich become rich simply because they work hard, follow the rules, and obey the law. If it would sound too cynical to say that the rich are rich because they do not work hard, violate the rules, and disobey the law, then a suspicious attitude toward the rich would be quite reasonable.

There is a big overlap between the rich and the entrepreneurial. Unfortunately, the governments, the entrepreneurs, the media, and the academics have done little work on establishing *the acceptance* of their richness. Too often the acceptance has been built on economic grounds. It seems that as long as entrepreneurs turn in a larger amount of tax, earn more hard cash in international trade, and offer jobs to more people, how they have accomplished those is a minor issue. Again, entrepreneurs play double gambles by using their economic contributions to justify their personal wealth. In the long run, this is a poor strategy for their own interest because such strategy entails high transaction costs and unnecessary investments in non-business activities. It is not enough simply to blame the poor suffering from the 'red eye' syndrome (being envious); a widely known and accepted standard of social stratification needs to be created and maintained, and its underlying rationale needs to be justified. However, entrepreneurs in China seem to have little motivation to actively enhance public acceptance of their strategies and behaviours. Too often this task is done by governments and the media, but entrepreneurs know that an honour granted by the government or a praising report in the media is not long-term legitimacy at all. While some legal and institutional procedures are being considered, entrepreneurs should organize themselves and some internal policing is in order. So far non-state entrepreneurs in China are not an organized body, with little power of helping themselves and bargaining with others.

One would easily think of China's authoritarian political system for explaining the lack of organized power among the private entrepreneurs. That, however, constitutes only a note of the context rather than an explanation. It is true that the Communist Party does not wish to see the entrepreneurs developing into a threatening opponent – no chance is given for political competition, but the entrepreneurs themselves should take some responsibility as well. What I would like to point out here is that the double gambles played by the entrepreneurs and the Chinese state have seriously undermined the institutional and organizational bases for organizing the entrepreneurs into independent political forces.

For the entrepreneurs, it is nearly impossible to establish explicit organizational connections with other private enterprises when following the strategies of wearing a 'red cap', obtaining sponsorship of a government agency, or making use of institutional holes. It is not merely that they do not want to share these secretive strategies with other private enterprises, nor that the strategies can only be practised by a single firm. What prevents private enterprises in China from forming alliances among themselves is that both administratively and strategically, they cannot help but rely on government agencies and state enterprises. In competing for limited resources, favourable rules, powerful connections, and market shares, private entrepreneurs naturally see each other as competitors, ignoring their shared positions and interests. Such an antagonistic view toward each other, reinforced by the desperation of not having a political party to represent their interests, makes almost all entrepreneurs apathetic to politics, except for a very small minority. Although many are members of the CCP, few are politically active. Most importantly, even among the few most active ones, political activities are absolutely an individual matter, not a collective concern to the whole group of entrepreneurs, because playing a double gamble requires individualized tactics tailored to each enterprise's own situation. Occasionally, sporadic proposals are made for changing a law or a state regulation regarding the private sector, but collective actions among the entrepreneurs are out of sight. Perhaps the history of private businesses in China is still too short for the formation of networks of trust.

For the Chinese state, it is critical to be proactive in order not to politically alienate the private entrepreneurs while their economic importance is growing. Leaders of the CCP are clearly aware of the fact that, sooner or later, private entrepreneurs will look for their political representatives to voice their concerns, preferences and even demands. Before, these voices were usually passed over to top leaders through informal or indirect channels, such as conversations with several selected private business owners, an industry conference, journalist reports, or academic studies. With a limited number of highly successful private entrepreneurs being elected as People's Representatives or members of the Political Consultant Assembly, formal channels have been enacted but only to a limited extent, as the relative number of this type of representatives remains very small, and they only have the opportunity to talk, not the power to make decisions. It is just a matter of time, however, that private business owners will no longer be satisfied with their political weakness and take actions to increase their political power, even though the actions are to be taken individually rather than collectively. Very likely, one such action is to join a non-Communist party in China. It is perhaps due to the fear of this scenario that Jiang Zemin proposed that the CCP accept private business owners as members. It is not difficult to see the proposal's logic: it is in the best interests of the CCP to incorporate the private entrepreneurs as part of the authoritarian regime rather than to compel them to become political activists in favour of a western style democracy.

Jiang's strategy works the best when private entrepreneurs are still busy competing for market shares and increasing their personal wealth. Within the CCP, some work needs to be done to square the circle of taking 'capitalists' as members of a Communist party. People in the West will be amazed again by how good the CCP is at blurring or crossing lines of ideological principles. In the near future, we shall see an increasing number of Communists who represent the interests of private business owners.

However, this scenario will create some confusion among ordinary people. If it is not too difficult a job to absorb private business owners into the ruling party, then it is not so easy to answer a series of questions that relate to the rising status of money, wealth, and power. Is China still a socialist nation? Is it right to have so much wealth concentrated in so few hands so quickly? Words like 'comrade' have been long outdated and replaced with 'Mr.' and 'Ms.', but does that mean we should now rank people by how much money or power they possess? What do we live for? Money and a luxurious life? Power over others? Attention from others? Where should our dignity and identity come from? What moral principles, if any, should we not give up under any circumstances? Entrepreneurs in China have helped to construct a much stronger economy, but in the meantime they have neglected, weakened, or even destroyed many values that ordinary Chinese people have held dear for so many years.

I am clearly aware of the complications of these issues and the risk of making general statements based on idiosyncratic cases. I do not think, however, that I have exaggerated the seriousness of the above questions. On the contrary, I believe that too little has been said about the moral responsibilities of the entrepreneurs or the moral consequences of their strategies and behaviours. All too often what is put under the limelight of media is their courage, smart and quick decisions, knowledge of the market and technology, and other personal charisma. Simultaneously, what is ignored, sidelined, or even concealed is their cunning manipulation of state policies, disrespect of employees' human rights, dishonesty to customers and clients, and fall into decadence, which only come to the attention of the public when a high-flyer entrepreneur is caught.

Obviously, entrepreneurs should not be the only ones responsible. The Chinese state, intellectuals and academics, and ordinary people should all have exercised greater effort in rebuilding not only the economy but also the ideology. Perhaps it is impossible for a society to have no ideology at all, as people have to rely on some stable references to do their thinking, so terms like 'ideological vacuum' and 'void of values' need specific definition. Since the 1970s, Communism and Maoism have lost their favour and traditional Chinese values have been seriously challenged. While strong in economic and political terms, Deng's pragmatism is ambiguous and weak on moral issues. Partly due to political censorship and partly due to the lack of sense of responsibility, philosophers and intellectuals in China have failed to offer a new set of moral values appealing to entrepreneurs and their employees. With no clear guidance from official sources, people, including the entrepreneurs, start to look for beliefs and choose by themselves: some are highly institutionalized, such as religions, either Chinese or foreign, others are semi-religious, such as *qigong* (breathing exercise) clubs, and still others are simply self-made principles wrapped up in rhyming words. It is not an ideological void; it is an ideological chaos.

The second generation

This book has focused on the first generation of entrepreneurs in China, that is, those who opened new businesses of their own around the end of the 1970s. As we have learnt from Chapter 5, most of them started their business careers when they were in their 40s and 50s. So, by now most of them have either retired or are approaching retirement. By 'the second generation' I do not actually mean their children – obviously, not all children of entrepreneurs become entrepreneurs, although some of them do. Nor do I exactly refer to those who started their businesses after the first generation, for example, those who 'stepped into the sea' in the early 1990s or later. Like much of the previous analysis, here the second generation is distinguished from the first mainly by the institutional context in which they operate. Thus, the concept is more conceptual than empirical.

In this relatively new context, the legitimacy of private entrepreneurship is basically settled. The Party has declared its full and comprehensive support of the private sector, and there is no need to worry about the capitalist nature of private enterprises anymore. Private businesses, as a form of private property, are to be protected by the State according to the amended Constitution; specific laws in this spirit are under construction. State regulations are moving in the direction of treating all types of enterprises in about the same way, although the process is slower in some areas (banking, key raw materials, state dominating industries, etc.) than in others. A variety of markets (raw materials, financial credits, labour, etc.) have gradually opened to private entrepreneurs. Academic researchers have done a lot of work documenting the development of private enterprises and have urged the institutional environment to become more liberal. Overall, people have accepted the existence of private enterprises as a matter of fact, taking them as part of China's economic landscape.

On the other hand, the market has become more competitive than ever before. For most products, the market has quickly shifted from the side of the seller to the side of the buyer. The demand is still high, but there is no shortage of supply anymore. Most of the time non-state enterprises find themselves competing with each other rather than with state enterprises, although some state enterprises have recovered from stagnation and turned themselves into competent and even formidable competitors. With China now a member of the WTO, people in China have started to feel the power of foreign companies. In the meantime, some entrepreneurs in China, no longer satisfied with working as a cheap supplier for a foreign brand, have focused their eyes on overseas markets and aimed to become a visible player in the international market.

How the interaction between institutional rules and the market will shape entrepreneurship in China in the following years is of course a phenomenon that I will be observing with great interest. In particular, I will watch their development in three fronts: strategy, internal organization, and social responsibilities. Some tentative observations are in order.

Before, I lamented the lack of strategic vision amongst private entrepreneurs in China. I understand that as a result of unpredictable and discriminating rules and the craving to get rich quickly. Now, state policies are moving in the direction of settling down, becoming less discriminatory against any particular type of business, and offering more extensive support to business activities. In other words, the institutional space for practising entrepreneurship in the dual domains of business and politics and playing institutional holes has been shrinking, although these practices and strategies will exist for a long time and perhaps take on some new forms. Entrepreneurs should be much less motivated to do so also because their personal material life has improved dramatically; there is no longer a need to take the risk of illegitimacy for the sake of getting out of poverty. If the first generation became entrepreneurial out of necessity, then the second generation should be entrepreneurial out of growth. That is, those who can take a longer view of their business development and lead a niche in industry would get ahead of those who are still in a rush to fill a market gap. This is a challenge to the second generation – leading entrepreneurs need to think over who they are industrially, what images they want to put forward to stakeholders and competitors, what principles they need to stick to, and how they can make their businesses sustainable. It is still necessary to monitor state policies and figure out responses, but the majority of entrepreneurial energy should now be invested in analyzing industrial directions, learning new technological breakthroughs, and increasing organizational effectiveness. Entrepreneurs in China must not fancy becoming one of the top 500 in the world in a few years. Rather, they should bury their heads into hard work.

The second generation will also have to do a much better job in organizing their firms. Again, for the purposes of taking advantage of institutional loopholes, avoiding external inspections and minimizing costs, entrepreneurs of the first generation cared little about organizational structures and procedures. They seemed to be ignorant of the long-term effects of well-designed organizational structures on reducing transaction costs. To them, formal procedures such as contracts and accounts were vulnerable parts of their businesses for others to attack rather than effective tools for enhancing competitiveness. In addition, they were occupied with an authoritarian mindset, not understanding the value of morale, trust, and culture in promoting organizational efficiency. Some members of the second generation will unconsciously pick up these 'bad mental habits', but if anyone has the ambition to stand out, then a new way of thinking has to be learnt. New entrepreneurs need to show that, unlike their opportunistic predecessors, they are organizational architects, not only entrepreneurial in identifying market opportunities but also smart at designing effective and efficient organizational structures. Perhaps this is a more demanding job than the previous one as forerunners in this aspect may find themselves isolated among peer business owners, and it takes quite a while for the positive effects of these practices to be felt.

In designing their firms, entrepreneurs must show that they have a strong sense of their social and moral responsibilities. Participation in government-sponsored programmes is the least effective way of promoting their image. Giving out money to people in poverty is of course honourable and admirable, but that can hardly escape the suspicion of exchanging money for reputation. It is more effective to show that they care through the social effects of their business. A most urgent matter is to sort out their relations with employees: Is there a properly written contract? Are the working conditions up to standards? Have any accidents been appropriately taken care of? Have any employee's human rights been violated? Beyond the enterprise, entrepreneurs should make every effort to clear up their own image, which has been tainted by a number of notorious cases. Selling false products, cheating clients and customers, polluting the environment, leading a disgraceful life, etc., should not be connected to entrepreneurs anymore. Entrepreneurs in China need to think more carefully about who they are, what they are doing, and how they make China a better society.

Appendix

An English Translation of Some Selected Questions Used in the National Survey of Privately Owned Businesses in China

The statistics reported in Chapter 5 were produced by analyzing the data collected in the National Survey of Privately Owned Businesses in China. To help the reader better understand them, I provide an English translation of selected survey questions in this appendix. To save space, I did not translate the letter of introduction.

The surveys were conducted in 1993, 1995, 1997, 2000, and 2002, respectively. It is neither necessary, nor desirable, to translate all the questions for each year – some questions are irrelevant to my study while others need to be improved to be useful. Also, it would take too much space to present the questionnaires in full. Questions in this appendix have been presented in the order they appear in Chapter 5, with the original formulations shown in *italics*. All questions here were used in more than one year, and I shall start with the ones used in the earliest year and then point out the changes made in the following years. In cases where I cannot find a proper corresponding expression in English, I have attached *pinyin* (the pronunciation system used in China) to the English translation.

1. Sex
Your sex: 1) Male; 2) Female.
Same formulation for all years.

2. Age
1993 *The month and the year of your birth:* _____
In the following years, only the year of birth was recorded.

3. Education
For 1993, 1995, 1997, and 2000, education was categorized into nine levels:
Your level of education: 1) Illiterate; 2) Primary school; 3) Secondary school; 4) Ordinary high school; 5) Vocational high school (technical school); 6) Specialist school; 7) College; 8) University undergraduate; 9) Postgraduate.
In the 2002 survey, these were reduced to five:
Your level of education: 1) Primary school; 2) Secondary school; 3) High school or vocational school; 4) University undergraduate; 5) Postgraduate.
In the meantime, the 2002 survey asked respondents to specify their highest degree obtained and to report whether they had any experience of studying abroad.

4.   Motivation in starting a new business

In 1993, the question was formulated as follows:

The most important reason that you initially wanted to establish your own enterprise (choose only one): 1) Could not maintain a good relationship with the head of the original work unit; 2) Original work unit did not allow full play of my capacity; 3) Earned too little at the original work unit; 4) Had no secure job; 5) Other (please specify) _____.

In 1995, the above first four choices were preserved, but the fifth was replaced with two new choices:

5) To realize my value; 6) Wanted to leave land (rural area)

The formulation used in 1997 differs from that in 1995 in two minor aspects. First, the wording for the third and the fourth items were modified.

3) To increase income; 4) Had no job or job not secure.

Second, a residual item was added: *Other (please specify) _____.*

No questions were asked on motivation in the following surveys.

5.   Ways of leaving the original work unit

The following question was used in 1993 and 1995 but disappeared in the following years:

The way in which you left your original work unit is: 1) resigned; 2) name expunged; 3) left voluntarily; 4) retired; 5) kept the position but no pay; 6) retired due to illness; 7) was expelled; 8) had no job before starting up the private business.

6.   The distribution of private enterprises in industries

The question in the 1993 survey is formulated as follows:

Among the following kinds of operations, what was the actual major business when you initially registered your enterprise? And what is the current major business of your enterprise? 1) Manufacturing; 2) Transportation; 3) Repair; 4) Commercial service; 5) Real estate; 6) Construction; 7) Catering; 8) Other service industries; 9) Scientific development; 10) Special industries (hotel, collectables, printing, etc.); 11) Information; 12) Planting and husbandry; 13) Advertising; 14) Culture and arts; 15) Other.

In the following surveys, a different scheme of categorization was followed:

1) Agriculture, forestry, husbandry, and fishing; 2) Mining; 3) Manufacturing; 4) Power; 5) Construction; 6) Geology and watering; 7) Transportation; 8) Service and catering; 9) Finance and insurance; 10) Real estate; 11) Social service; 12) Hygiene and sports; 13) Education and culture; 14) Science and technology; 15) Other.

7.   Start-up capital

The following question was posed to the respondents in 1993 and 1995:

How did you obtain the initial capital for starting up your enterprise? (Please select three items from below according to the order of their importance.)

Most important	Second important	Third important

1) *Inheritance; 2) Savings from work or business; 3) Capital gain; 4) Overseas investment; 5) Borrowed from relatives and friends; 6) Bank loan; 7) Loan (from credit association); 8) Loan (from collective entity); 9) Loan (from other people); 10) Other _____ (Please specify).*

8. Level of difficulty in acquiring bank loans

The following question was asked firstly as a supplementary question in 1997 and then repeated in 2000:

[How would you evaluate] the level of difficulty for your enterprise in acquiring [bank] loans?

a) Very difficult; b) Difficult; c) Sometimes difficult, sometimes easy; d) Easy; e) Very easy.

9. The major barrier for acquiring bank loans

The 2000 and 2002 surveys included a question on this issue, but the formulations were not exactly the same. Here is the question used in 2000:

If you had any difficulties [in acquiring bank loans], what was the reason? a) Conditions on mortgage and guarantees of repayment were too harsh; b) Not willing to reveal financial information; c) Evaluation of credit ranking too restrictive; d) Interest rate too high; e) The amount of loan not sufficient; f) Period of loan too short; g) Other (please specify) _____.

In the 2002 survey '*Discrimination against private ownership*' was added as the first item. In addition, item b above was modified as '*The requirement of revealing financial information too demanding*'. All other items were retained.

10. Ownership

Respondents were asked to report the ownership structure of their enterprise in all surveys, but the items have changed. The following three items were included throughout the years: *1) Sole ownership; 2) Partnership; 3) Limited liability company*. In 1993, the residual item '*Other*' was included as well, which was omitted in the following years. In 2000 and 2002, the category '*Shareholding company*' was added.

11. Registration

The 1993 survey asked respondents to report the year and month of the initial registration but did not ask what the enterprise was exactly registered as. From 1995, the following question was included:

What was the nature [of your enterprise] at its initial registration? 1) State-owned enterprise; 2) Urban or town collective enterprise; 3) Rural collective enterprise; 4) Cooperative enterprise; 5) Shareholding enterprise; 6) Three capital (san zi) enterprise [overseas companies and joint ventures]*; 7) Private enterprise; 8) Individual business (getihu); 9) Other (please specify) _____.*

12. The total number of employees

In a table – too large to be reproduced here, respondents were asked to report *the total number of employees in their enterprise at the initial opening of the business* and *at the end of the year prior to the survey year*, respectively. Note that investors were not included. Further, employees were categorized into three groups: *'production workers'*, *'managerial staff'*, and *'technical personnel'*.

13. Recruitment of employees

In the 1993 and 1997 surveys, interviewers asked their respondents to tick *'the most important source'* of *major managers*, *technicians*, and *workers*, respectively, in the following table:

	(1) State-owned enterprise	(2) Collective enterprise	(3) Graduates from schools and colleges	(4) Other private enterprise	(5) Previously unemployed	(6) Peasant farmers	(7) Other (please specify)
Major managers							
Technicians							
Workers							

14. The entrepreneur as the owner and the manager

In the surveys of 2000 and 2002, owners of private business were asked *'Are you the chief executive officer or head of the enterprises as well? Yes or no?'*

15. The decision-maker

The following question was used in all surveys:
In your enterprise, who makes crucial decisions? (Please tick only one item): 1) Yourself; 2) Board of Directors; 3) You and top managers; 4) You and other organizations. Since 1997, a residual item was offered *'Others (please specify)'*, but as few ticked this item, it has been combined with *'You and other organizations'* as an overall residual category.

16. Family management of the business

The following question was included in the questionnaires of the 1997 and the 2002 surveys:
Based on your experience, with which of the following statements do you agree? (Please choose only one.) 1) For the development of this enterprise, it must be managed by myself or my family member. 2) For the development of this enterprise, it can be managed by other more capable person as well. 3) Other (please specify) _____

17. Major customers and suppliers

In 1993, the following two questions were asked:
Your raw materials or supplies mainly come from (choose only one item): 1) State-owned enterprise; 2) Official trading market; 3) Civil or private enterprise; 4) Other (please specify) _____.
The major target of your sales or services is (multiple choices allowed): 1) State-owned enterprise; 2) Private, civil, or town-and-village enterprise; 3) Directly to customers; 4) Export; 5) Other (please specify) _____.

In 1995 and 1997, the two questions were combined into a table and only one choice was allowed for both questions:

Your main supplier and the major target of your sales and services are (choose only one for each):

	1) SOE	2) Private or TVE	3) Trading market	4) Overseas	5) Other
A. Supplies					
B. Sales or services					

18. Perceived difficulty in obtaining business resources

Questions on this issue were firstly included in 1993:

Has your enterprise encountered any difficulties in the following items, and if it has, what are the major reasons (please tick in the cell that applies):

	Not difficult	Somehow difficult	Very difficult
Purchase raw materials			
Obtain water for production			
Obtain electricity for production			
Expansion of premises for production and operation			
Recruitment of technicians			
Sales			
Transportation			

Here, I have omitted the reasons due to the large number of missing values.

In the 1995 survey, the following items were added: *Recruitment of managers, Obtain capital for production,* and *Other.* Even more items were included in the 2000 survey: *Development of new projects, Search for customers of service, Tax too heavy, Too many fees, Too many imposed collections of fees and charges, Instability of employees, Personal and family security.*

19. Major helper for production and management

Questions about this subject were asked in 1995 and 1997 with some changes of the items provided. In 1995, the questions were formulated as follows:

If you have any problem in the following items, who do you believe will be the most helpful (choose only one respectively for each item).

As the table is too big to be put here, I shall list the row items and the column helpers separately. The items in the rows include:

A) Lack of capital; B) Sales of products stagnant; C) Management difficulties; D) Lack of technology; E) Preparation of expanding business scale; F) Legal rights ruined; G) Personal and relatives' security threatened. In 1997, items C and E were replaced with *Lack of business premises* and *Electricity and water.*

The helpers in the columns include:

1) Party or government leaders; 2) Administrative departments of government; 3) Association of individual businesses or private enterprises; 4) Association of Businesses (gong shang lian) and trade unions; 5) Other business owners; 6)

Relatives; 7) Friends; 8) Other influential persons; 9) Legal procedures and the media; 10) Search for new market or change of product.

In 1997, item 2) was changed to *Financial institutions*, and item 9) was split into two separate items, *Legal procedures* and *Support from the media*. The last item was changed to *Resolve through negotiations among ourselves.*

20. Feeling of competitiveness and competing strategies

The 1997 survey included some supplementary questions, two of which are:

A. Are your major product, commodities or services facing fierce competition in the market? 1) Very fierce; 2) Somewhat fierce; 3) Not fierce.

B. Facing market competition, what is the major strategy that you have adopted? (Please select three items according to their importance and put the item number in the following table)

	Most important	Second important	Third important
Item number			

1) Offer lower price to customers; 2) Increase the kickbacks to sales intermediaries; 3) Make more advertisements; 4) Adopt other methods for enhancing the reputation of the enterprise and the product; 5) Improve product quality; 6) Improve after-sale service; 7) Improve management and reduce costs; 8) Develop new products; 9) Change to other industries; 10) Other (please specify) _____.

These were repeated without any change in the 2000 survey.

21. Business disputes

Survey researchers in China started to include questions on this issue in 1995.

Up to now, the disputes that your enterprise has experienced and their solutions (Choose only one item for each question):

A. Which kind of disputes have happened most frequently? 1) With suppliers (such as low quality, delay of delivery, etc.); 2) With purchasers (such as delay of payment or no payment at all, etc.); 3) With customers (such as quality of product or service, price, etc.); 4) With administrative department of government.

In the 1997 survey, a fifth item was added: *5) With local residents or organizations.*

In the 2000 survey, the residual item was added: *6) Other (please specify) _____.*

B. How were these disputes usually resolved? 1) Ignore; 2) Try to negotiate and reconcile; 3) Bring the case to local government or upper level administrative department; 4) Bring to court; 5) Resolve through personal relations.

The residual item was added in 1997 and 2000: *6) Other (please specify) _____.*

C. Were you usually satisfied with the result? 1) Very unsatisfied; 2) Somewhat unsatisfied; 3) Quite satisfied; 4) Very satisfied.

An intermediary category was added in 1997 and 2000, making it a five-point scale:

1) Very unsatisfied; 2) Somewhat unsatisfied; 3) Hard to say; 4) Quite satisfied; 5) Very satisfied.

The formulation was changed quite dramatically in 2002 with a new table. The kinds of disputes had only two categories: *1) Ordinary economic disputes; 2) With administrative departments.*

The number of ways in which the disputes were resolved not only increased to eleven but also the contents were modified: *1) Tolerate in silence; 2) Try to negotiate and reconcile among ourselves; 3) Ask local government or upper level administrative department to solve the problem; 4) Ask an institution to arbitrate or make a lawsuit; 5) Report to People's Representatives or Representatives of the People's Assembly of Political Consultations; 6) Report to the government through Association of Businesses and Association of Private Enterprises; 7) Seek for support of Party or government leaders through personal connections; 8) Resolve among ourselves through personal connections; 9) Associate with one another spontaneously and try to resolve; 10) Report to newspapers or other mass media; 11) Other (please specify)* _____.

Finally, satisfaction with the result had only two categories: *1) Quite satisfied; 2) Not satisfied.*

22. Types of insurance offered to employees

Questions about employee welfare were grouped together in the surveys and the information provided referred to the year prior to the survey year. For example, here is the question used in 1995:

Employee income and welfare in your enterprise in 1994: 1) Employee average annual income _____; *2) Medical expense and medical insurance (per person, per year)* _____; *3) Labour insurance (per person, per year)* _____; *4) Retirement insurance (per person, per year)* _____; *5) Life insurance (per person, per year)* _____. In the following years, respondents could put in 0 if no insurance was provided.

23. Written rules

The following was included as a supplementary question in 1997 and then repeated in 2000.

Has your enterprise put the following rules and regulations in writing? 1) Enterprise (company, factory) organizational constitutions (or Board of Directors Constitution)? 2) Constitutions of personnel, employment, and management; 3) Labour contracts; 4) Regulations of salary and welfare; 5) Managerial regulations of roles and responsibilities; 6) Regulations of financial management; 7) Regulations of sales and supplies; 8) Other major rules (please specify) _____.

24. Organizations within private enterprises

The 1993 and 1995 surveys included the following question:

Does your enterprise have the following organizations? 1) Branch committee of the Chinese Communist Party; 2) Labour union; 3) Congress of employee representatives; 4) Board of directors; 5) Managers' committee.

It disappeared in the 1997 survey but came back with different categories in 2000 and 2002: *1) Congress of shareholders; 2) Board of directors; 3) Board of inspectors; 4) CCP committee; 5) Labour union; 6) Congress of employee representatives.*

25. Organizational memberships
The question on this subject remained the same until 2002:
Have you joined the following organizations? (tick as many as applicable) 1) Association of Individual Business Owners; 2) Association of Private Enterprise Business Owners; 3) Clubs of Private Business Owners; 4) Trade Unions; 5) Association of Businesses (Gong Shang Lian); 6) CCP; 7) Communist Youth League; 8) Democratic Parties.
In 2002, these were reduced into four categories: *1) CCP; 2) Communist Youth League; 3) Democratic Parties; 4) Association of Businesses (Gong Shang Lian).*

26. Congressional memberships
In China, Congress of People's Representatives is the highest legislative body. A less powerful political body is People's Assembly of Political Consultations, expected to provide a platform for the voices from non-Communist political parties and groups. Starting from 1995, owners of private enterprises were asked to report their memberships of these two political entities. First, there was a question about membership: *Are you a People's Representative? 1) Yes; 2) No.* The second question pertains to the level of membership: *If you are a People's Representative, at which level? 1) County (city); 2) Province; 3) Nation.* In 2000 and 2002, '*Township*' was added as the lowest level. The third question further asked the respondents whether they took any leading position: *Are you in one of the following positions: 1) Director; 2) Deputy-Director; 3) Member of the Standing Committee.* These questions were repeated for People's Assembly of Political Consultations.

27. Perceived support of governmental agencies
The following question was asked in the 1993 survey:
Do you think that the following institutions and departments are helpful to your enterprise?

	Supportive	So-so	Not supportive
1. Local government			
2. Police			
3. Environment agency			
4. Quality inspection			
5. Taxation			
6. Price control			
7. Hygiene inspection			
8. Customs			
9. Media and publications			
10. Personnel			
11. Business administration			
12. Measurement			

It was only repeated in 1995 with fewer institutions listed: '*Media and publications*' and '*Personnel*' were eliminated.

28. Perceived social problems

In 1995 and 1997, private business owners in China were asked about social problems on their minds:

Among the social problems listed below, which one do you think is the biggest at present? 1) Inequality of redistribution; 2) Exchange of power and money; 3) Deterioration of security; 4) Indiscriminating charges, fees, and involuntary donations; 5) Government officials and military officers involving in businesses; 6) Blackmail and extortion; 7) Other (please specify) _____.

The only difference between the two years is that the 1995 survey did not have the residual category.

29. Profits and indiscriminating charges

In every survey, the respondents were asked to report the total amount of profits in the year prior to the year in which the survey was conducted. Then, they were asked to report the components of expenditure for that year, including indiscriminating charges, fees, and involuntary donations in ten thousand yuan. The 1995 survey was different from others as it asked the respondents to report proportions rather than the total amount.

30. Self-assessed social, economic, and political statuses

The following question remained the same for all the surveys:

Compared with other members of our society, where do you think you are on the three social ladders listed below? (Please tick or circle the number on each of the three ladders, with 1 the highest and 10 the lowest.) 1) Income; 2) Social reputation; 3) Political participation.

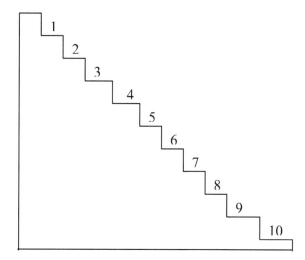

Bibliography

Aldrich, Howard, 'Entrepreneurship', pp. 454–455 in Neil Smelser and Richard Swedberg (eds), *The Handbook of Economic Sociology*, 2nd edition (Princeton University Press and Russell Sage Foundation, 2005).

Ash, Robert F. and Kueh, Y.Y. (eds), *The Chinese Economy under Deng Xiaoping* (Oxford University Press, 1996).

Bates, Robert (ed.), *Toward a Political Economy of Development: A Rational Choice Perspective* (University of California Press, 1988).

Baumol, William J., 'Entrepreneurship in Economic Theory', *American Economic Review*, 58/2 (1968): 64–71.

__, *Entrepreneurship, Management, and the Structure of Payoffs* (Cambridge, MA: MIT Press, 1993).

Becker, Markus and Knudsen, Thorbjørn, 'The Entrepreneur at the Crucial Juncture in Schumpeter's Work: Schumpeter's 1928 Handbook Entry *Entrepreneur*', *Austrian Economics and Entrepreneurial Studies, Advances in Austrian Economics*, 6 (2003): 199–233.

Bian, Yanjie, 'Institutional Holes and Job Mobility Processes: Guanxi Mechanisms in China's Emergent Labour Markets', pp. 117–135 in Thomas Gold, Doug Guthrie, and David Wank (eds), *Social Connections in China: Institutions, Culture, and the Changing Nature of Guanxi* (Cambridge University Press, 2002).

Bickford, T.J., 'The Chinese Military and Its Business Operations: The PLA as Entrepreneur', *Asian Survey*, 34/5 (1994): 460–474.

Biggart, Nicole Woolsey, 'Institutionalized Patrimonialism in Korean Business', pp. 113–133 in Craig Calhoun (ed.), *Business Institutions*, vol.12 of *Comparative Social Research* (JAI Press, 1991).

Birley, S., 'New Ventures and Employment Growth', *Journal of Business Venturing*, 2/2 (1987): 155–165.

Brown, David, Qi, Hantang and Zhang, Yong, 'Insights into Strategy Development in China's TVEs', pp. 72–86 in David H. Brown and Alasdair I. MacBean (eds), *Challenges for China's Development: An Enterprise Perspective* (Routledge, 2005).

Bruun, Ole, *Business and Bureaucracy in a Chinese City: An Ethnography of Private Business Household in Contemporary China* (University of California Press, 1993).

Buchanan, James, *What Should Economists Do?* (Indianapolis, IN: Liberty Press, 1979).

Burawoy, Michael, et al., *Ethnography Unbound: Power and Resistance in the Modern Metropolis* (Berkeley: University of California Press, 1991).

Burns, John, 'The People's Republic of China at 50: National Political Reform', *The China Quarterly*, 159 (1999): 580–594.

Burt, Ronald, *Structural Holes* (Harvard University Press, 1992).

Byrne, David, *Interpreting Quantitative Data* (London: Sage Publications, 2002).

Casson, Mark, 'Entrepreneur', in J. Eatwell, M. Milgate and P. Newman (eds), *The New Palgrave: A Dictionary of Economics* (London: McMillan, 1987).

Central Committee of the Chinese Communist Party, *A Collection of Important Documents Since the Third Plenum* (in Chinese) (Beijing: People's Press, 1991).

__, 'Some Issues Regarding Current Economic Policies in Rural Areas', quoted and translated from Zhang and Ming (1999).

Chang, Sea-Jin, *The Rise and Fall of Chaebols: Financial Crisis and Transformation of Korean Business Groups* (Cambridge University Press, 2003).

Chau, Theodora Ting, 'Approaches to Succession in Eastern Asian Business Organizations', *Family Business Review*, 4/2 (1991): 161–189.

Chen, Jianbao and Jefferson, G.H. 'Development of the Hengdian Township Enterprise Group: A Case Study', pp. 279–287 in Gary H. Jefferson and Inderjit (Hg.) Singh (eds), *Enterprise Reform in China: Ownership, Transition, and Performance* (Oxford University Press, 1999).

Cheung, Peter T.Y., Chung, Jae Ho, and Lin, Zhimin, *Provincial Strategies of Economic Reform in Post-Mao China: Leadership, Politics, and Implementation* (Armonk, NY: M.E. Sharpe, 1998).

Cheung, Tai Ming, *China's Entrepreneurial Army* (Oxford University Press, 2001).

Chu, Xiaoping, 'A Study of Family Business: A topic of modern significance' (*jia zu qi ye yan jiu: yi ge ju you xian dai yi yi de hua ti*), *Social Science in China* (*zhong guo she hui ke xue*, No. 5, 2000).

Czarniawska-Joerges, Barbara, *Economic Decline and Organizational Control* (New York: Praeger, 1989).

De Vecchi, Nicoló and Stone, Anne, *Entrepreneurs, Institutions, and Economic Change: The Economic Thought of J.A. Schumpeter (1905–1925)* (Edward Elgar, 1995).

Deng, Xiaoping, *Selected Works*, volumes 1–3 (*People's Daily* Online, http://english. peopledaily.com.cn/dengxp).

Dickson, Bruce, *Red Capitalists in China: The Party, Private Entrepreneurs, and Prospects for Political Change* (Cambridge, England: Cambridge University Press, 2003).

DiMaggio, Paul, 'Introduction: Making Sense of the Contemporary Firm and Prefiguring Its Future', in *The Twenty-First Century Firm: Changing Economic Organization in International Perspective* (Princeton University Press, 2001).

__(ed.), *The Twenty-First Century Firm: Changing Economic Organization in International Perspective* (Princeton University Press, 2001).

Dong, Fureng, *An Economic History of the People's Republic of China* (in Chinese) (Joint Publishing Hong Kong, Co., Ltd, 2001).

Eckstein, Harry, 'Case Study and Theory in Political Science', pp. 79–138 in F.I. Greenstein and N.W. Polsby (eds), *The Handbook of Political Science* (Reading: Addison-Wesley, 1975).

Fu, Jian, 'Private Enterprises and the Law', pp. 166–177 in Ross Garnaut and Ligang Song (eds), *China's Economic Transformation: The Rise of the Private Economy* (RoutledgeCurzon, 2003).

Gan, De'an, et al., *A Study of Family Business in China* (*zhong guo jia zu qi ye yan jiu*, Beijing: China Social Sciences Publishing House, 2002).

Garnaut, Ross and Song, Ligang (eds), *China's Economic Transformation: The Rise of the Private Economy* (RoutledgeCurzon, 2003).

George, Alexander L. and Bennett, Andrew, *Case Studies and Theory Development in the Social Sciences* (MIT Press, 2005).

Gersick, Kelin E., et al. (eds), *Generation to Generation: Life Cycles of the Family Business* (Boston, Mass: Harvard Business School Press, 1997).

Gilley, Bruce, *Model Rebels: The Rise and Fall of China's Richest Village* (University of California Press, 2001).

Gold, Thomas, 'Back to the City: The Return of China's Educated Youth', *The China Quarterly*, 84 (1981): 755–770.

__, 'Urban Private Business and China's Reforms', pp. 84–103 in Richard Baum (ed.), *Reform and Reaction in Post-Mao China: The Road to Tiananmen* (Routledge, 1991).

__, Doug Guthrie, and David Wank (eds), *Social Connections in China: Institutions, Culture, and the Changing Nature of Guanxi* (Cambridge University Press, 2002).

Goldman, Merle and MacFarquhar, Roderick (eds), *The Paradox of China's Post-Mao Reforms* (Cambridge, Massachusetts and London, England: Harvard University Press, 1999).

Gore, Lance, *Market Communism: The Institutional Foundations of China's Post-Mao Hyper-growth* (Oxford University Press, 1999).

Granovetter, Mark, 'Business Groups', in Neil Smelser and Richard Swedberg (eds), *The Handbook of Economic Sociology*, 1st and 2nd editions (Princeton University Press, 1994 and 2005).

Greenwood, R. and Hinings, C.R. 'Understanding Radical Organizational Change: Bringing Together the Old and the New Institutionalism', *Academy of Management Review*, 21/4 (1996): 1022–1054.

Guthrie, Douglas, 'Entrepreneurial Action in the State Sector: The Economic Decision of Chinese Managers', pp. 159–190 in Victoria Bonnell and Thomas Gold, *The New Entrepreneurs of Europe and Asia: Patterns of Business Development in Russia, Eastern Europe, and China* (M.E. Sharpe, 2002).

Harwood, Edwin, 'The Sociology of Entrepreneurship', in Calvin A. Kent, Donald L. Sexton, and Karl H. Vesper (eds), *Encyclopaedia of Entrepreneurship* (Englewood Cliffs, New Jersey: Prentice-Hall, 1982).

He, Wei; Wei, Jie; Shen, Weiguang, *Zhu Ming Zhuan Jia Xue Zhe Lun Heng Dian* (*Observations by Prominent Scholars on Hengdian*, People's Press, 1994).

Hedström, Peter and Richard Swedberg, 'Social Mechanisms: An Introductory Essay', pp. 1–31 in Peter Hedtröm and Swedberg, Richard (eds), *Social Mechanisms: An Analytical Approach to Social Theory* (Cambridge University Press, 1998).

Higgins, Benjamin, *Economic Development: Principles, Problems, and Policies*, revised edition (London: W.W. Norton and Company, 1968).

Jia, Ting (ed.), *Biographies of Well-Known Private Entrepreneurs in Contemporary China* (*Dang Dai Zhong Guo Zhi Ming Si Ying Qi Ye Jia Lie Zhuan*) (Beijing: Zhong Guo Cheng Shi Jing Ji She Hui Chu Ban She, 1989).

Johansson, Dan, 'Economics without Entrepreneurship or Institutions: A Vocabulary Analysis of Graduate Textbooks', *Economic Journal Watch*, 1/3(2004): 515–538.

Kirzner, Israel, 'Entrepreneurial Discovery and the Competitive Market Process: An Austrian Approach', *Journal of Economic Literature*, XXXV (1997): 60–85.

Knight, Frank, *Risk, Uncertainty and Profit* (Boston, Massachusetts: Houghton Mifflin, 1921).

Knight, J. and Song, L., 'Towards a Labour Market in China', *Oxford Review of Economic Policy*, 11 (1995): 97–117.

Kornai, János, *The Socialist System* (Princeton University Press, 1992).

Kraus, Willy, *Private Business in China: Revival between Ideology and Pragmatism* (Hurst and Company, 1991).

Krug, Barbara (ed.), *China's Rational Entrepreneurs: The Development of the New Private Business Sector* (RoutledgeCurzon, 2004).

__, and Mehta, Judith, 'Entrepreneurship by Alliance', in Barbara Krug (ed.), *China's Rational Entrepreneurs: The Development of the New Private Business Sector* (RoutledgeCurzon, 2004).

Li, Xinchun, 'Family Institutions and Enterprise Management in China' ('*zhong guo jia zu zhi du yu qi ye zu zhi*'), *Quarterly Journal of Social Science in China* (Hong Kong, Spring, 1998).

Li, Zhenjie, *Si Ying Qi Ye Tou Shi* (*Private Enterprises in Perspective*, in Chinese) (Beijing: Economics and Management Press, 1999).

Lin, Nan, 'Local Market Socialism: Local Corporatism in Action in Rural China', *Theory and Society*, 24 (1995): 301–354.

Linnemann, Maja, *Women Business Owners in China: Results of a Survey* (Bremen: Institute for World Economics and International Management, 1998).

Liu, Peifeng, *Si Ying Qi Ye Zhu* (*Owners of Private Enterprises*) (Beijing: Social Science Documentation Publishing House, 2005).

Liu, Yia-Ling, 'Reform From Below: The Private Economy and Local Politics in the Rural Industrialization of Wenzhou', *The China Quarterly*, 130 (1992): 293–316.

Lu, Ding and Tang, Zhimin, *State Intervention and Business in China: The Role of Preferential Policies* (Edward Elgar, 1997).

Malik, Rashid, *Chinese Entrepreneurs in the Economic Development of China* (Praeger, 1997).

Mao, Zedong, 'Report to the Second Plenary Session of the Seventh Central Committee of the Communist Party of China' (5 March 1949) http://www.marxists.org/reference/archive/mao/selected-works/volume-4/mswv4_58.htm.

March, James G. and Olsen, Johan P., *Rediscovering Institutions: The Organizational Basis of Politics* (The Free Press, 1989).

Marx, Karl, 'Critique of the Gotha Program', pp. 525–541 in Robert C. Tucker (ed.), *The Marx-Engels Reader*, 2nd edition (W.W. Norton and Company, 1978).

McNulty, P.J., 'Competition: Austrian Conceptions', in J. Eatwell, M. Milgate and P. Newman (eds), *The New Palgrave: A Dictionary of Economics* (London: McMillan, 1987).

Merton, Robert, 'Notes on Problem-Finding in Sociology', pp. 17–42 in *Social Research and the Practicing Professions* (Cambridge, Massachusetts: Abt Books, 1982), originally published in Robert K. Merton, Leonard Broom, and Leonard S. Cottrell, Jr. (eds), *Sociology Today: Problems and Prospects* (New York: Basic Books, Inc., 1959).

__, 'Sociological Ambivalence', pp. 3–31 in his *Sociological Ambivalence and Other Essays* (The Free Press, 1976).

Mises, Ludwig von, *Human Action: A Treatise on Economics* (Irvington: Foundation for Economic Education, 1996).

Mou, Qizhong, *Le Guan De Zhong Guo Jing Ji* (*An Optimistic View of China's Economy*, Land Research Institute, 1997).

Naughton, Barry, 'Deng Xiaoping: The Economist', *China Quarterly*, 135 (1993): 491–514.

Nee, Victor, 'A Theory of Market Transition: From Redistribution to Markets in State Socialism', *American Sociological Review*, 54/5 (1989): 663–681.

__, 'Organizational Dynamics of Market Transition: Hybrid Forms, Property Rights, and Mixed Economy in China', *Administrative Science Quarterly*, 37 (1992): 1–27.

__, and Su, Sijin, 'Institutions, Social Ties and Commitment in China's Corporatist Transformation', pp. 111–134 in J. McMillan and B. Naughton (eds), *Reforming Asian Socialism: The Growth of Market Institutions* (Ann Arbor: University of Michigan Press, 1996).

__, and Yang, Cao, 'Path Dependent Social Transformation: Stratification in Hybrid Mixed Economies', *Theory and Society*, 28 (1999): 799–834.

__, and Mary Brinton, *The New Institutionalism in Sociology* (Stanford University Press, 2001).

__, 'The New Institutionalisms in Economics and Sociology', in Neil Smelser and Richard Swedberg (eds), *The Handbook of Economic Sociology*, 2nd edition (Princeton University Press and Russell Sage Foundation, 2005).

Nolan, Peter, *China at the Crossroads* (Cambridge: Polity Press, 2003).

__, *China's Rise, Russia's Fall: Politics, Economies, and Planning in the Transition from Stalinism* (St. Martin's Press, 1995).

__, 'China's Post-Mao Political Economy: A Puzzle', *Contributions to Political Economy*, 12 (1993): 71–87.

North, Douglas, *Structure and Change in Economic History* (W.W. Norton & Co., Ltd 1981).

__, *Institutions, Institutional Change, and Economic Performance* (Cambridge University Press, 1990).

__, 'Institutions', *Journal of Economic Perspectives*, 5 (1991): 97–112.

__, 'Economic Performance Through Time', *American Economic Review*, 84/3 (1994): 359–368.

__, *Understanding the Process of Economic Change* (Princeton University Press, 2005).

Oi, Jean, 'Fiscal Reform and the Economic Foundations of Local State Corporatism in China', *World Politics*, 45/1 (1992): 99–126.

__, 'The Role of the Local State in China's Transitional Economy', *The China Quarterly*, 144 (1995): 1132–1149.

__, *Rural China Takes Off: Institutional Foundations of Economic Reform* (University of California Press, 1999).

Oliver, Christine, 'Strategic Responses to Institutional Processes', *Academy of Management Review*, 16 (1991): 145–179.

Orrù, Marco, Woolsey Biggart, Nicole and Hamilton, Gary, 'Organizational Isomorphism in East Asia', pp. 361-389 in Walter Powell and Paul DiMaggio (eds), *The New Institutionalism in Organizational Analysis* (University of Chicago Press, 1991).

Ostrom, Elinor, *Crafting Institutions for Self-governing Irrigation Systems* (San Francisco, California: Institute for Contemporary Studies Press, 1992).

__, Schroeder, Larry, and Wynne, Susan, *Institutional Incentives and Sustainable Development: Infrastructure Policies in Perspective* (Boulder; Oxford: Westview Press, 1993).

Peaple, Andrew, 'China Overtakes UK As World's 4th Largest Economy', *Dow Jones Newswires* (26 January 2006).

Pearson, Margaret, *China's New Business Elite: The Political Consequences of Economic Reform* (University of California Press, 1997).

Pei, Minxin, *From Reform to Revolution: The Demise of Communism in China and the Soviet Union* (Cambridge: Harvard University Press, 1994).

Peng, Mike W. and Heath, P., 'The Growth of the Firm in Planned Economies in Transition: Institutions, Organizations, and Strategic Choices', *Academy of Management Review*, 21/2 (1996): 492–528.

__, and Luo, Y. 'Managerial Ties and Firm Performance in a Transition Economy: The Nature of a Macro-Micro Link', *Academy of Management Journal*, 43/3 (2000): 486–501.

Peng, Xizhe, 'Education in China', pp. 115–133 in Peng, Xizhe with Guo, Zhigang (eds), *The Changing Population of China* (Blackwell, 2000).

Pettigrew, Andrew, 'On Studying Organizational Culture', *Administratively Science Quarterly*, 24 (1979): 570–581.

Powell, Walter and DiMaggio, Paul (eds), *The New Institutionalism in Organizational Analysis* (University of Chicago Press, 1991).

President's Commission, *Entrepreneurship and Its Impact on the U.S. Economy* (Washington, DC: President's Commission on Industrial Competitiveness, 1984).

Ragin, Charles C., *The Comparative Method: Moving Beyond Qualitative and Quantitative Strategies* (Berkeley, Los Angeles, and London: University of California Press, 1987).

Reynolds, P.D., 'New Firms: Societal Contribution Versus Survival Potential', *Journal of Business Venturing*, 2/3 (1987): 231–246.

Reynolds, Paul and White, Sammis, *The Entrepreneurial Process: Economic Growth, Men, Women, and Minorities* (Westport, CN: Quorum Books, 1997).

Rosen, Sherwin, 'Austrian and Neoclassical Economics: Any Gains from Trade?', *Journal of Economic Perspectives*, 11/4 (1997): 139–152.

Ruef, Martin, 'Origins of Organizations: The Entrepreneurial Process', *Entrepreneurship (Research in the Sociology of Work)*, 15 (2005): 63–100.

Sautet, Frederic, 'The Role of Institutions in Entrepreneurship: Implications for Development Policy' (Mercatus Center, George Mason University, February 2005).

Schoonhoven, Claudia Bird and Romanelli, Elaine (eds), *The Entrepreneurship Dynamic: Origins of Entrepreneurship and the Evolution of Industries* (Stanford, California: Stanford University Press, 2001).

__, 'Emergent Themes and the Next Wave of Entrepreneurship Research', pp. 383–408 in Claudia Bird, Schoonhoven, and Elaine, Romanelli (eds), *The Entrepreneurship Dynamic*.

Schumpeter, Joseph, *The Theory of Economic Development*, 2nd edition (Cambridge: Harvard University Press, [1926] 1934).

__, *Capitalism, Socialism and Democracy* (New York: Harper and Row, 1942 [1975]).

__, 'Economic Theory and Entrepreneurial History', in Richard V. Clemence (ed.), *Essays on Entrepreneurs, Innovation, Business Cycles, and the Evolution of Capitalism* (Addison-Wesley Press, Inc., 1949 [1951]). Reprinted from *Change and the Entrepreneur*, pp. 63–84.

__, *History of Economic Analysis* (London: Allen & Unwin, 1954).

__, *Business Cycles: A Theoretical, Historical, and Statistical Analysis of the Capitalist Process* (New York: McGraw-Hill, 1939; reprinted by Porcupine Press, 1982).

__, 'Comments on a Plan for the Study of Entrepreneurship', reprinted pp. 406–428 in Richard Swedberg (ed.), *The Economics and Sociology of Capitalism* (Princeton University Press, 1991).

__, 'Entrepreneur', translated by Markus C. Becker and Thorbjørn Knudsen, *Austrian Economics and Entrepreneurial Studies*, *Advances in Austrian Economics*, 6 (2003): 235–265.

Scott, W. Richard (ed.), *Institutional Environments and Organizations: Structural Complexity and Individualism* (Thousand Oaks, CA: Sage, 1994).

Shane, Scott, 'Cultural Influences on National Rates of Innovation', *Journal of Business Venturing*, 8 (1993): 59–73.

__, *A General Theory of Entrepreneurship: The Individual-Opportunity Nexus* (Edward Elgar, 2003).

Shaver, K.G. and Scott, L.R., 'Person, Process, Choice: The Psychology of New Venture Creation', *Entrepreneurship Theory and Practice*, 16/2 (1993):16–22.

Shen, Weiguang; Song, Jian; Xu, Lijun; Fan, Xiaoping; Zhou, Ying; Zhang, Haibo, *Hengdian Mou Shi* (*The Hengdian Model*, Beijing: People's Press, 1993).

__, Xu, Lijun; Sun, Shiyan; Lu, Cansong, *Heng Dian She Tuan Jing Ji Mou Shi Yan Ju* (*A Study of Hengdian's Model of Community Economy*, Beijing: People's Press, 1994).

__, Zhang, Haibo; Zhang, Min, *Heng Dian De Jing Shen Wen Ming Jian She* (*The Construction of Spiritual Civilization at Hengdian*, Beijing: People's Press, 1994).

__, He Wei and Wei Jie, also compiled a collection of comments and short essays by some of the most prominent economists in China on Hengdian – *Zhu Ming Zhuan Jia Xue Zhe Lun Heng Dian* (*Observations by Prominent Scholars on Hengdian*, People's Press, 1994).

Shi, Qingqi, 'Zhong Guo Fu Nu Chuang Ye Yu Nu Qi Ye Jia Fa Zhan Yan Jiu' ('A Study of Enterprises Started by Women and the Development of Female Entrepreneurs in China'), *2001 Zhong Guo Nu Qi Ye Jia Fa Zhan Bao Gao* (*2001 Report on the Development of Female Entrepreneurs in China*, Beijing: Geology Press, 2002), pp. 3–10.

Smelser, Neil and Swedberg, Richard, 'Introduction' to *Handbook of Economic Sociology*, 2nd edition (Princeton University Press and Russell Sage Foundation, 2005).

Solinger, D.J., 'Urban Entrepreneurs and the State: The Merger of State and Society', pp. 121–141 in Arthur Lewis Rosenbaum (ed.), *State and Society in China: The Consequences of Reform* (Boulder, CO: Westview Press, 1992).

Stake, Robert, *The Art of Case Study Research* (Sage Publications, 1995).

Stark, David, 'Recombinant Property Forms in Eastern European Capitalism', *American Journal of Sociology*, 101 (1996): 993–1027.

__, and Bruszt, László, *Postsocialist Pathways: Transforming Politics and Property in East Central Europe* (Cambridge University Press, 1998).

__, 'Ambiguous Assets for Uncertain Environments: Heterarchy in Postsocialist Firms', pp. 69-104 in Paul DiMaggio (ed.), *The Twenty-First Century Firm* (Princeton University Press, 2001).

__, and Vedres, Balázs, 'Social Times of Network Spaces: Network Sequences and Foreign Investment in Hungary', *American Journal of Sociology*, 111/5 (2006): 1367–1411.

Stiglitz, Joseph, *Whither Socialism?* (The MIT Press, 1994).

Stinchcombe, Arthur, *Stratification and Organization: Selected Papers* (Cambridge: Cambridge University Press, 1986).

__, 'On the Virtues of the Old Institutionalism', *Annual Review of Sociology*, 23 (1997): 1–18.

__, *When Formality Works: Authority and Abstraction in Law and Organizations* (University of Chicago Press, 2001).

Sun, Shiyan, *Wen Hua Li: Heng Dian De Qi Shi* (*The Power of Culture: Lessons from Hengdian*, Beijing: School of the Chinese Communist Party Press, 1995).

__, *Shi Chang Xing Gong You Zhi: Hengdian Chan Quan Zhi Du Xi Tong Kao Cha* (*A Market Type Public Ownership: A Systematic Investigation on the Hengdian Model's Property Ownership Institutions*), Shanghai: San Lian Press, 1998).

Swedberg, Richard, 'The Man and His Work', 'Introduction' to Richard Swedberg (ed.), *The Economics and Sociology of Capitalism* (Princeton University Press, 1991).

__, (ed.), *Entrepreneurship: The Social Science View* (Oxford University Press, 2000).

Tilly, Charles, 'Review of *Understanding the Process of Economic Change*', *Perspectives of Politics*, 4/3 (2006): 616–617.

Tsai, Kellee, *Back-Alley Banking: Private Entrepreneurs in China* (Cornell University Press, 2004).

Tucker, Robert C. (ed.), *The Marx-Engels Reader*, 2nd edition (New York & London: W.W. Norton & Company, 1978).

Twitchett, Denis and Fairbank, John K. (eds), *The Cambridge History of China*, Vol. 14, *The People's Republic 1949–1979, Part 1: The Emergence of Revolutionary China, 1949–1965* (Cambridge University Press, 1987).

Van de Ven, Andrew, Polley, Douglas, Garud Raghu, and Venkataraman, Sankharan, *The Innovation Journey* (New York, Oxford University Press, 1999).

Walder, Andrew, 'Local Government as Industrial Firms: An Organizational Analysis of China's Transitional Economy', *American Journal of Sociology*, 101/2 (1995): 263–301.

__, (ed.), *The Waning of the Communist State: Economic Origins of Political Decline in China and Hungary* (Berkeley, California; London: University of California Press, 1995).

Wank, David, *Commodifying Communism: Business, Trust, and Politics in a Chinese City* (Cambridge University Press, 1999).

Weber, Max, *Economy and Society* (University of California Press, 1978).

White, Gordon, *Riding the Tiger: The Politics of Economic Reform in Post-Mao China* (Macmillan, 1993).

White, Lynn T., III, *Unstately Power (I): Local Causes of China's Economic Reforms* (M.E. Sharpe, 1998).

Williamson, Oliver, *Markets and Hierarchies: Analysis and Antitrust Implications* (New York, Free Press, 1975).

__, *The Economic Institutions of Capitalism: Firms, Markets, and Relational Contracting* (The Free Press, 1985).

Wong, John, Rong Ma, and Mu Yang (eds), *China's Rural Entrepreneurs: Ten Case Studies* (Singapore: Times Academic Press, 1995).

Wu, Jinglian, *Understanding and Interpreting Chinese Economic Reform* (Thomson/South-Western, 2005).

Xia Xiaolin, 'Si Ying Bu Men: Lao Zi Guan Xi He Xie Tiao Ji Zhi' ('The Private Sector: Employment Relations and Mechanisms of Mediation'), *Guan Li Shi Jie* The World of Management, 6 (2004), http://theory.people.com.cn/GB/40555/3833168.html#.

Xu, Wenrong, *Heng Dian Zhi Lu* (*The Road of Hengdian*) (Beijing: People's Press, 1994).

__, *Collected Works* (three volumes, People's Press, 2005).

Yang, Mayfair, 'The Resilience of Guanxi and its New Deployment: A Critique of Some New Guanxi Scholarship', *The China Quarterly*, 170 (2002): 459–476.

Yao, Xiantao and Wang, Lianjuan, *The Current Situation, Problems, and Strategies of Family Businesses in China* (*zhong guo jia zu qi ye xian zhuang wen ti yu dui ce*, Beijing: Enterprise Management Publishing House, 2002).

Young, Susan, *Private Business and Economic Reform in China* (M.E. Sharpe, 1995).

Yuan, Guanghou, *Shang Hai Ju Zi Mou Qizhong* (*Mou Qizhong: A Business Giant*) (Beijing: Zu Jia Chu Ban She, 1994).

Zhang, Houyi and Ming Lizhi (eds), *Zhongguo Siying Qiye Fazhan Baogao (1978– 1998)* (*Report of the Development of Private Business in China*) (Beijing: Social Science Documentation Publishing House, 1999).

Zheng, Shiping, *Party vs. State in Post-1949 China: The Institutional Dilemma* (Cambridge University Press, 1997).

Index